CULTURE**SHOCK!**

A Survival Guide to Customs and Etiquette

D1481591

BRAZIL

Volker Poelzl

Marshall Cavendish
Editions

This edition published in 2006 by:
Marshall Cavendish Corporation
99 White Plains Road
Tarrytown, NY 10591-9001
www.marshallcavendish.us

Other Marshall Cavendish Offices:
Marshall Cavendish International (Asia) Private Limited. 1 New Industrial Road, Singapore 536196 ▪ Marshall Cavendish Ltd. 119 Wardour Street, London W1F 0UW, UK ▪ Marshall Cavendish International (Thailand) Co Ltd. 253 Asoke, 12th Flr, Sukhumvit 21 Road, Klongtoey Nua, Wattana, Bangkok 10110, Thailand ▪ Marshall Cavendish (Malaysia) Sdn Bhd, Times Subang, Lot 46, Subang Hi-Tech Industrial Park, Batu Tiga, 40000 Shah Alam, Selangor Darul Ehsan, Malaysia

Marshall Cavendish is a trademark of Times Publishing Limited

ISBN 10: 0-7614-2490-3
ISBN 13: 978-0-7614-2490-1

Please contact the publisher for the Library of Congress catalog number

Printed in Singapore by Times Graphics Pte Ltd

Photo Credits:
All photos by Volker Poelzl except pages 58, 101, 219 (Daniela Norberto).
▪ Cover photo: Photolibrary.com

All illustrations by TRIGG

ABOUT THE SERIES

Culture shock is a state of disorientation that can come over anyone who has been thrust into unknown surroundings, away from one's comfort zone. *CultureShock!* is a series of trusted and reputed guides which has, for decades, been helping expatriates and long-term visitors to cushion the impact of culture shock whenever they move to a new country.

Written by people who have lived in the country and experienced culture shock themselves, the authors share all the information necessary for anyone to cope with these feelings of disorientation more effectively. The guides are written in a style that is easy to read and covers a range of topics that will arm readers with enough advice, hints and tips to make their lives as normal as possible again.

Each book is structured in the same manner. It begins with the first impressions that visitors will have of that city or country. To understand a culture, one must first understand the people—where they came from, who they are, the values and traditions they live by, as well as their customs and etiquette. This is covered in the first half of the book.

Then on with the practical aspects—how to settle in with the greatest of ease. Authors walk readers through topics such as how to find accommodation, get the utilities and telecommunications up and running, enrol the children in school and keep in the pink of health. But that's not all. Once the essentials are out of the way, venture out and try the food, enjoy more of the culture and travel to other areas. Then be immersed in the language of the country before discovering more about the business side of things.

To round off, snippets of basic information are offered before readers are 'tested' on customs and etiquette of the country. Useful words and phrases, a comprehensive resource guide and list of books for further research are also included for easy reference.

CONTENTS

FOREWORD

Spending time in a foreign country is both a rewarding and challenging experience. On one hand, travellers feel the enthusiasm of explorers, and on the other hand, they find themselves overwhelmed by a new and foreign environment. My first visit to Brazil was no exception. I was a newcomer in São Paulo, excited about the novelties around me, but also confused by this unfamiliar culture and people in the world's third largest city. These first impressions have remained fresh in my memory and have helped me write this book. When researching and compiling information, I often recalled my first experiences in Brazil, and kept asking myself: what facts about the people, their customs and behaviour would have eased my transition into Brazilian culture? What insights would have prepared me a little better for the challenges I would encounter? This book is the result of trying to answer these questions and to provide important cultural survival tools for the reader's own first steps into the 'land of samba and the tambourine.'

In addition to consulting numerous written sources, I had the opportunity to talk with many Brazilians about their country and culture. Among them were politicians, businesspeople, musicians, artists, poets, ranchers, peasants, housewives, as well as indigenous people. I have also talked with foreigners living in Brazil and listened to their stories. But during my extensive research and travels, I have come to realise that Brazil is not easily defined nor explained. There are so many different Brazils that are lived, loved, and suffered every day, that it is impossible to grasp it all and describe it in one book. Instead, what I would like to provide for the reader here is a glimpse of this immensity that characterises Brazil, a glimpse of the complexity and diversity of its culture that is so marvellously expressed in Brazilian art, music, and writing, and more than anything else, in the way Brazilians live their daily lives.

A view of Rio de Janeiro.

INTRODUCTION

'São Paulo or Rio. Naked Savages or the Amazon...
It is between these antagonistic extremes,
that the real Brazil lies...'
—Gilberto Freyre, *New World in the Tropics*

Brazil is a complex and fascinating country. It is not only South America's largest nation, but also the most varied and diverse in geography, climate, population and culture. Brazil is home to steaming jungles and dry steppes, pristine beaches and lofty mountain peaks. It builds airplanes and sends satellites into space, while in the remote Amazon jungle, native tribes still practice their Stone Age traditions. Brazil's cities delight with the gems of their colonial past, whilst at the same time take pride in the accomplishments of their modern architecture. Wherever one travels, wherever one lives, one encounters a diversity that is at once dazzling and enlightening, confusing and delightful.

Brazilians are a people from many different backgrounds. Their varied heritage and traditions contribute to the country's enormous wealth of cultural manifestations. The Brazilian language, for example, although essentially Portuguese, has been enriched by many indigenous and African words. Indigenous influences are also apparent in place names and food items, as well as mythology and religious practices. Portuguese Catholicism introduced street processions into Brazil, but it was the African slaves who provided the rhythmic percussion for the dances and pageants. Many dishes, especially in North-eastern Brazil, contain ingredients of African origin. It is this fusion of races, cultures, and languages that makes Brazil such a vibrant country. It is also a young and dynamic nation with an admirable ability to overcome hardship and face the future with all-encompassing optimism and hope.

Although this book is not an exhaustive discussion of Brazilian culture and life, I hope to share a little of the Brazilian spirit with you. The first few chapters are a general introduction to Brazil, its geography, history, political system, economy, people, religious beliefs and social realities. These are followed by an in-depth look at Brazilian food, language, customs, etiquette, and at how Brazilians live and spend their time. The final chapters provide specific information about settling in Brazil, employment, business, and how to deal with the various aspects of everyday life. An appendix provides a listing of useful resources, contacts and readings.

Expect your Brazilian experience to have ups and downs, but never to be predictable, repetitive or boring. This is the true Brazilian way. As poet Vinicius de Moraes, one of the best interpreters of the Brazilian soul wrote:

'A vida vem em ondas como o mar.' ('Life comes in waves like the sea'.)

ACKNOWLEDGEMENTS

This book would not have been possible without the assistance of my friends both in Brazil and the United States. I would especially like to thank Dani for her companionship on my extended explorations of Brazil over the past seven years. I am also indebted to Gilson and Irene (São Paulo), José Norberto and Elsa (Cacoal), Hélder and Simone (Porto Velho), Paulinho and Élina (Cuiabá), Franklin and 'Meire' (Crato), Alessandra, Rachel, Alan, Ricardo, Mauro and Clayton (Recife), Laura (Rio de Janeiro), Zulmira and Camila (Curitiba) for their hospitality and help during the final stages of my research. Thanks also to Vicky, Hélio, and Nick for providing useful insights and information.

I would like to thank my friends Tim, Paula, and Lee for their support while writing this book. Thanks also to my Tucson Arizona coffeehouse friends, who provided the necessary diversion while I was working on finishing the manuscript. I am also grateful to Patricia for her hospitality and help with the logistics of repeated Brazil trips, and to Shellie for sharing her beautiful house with me.

I also appreciate the assistance from the tourist offices in São Paulo and Belo Horizonte, the friendly staff at Bahiatursa in Salvador, and Tânia from the Museu Histórico in Crato, Ceará.

To the Norberto family,
in gratitude for their hospitality and friendship.

MAP OF BRAZIL

FIRST IMPRESSIONS

CHAPTER 1

'On this day, in the afternoon, we sighted land!
First a large mountain, very high and round,
and other lower mountains to the south;
and flat land, with large forests ...'
—Pero Vaz de Caminha,
in a letter to Portuguese King Manuel I,
reporting the discovery of Brazil in 1500.

BRAZIL AT FIRST SIGHT

Just as the discoverer of Brazil, Pedro Cabral, knew little about what lay behind the first view of Brazil's coast, newcomers to Brazil will find a flood of new impressions that make it difficult to make sense of it all. No matter where you first set foot in Brazil, you will soon be surprised by the country's inherent diversity, dynamism and contradictions. First impressions are often tainted by our prejudices and fears, and it is only all too easy to let initial difficulties loom too big in our minds and taint our future perceptions. In this sense, first impressions of Brazil have to be taken with a grain of salt, and you can count on your first impressions to be debunked and contradicted before too long. What I have found to be important is to quickly go beyond the first impressions and move toward a more informed perception of the manifold realities of Brazilian life. Brazil is in many ways overwhelming at first, and it takes a little patience and time to sort things out and get a firm grip on the country's reality.

I remember arriving in the centre of São Paulo coming from the airport. The amount of traffic, noise, exhaust fumes, and the number of peddlers and street vendors crowding the streets was overwhelming. What struck me the most were the many homeless people living on the streets, and the throngs of children begging or selling knick-knacks. Eventually I learned to put these first experiences and observations into context, as my views gradually expanded and changed, but this took some time. It was not until a few months after my arrival, that I began to discover and enjoy São Paulo's unrivaled cultural life and cosmopolitan diversity. Brazil is a very dynamic society, and in the years since my first visit, I noticed how my first impressions of São Paulo no longer corresponded to the reality today. New laws had been introduced to regulate street commerce more strictly, and new government programmes had encouraged many poor families to send their children to school, instead of having them beg in the streets.

For all the wealth in the upscale suburbs, there is also much poverty in the dozens of shantytowns I saw along the motorways. But São Paulo with its 16 million inhabitants is not representative of Brazilian cities. After the shock of arriving in the world's third-largest city, it took me some time to discover that Brazil's mid-sized cities nowhere resembled the dense urban jungle of São Paulo. There were far fewer shantytowns, there were very few homeless families and children on the streets, and the city centres were not nearly as overcrowded with unemployed workers hawking contraband merchandise.

Similarly, the neat Swiss-style towns in the mountains outside Rio de Janeiro are not typical examples of Brazilian towns, as they are more reminiscent of Central Europe than of Brazil.

Without any doubt your first impressions will greatly vary depending on where you go. Arriving in São Paulo, I landed in Brazil's economic powerhouse.

Brazil is a land of contrasts and extremes, and first impressions are only a first step toward a better understanding, a starting point, from which to begin one's exploration of Brazil's wealth of culture, regions and people. Every impression and every experience forms only a small piece in the large mosaic that constitutes Brazil.

The locals are known to be hard-working and ambitious, which is evident in the city's economic wealth. Living in Copacabana Beach in Rio de Janeiro later on, I discovered a very different aspect of Brazilian life. The inhabitants of Rio de Janeiro prefer the beach over the office. In São Paulo's central business district most people were dressed formally, whereas in Rio de Janeiro everybody seemed to be tanned and people dressed much more casually. Your first impressions also greatly depend on how much you immerse yourself in Brazilian culture and public life. I knew foreigners in Brazil, who never took a public bus, and only dined, socialised and shopped at well-guarded shopping centres and upscale suburbs. Brazilians love crowds and enjoy socialising in sidewalk bars, town squares, and the outdoors in general, and the glitzy gallerias on the outskirts and wealthy suburbs form an atypical bubble within the otherwise very different public life in Brazil.

ABOUT THE LAND

Not unlike the early explorers, newcomers to Brazil will be mesmerised by the lush and abundant vegetation. Not only are Brazil's Amazon region and the coastal mountains covered with tropical forest, but even in cities small pockets of jungle form wherever there is a patch of open land. From the complex beauty of a passion flower to the massive grandeur of the Amazon's silk cotton tree, it is an immense joy to experience the diversity of Brazil's natural environment. I still remember when I first saw a pair of macaws flying overhead into the sunset, and when I first watched a toucan pick palm nuts with its huge bill. I also still remember clearly my first encounters with caimans, snakes and iguanas, which all gave me the impression that Brazil's jungles are this vast and untouched ecosystem, where animals live as undisturbed as ever.

But I soon learned that Brazil's exuberant and lush natural environment is severely threatened. Travelling all over the Amazon, I discovered that the imposing Amazon rain forest is being choked by a growing belt of cattle ranches and soybean farms, and that deforestation is the way of life in the Amazon. But neither the white sandy beaches, nor the dense amazon jungle tell the whole story of Brazil's natural environment. It took me a several years to finally travel to all regions in Brazil and see the bone-dry, bleached scrublands of the drought-ridden interior of North-eastern Brazil, the lush pine forests of the south, as well as the many deserted beaches along the coast, that stretch as far as the eye can see. Brazil has been nicknamed 'the gentle giant', and the country is indeed a giant in every aspect, a giant that takes time to be explored and understood.

ABOUT THE PEOPLE

Brazilians are outgoing and extroverted. I spoke Spanish and knew some Portuguese when I first arrived, and I quickly found myself invited to a drink, play music on the beach or have lunch at someone's home. But some foreigners from less extroverted cultures might first interpret people's friendliness and outgoing nature as an infringement of privacy. Similarly, the perceived lack of personal space can also be a challenge in the beginning. Brazilians touch each other all the time, and riding on a crowded bus on a hot day in the Amazon city of Manaus can become a strangely intimate experience, with sweaty, scantily clad bodies standing close together.

Coming into town from the airport, most people's first encounters with Brazilians are with taxi drivers, who, like their colleagues in many countries like to overcharge inexperienced foreigners. A few years ago, the tourist office in Rio de Janeiro offered hospitality courses for taxi drivers, since officials realised that most foreigners' first contacts are with taxi drivers at the airport, and that these first impressions

Brazil is a young country, and children are found playing everywhere.

are important and should be positive. I have found Brazilians to be extremely generous, friendly and hospitable, and the attitudes of some taxi drivers do not reflect how Brazilians treat foreigners in general.

But despite these outgoing and open people, my first impressions of Brazilians were marked by the fact that I was in Brazil by myself and that I had trouble understanding Portuguese. It took me some time before I felt comfortable with the language, and no longer felt a stranger and outsider, isolated from sharing experiences with the Brazilians because of the language barrier. But once I spoke the language better, I found that it was the Brazilians themselves who most helped me to cope with the many new impressions and experiences. Thanks to these friendly and outgoing people, foreigners do not feel like outsiders for very long, as they are quickly taken in and welcomed by Brazilians. After a few months in Brazil, I saw the door gradually open to a better understanding of this complex and fascinating country, mostly with the help of my new Brazilian friends.

Looking back at my first experiences in Brazil, I realise that my first impressions have blended with many other observations since then. Brazil continues to be an ever-changing mosaic, and every time I return to Brazil, I have to leave old impressions and preconceived opinions behind, and be once again open for new experiences.

A LOOK AT BRAZIL

'... this land is blessed with great fertility, excellent climate,
benign skies, general wholesomeness, healthful air, and
a thousand other virtues that must be added to these.'
—Ambrósio Fernandes Brandão,
Dialogues of the Great Things of Brazil, 1618

GEOGRAPHY

Brazil extends over 8.5 million sq km (3.3 million sq miles) and covers 47.3 per cent of the South American continent. It is the fifth largest country in the world, slightly smaller than the US and 35 times bigger than the United Kingdom. Brazil has 14,691 km (9,129 miles) of land boundaries and borders all South American nations except Chile and Ecuador. The coastline of 7,491 km (4,655 miles) along the Atlantic Ocean is one of the longest of any country. Brazil is divided into five geographic regions with distinct topographic, cultural and economic characteristics.

The South

Brazil's south consists of the states of Paraná, Santa Catarina, and Rio Grande do Sul. This region is characterised by an inland plateau and low mountains that form the southern end of the coastal mountain range, the Serra do Mar. Brazil's southernmost state, Rio Grande do Sul, also shares the pampa, a vast grass-covered plain that extends into Uruguay and Argentina.

The South is home to one of Brazil's most spectacular natural wonders—the Iguaçu Falls, as well as the Itaipu Dam, the country's most ambitious hydroelectric power plant, and among the world's biggest dams. Southern Brazil was once covered by dense pine forests, but the inland plateau is today largely deforested and has become a centre of agro-industry and Brazil's major grain belt. The pampa is an important cattle-raising region.

During the 19th and early 20th century, the region's mild climate attracted large numbers of German, Italian and Polish immigrants who established small and prosperous family farms. Today, Brazil's South continues to treasure its distinct European heritage, which is expressed in its architecture, culinary specialities, festivals and music. The state capitals Curitiba, Florianópolis and Porto Alegre are considered Brazil's most livable cities and have become national role models for city planning, environmental protection and economic development.

The South-east

The South-east consists of the states of Espírito Santo, Minas Gerais, Rio de Janeiro and São Paulo. It is characterised by two distinct regions, the hot and humid coastal plain, and the Atlantic plateau further inland with an average elevation of 500–900 m (1,640–2,950 ft). This upland is separated from the coast by the Serra do Mar, a mountain range that reaches from the state of Espírito Santo to the state of Santa Catarina, and is home to some of Brazil's tallest peaks. The mountains drop down to the coast in a steep escarpment,

Ipanema Beach in Rio de Janeiro, bordered by the coastal mountains.

which forms the largest remaining continuous area of the Atlantic rain forest, which once covered the entire region. The coastal mountains are characterised by large granite outcrops such as the Pão de Açucar (Sugar Loaf Mountain) in Rio de Janeiro.

The South-east is home to Brazil's best developed industrial complex and has the most advanced agriculture in the country. Coffee, orange juice and grains are produced for export, as well as dairy products and meat for domestic consumption. The South-east has the highest income level and standard of living in Brazil, but urban areas are increasingly marked by crime and social problems. The largest cities are São Paulo, Rio de Janeiro and Belo Horizonte.

The Central West

The Central West consists of the states of Mato Grosso, Mato Grosso do Sul, Goiás and the Distrito Federal (Federal District) of Brasília. This region covers most of Brazil's large central plateau, the planalto central. It has an average altitude of 600–1,000 m (1,968–3,280 ft) and is crossed by several mountain ranges and river valleys. The Paraná and the Paraguay River are the region's largest rivers and reach the Atlantic Ocean through the River Plate (Rio da Prata) in Argentina.

The vast expanse of savanna, known as *cerrado*, that once covered most of the Central West, has been drastically reduced by the introduction of industrial farming. Agro-industry and cattle raising are the region's most important economic activities.

During its annual floods, the Paraguay River inundates the low-lying basin of the Pantanal, the region's most important tourist destination. The largest cities are Brasília, Goiânia, Campo Grande and Cuiabá.

The North-east

North-eastern Brazil is made up by the states of Maranhão, Piauí, Ceará, Rio Grande do Norte, Paraíba, Pernambuco, Alagoas, Sergipe and Bahia. The region is characterised by several different topographic zones. A coastal plain 200 km (124 miles) wide, known as *zona da mata* (forest zone), stretches from Rio Grande do Norte to Bahia. It is a humid and fertile region, once covered by the Atlantic rain forest, hence its name. Today, most of the *zona da mata* has given way to sugar cane and citrus plantations. Further inland, behind the coastal plain lies the *agreste*, a hilly region devoted mainly to cattle-raising. It is a transitional zone between the lush coast and the semiarid highlands of the interior, known as the *sertão*. The *sertão* stretches across most north-eastern states and is periodically affected by drought, causing widespread misery and migration.

The North-east is Brazil's poorest region. Fifty per cent of the families have a monthly income of about half the minimum wage. Sugar cane and citrus plantations are important sectors of the economy, as well as oil exploration and tourism.

The São Francisco River with a length of 2,896 km (1,800 miles) is the largest river in the North-east. It has its source in the Serra da Canastra, a mountain range in the western part of Minas Gerais, from where it flows north through the *sertão* region of five states toward its confluence with the Atlantic Ocean. The Sobradinho Dam is the region's largest hydroelectric power plant and provides water for citrus plantations and the surrounding cities. The largest cities in the North-east are Salvador, Recife and Fortaleza.

The North

This region is also known as Amazônia and covers the Brazilian part of the vast Amazon basin with its major tributaries. Six states make up this sparsely populated region: Rondônia, Acre, Amazonas, Roraima, Pará, Amapá and Tocantins. Most of Amazônia is covered by the Amazon rainforest, which is home to many large Indian reservations. The Amazon river is the world's most extensive river system with a length of about 6,500 km (4,040 miles). It is also the world's largest river in volume, discharging one fifth of the world's freshwater into the sea. The force of the Amazon's water entering the Atlantic Ocean is so great that there is still freshwater 161 km (100 miles) off the coast. The river is navigable by ocean-going vessels all the way to the Peruvian city of Iquitos, 3,885 km (2,414 miles) upstream. The Amazon basin is bordered to the south by the planalto central, the central highlands, and to the north by the Guyana Plateau with its eroded mountain formations and mesas. The highest point in Brazil, Pico da Neblina (3,014 m or 9,889 ft), is part of this highland. It is a remote table mountain near the border with Venezuela.

The most important economic activities in northern Brazil are extractivism (Brazil nuts, rubber latex), timber, and mining. The Carajás mining project in the state of Pará contains the world's largest deposit of iron ore as well as several other important ores. There are also large cattle ranches and expanding soybean fields in the southern Amazon, which has led to widespread deforestation. The region's rising energy needs have led to the construction of several large hydroelectric projects, often flooding Indian reservations and vast areas of rain forest. The region's largest cities are Manaus and Belém.

THE NATURAL ENVIRONMENT

'At times I was so delighted with the fragrance
of the trees and flowers and with the taste of the fruits and
roots that I thought to myself that I was close to
the earthly paradise.'
—Amerigo Vespucci in a letter to Lorenzo di Medici, 1502

Brazil's natural beauty and lush vegetation has enchanted visitors ever since the Portuguese first landed there in 1500. The Portuguese observed with amazement that the natives didn't grow food, but simply harvested what the forest provided. Early settlers admired the parrots with their rainbow-coloured plumage, and described with fascination the unusual creatures and plants they found in the new land, such as the tapir, armadillo, anteater and caiman. Jean de Léry, a French Protestant missionary who visited Brazil in 1556, devoted an entire chapter of his travelogue to the 'animals, kinds of venison, big lizards, snakes, and other monstrous beasts of America.'

Fauna and Flora

Brazil has over 400 species of mammals. Among the largest and most feared is the jaguar. It was once common throughout

Macaws are commonly seen in the Amazon region.

Brazil, but today it can only be found in remote areas of the Amazon and Central West. Other large mammals are the anteater, sloth, tapir, river dolphin, manatee and capybara. Brazil's forests are home to 30 different kinds of monkeys, among them the howler monkey, spider monkey and squirrel monkey. There are also nearly 1,600 bird species, more than in any other country. Among Brazil's largest flying birds are harpy eagles, caracaras, hawks, vultures, egrets and herons. The flightless rhea, a large running bird and relative of the ostrich, finds its home in the savannas of the Central West. The macaws are among Brazil's most beautiful birds. It is an impressive spectacle when they cross the evening sky with their colourful plumage and characteristic call: '*ara–ara*'.

Brazil is also home to over 400 species of reptiles, among them turtles, lizards, snakes, crocodilians, 500 species of amphibians, as well as over 2,000 species of freshwater fish. Brazil's biggest freshwater fish is the pirarucu, a primitive fish with large hard scales and a single lung. It can grow up to 2 m (6.6 ft) long and weigh up to 125 kg (276 lbs). Brazil's largest group of creatures is also the least visible. There are one million known invertebrates, 700,000 of which are insects. The best-known are the various species of tarantulas, mosquitoes, ants, millipedes, moths and butterflies such as the Blue Morpho.

Brazil's plant life is no less diverse than its fauna. The climatic variations and Brazil's different soil and drainage conditions are reflected in the breathtaking diversity of its vegetation. There are an estimated 55,000 different plant species, the highest number of any country in the world. No matter where you are in Brazil, you will be overwhelmed by the variety of beautiful flowers, flowering shrubs, bromeliads, cacti, palms and the imposing tree giants of the rainforest with their enormous roots and lofty canopies.

The Amazon Rainforest

With a total size of over 5.5 million sq km (2.1 million sq miles), the Amazon rain forest is the world's largest tropical forest. Sixty per cent of this vast ecosystem is on Brazilian soil where it covers 40 per cent of the national territory. The forest vegetation is characterised by broad-leaved evergreen trees, which depend on frequent rainfall to reach their enormous heights of up to 60 m (197 ft). The Amazon is considered the largest gene reserve in the world, with an estimated 10 per cent of all plant and animal species. In a few hectares of the Amazon rainforest, there are more species of plants and insects than in all of Europe. There are over 400 different types of hardwoods and many of them are used commercially for their timber, sap or fruit.

Due to human impact from settlements, as well as mining and logging activities, the Brazilian Amazon rainforest has lost about 14 per cent of its original area to deforestation, an area of about the size of France. Since 1978, an average of about 18,500 sq km (7,150 sq miles) of primary rainforest have been destroyed every year, with 26,000 sq km (10,000 sq miles) of deforestation in 2004 alone. The regions with the highest degree of ongoing deforestation are the states of Mato Grosso, Rondônia and Pará.

The Cerrado

The *cerrado* is the characteristic vegetation of central Brazil, where soils are sandy and nutrient-poor. It is an extensive savanna interspersed with bush forest. Tall vegetation is limited to gallery forest along rivers and ravines, where enough moisture collects to sustain abundant growth. Due to farming and settlement, the *cerrado* has suffered substantially from human impact. Only 20 per cent of the original savanna ecosystem remains today.

Pantanal

The low-lying *pantanal* is the world's largest seasonal floodplain and is part of the Paraguay River basin. It covers 150,000 sq km (57,915 sq miles) and its characteristic vegetation is extensive grasslands interspersed with shrubs and trees on higher elevations. The *pantanal* is one of Brazil's best-known ecological treasures. It is home to diverse fauna and flora, and attracts a large number of visitors every year. Among the region's most prominent inhabitants are the caimans, often seen sunbathing along the meandering river channels.

The Atlantic Rainforest

Brazil's coastal regions and adjacent mountain ranges are home to the Mata Alântica (Atlantic Rain Forest), which was once a wide and dense belt of tropical forest stretching from Rio Grande do Norte to Santa Catarina. It covered an area of

A caiman, a common denizen of Brazil's rivers.

approximately 1.2 million sq km (463,323 sq miles), about 15 per cent of Brazil's total territory. Extensive sugar cane and coffee plantations, as well as urban growth have lead to rapid deforestation and today, only about seven per cent of its original expanse remains. As a result, many animal and plant species are threatened by extinction, among them most primate species such as the muriqui, tamarin and marmoset. Predatory logging practices in the past have almost completely wiped out the once abundant brazilwood and jacaranda trees.

The Caatinga

The caatinga is a seasonal shrub forest that grows mainly in the *sertão*, the North-east's dry interior. The vegetation is well-adapted to rocky soils and periods of drought that frequently affect the region. Most of the shrubs are spindly and have very small leaves or no leaves at all. Cacti are also common in the caatinga and often grow very tall.

Pine Forest

Brazil's south, with its slightly cooler climate is home to open subtropical forests. The most prominent tree species is the araucária pine which once covered the entire highlands of the state of Paraná, Santa Catarina and Rio Grande do Sul. Due to the region's expanding agro-industry, only small pockets of araucária forest remain today.

CLIMATE

'This land is healthful and has good climes, and the people find themselves in good health and live many years.'
—Pero de Magalhães Gândavo,
Tratado da Terra do Brasil (ca. 1570)

Most of Brazil lies between the equator and the tropic of Capricorn, and is characterised by a hot and humid climate. Since Brazil is situated south of the equator (except its northernmost corner), the seasons are reversed. The Brazilian winter lasts from June through September and the summer from December through March. Brazil is divided into six different climate zones with distinct regional characteristics.

Equatorial Climate

The equatorial climate zone covers the entire Amazon river basin. It has the highest precipitation in Brazil, with annual rainfall of around 2,000 mm (79 inches), which is evenly distributed throughout the year. Belém, the capital of the state of Pará, is one of the rainiest cities in the world with over 2,500 mm (98 inches) of rain per year. Temperatures don't vary much between the coldest and warmest months. The high temperatures rarely exceed 35°C (95°F). Due to the frequent rains, the humidity in the Amazon is high, averaging around 70 per cent.

Tropical Climate

The tropical climate zone covers the southern Amazon basin and most of central Brazil, as well as the state of Maranhão. It is characterized by a distinct dry season during the winter (from June to September) with little precipitation and a rainy season in the summer with abundant rainfall of around 1,500 mm (59 inches) from December through March. The seasonal variation in temperature is low. Temperatures can reach a high of 35°C (95°F).

Atlantic Tropical Climate

The Atlantic tropical climate zone extends along the coast from the state of Rio Grande do Norte to the state of Paraná. The proximity of the ocean brings moisture all year and leads to frequent rainfall. The period of the highest rainfall is in the winter in the North-east and in the summer in the South-east. High temperatures in the summer are around 30°C (86°F), but can climb to 38°C (100°F) in Rio de Janeiro.

Semiarid Climate

The inland region of the North-east, known as the *sertão*, is Brazil's hottest and driest region. Temperatures can reach more than 38°C (100°F). Rainfall is scarce and occurs irregularly throughout the year. This region is also referred to as the *polígono da seca* (polygon of drought) because it is periodically affected by drought that can last for several years.

Highland Tropical Climate

The highland tropical climate is prevalent in regions above an elevation of 800 m (2,624 ft), mainly on the inland plateau of the south-eastern states of São Paulo and Minas Gerais. The temperature is cooler than in lower elevation and frost may occur in the winter. Average high temperatures in Belo Horizonte are around 29°C (84°F) in the summer, and the average lows in the winter are around 16°C (60°F). In São Paulo, the average high temperature in the summer is around 30°C (86°F) and the average lows in the winter are around 13°C (55°F).

Subtropical Climate

The subtropical climate zone covers Brazil's southern states of Paraná, Santa Catarina and Rio Grande do Sul. It is characterised by hot summers, reaching 30°C (86°F) and cool winters with average lows around 10°C (50°F). Temperatures in the winter can fall below freezing, but snow is rare. Rainfall occurs throughout the year.

TIME ZONES

Brazil has four time zones. The islands of the Fernando de Noronha Archipelago in the Atlantic Ocean are two hours behind Greenwich Mean Time (GMT). All of the Atlantic and central states including major cities such as São Paulo, Rio de Janeiro, Salvador, Belo Horizonte and Brasília, are three hours behind GMT. The states of Mato Grosso, Mato Grosso do Sul, Rondônia, most of Amazonas, Roraima and the western half of the state of Pará are four hours behind GMT. The state of Acre and the south-western corner of the state of Amazonas are five hours behind GMT. The central and southern states observe daylight saving time, which is in effect from October through February. Clocks go back one hour during this period.

POPULATION

Brazil is Latin America's most populous country with over 185 million inhabitants. Most of the population lives along the Atlantic coast, while inland areas are sparsely settled. The South and South-east are the most densely populated regions. They cover only 18 per cent of Brazil's territory, but account for about three quarters of the population. Due to Brazil's vast size, the population density is low.

Population Growth

Brazil's population currently grows by over two million people each year, but the growth rate has been declining for the past few decades, dropping from three per cent per year in the 1950s to currently 1.4 per cent per year.

Age Distribution

During the last 50 years, the age distribution of Brazil's population has changed significantly. In 1940, over half of Brazil's population was younger than 17 years, but by the late 1990s, this figure had fallen considerably. Projections for the year 2020 indicate that only a quarter of the population will be younger than 17 years. In contrast, the population of

senior citizens over 60 years old has been on the rise. Life expectancy has also increased, further contributing to the ageing of Brazil's population.

URBANISATION
While Brazil was predominantly a rural country until the mid 20th century, 82 per cent of Brazil's population live in cities today. Seven of the 10 largest cities saw their population double from 1970–1995. This was in part due to heavy migration from rural areas to the cities. Migration to Brazil's large cities slowed down during the 1990s and turned toward developing regions mainly in the Central West.

A Country of Immigrants
Brazil's population is a colourful blend of Amerindians, European settlers and the descendants of African slaves. More than half of Brazil's population is white, including descendants of Portuguese, German, Italian, Spanish and Polish immigrants. Widespread miscegenation has resulted in a large population of mixed ethnic origins, accounting for about 40 per cent of the population. Brazil's blacks make up about 5 per cent of the population and less than 1 per cent are minority groups such as Japanese and Amerindians. Besides the main immigrant groups from Europe, there were also settlers from the Near East, especially Syria and Lebanon, who came to Brazil between the late 19th and the mid 20th centuries. Starting in 1908, a large wave of immigrants arrived from Japan to work on the rapidly expanding coffee plantations. The city of São Paulo is today home to approximately 750,000 Japanese Brazilians known as Nikkei, who make up the largest Japanese community outside Japan.

THE PAST AND THE PRESENT
'Antes dos Portugueses descobrirem o Brasil,
o Brasil tinha descoberto a felicidade.'
(Before the Portuguese discovered Brazil,
Brazil had discovered happiness.)
—Oswald de Andrade, Manifesto Antropófago, 1928

Prehistory

Archeological finds have shown that the presence of Paleo-Indians in Brazil goes at least as far back as 9,000–11,000 years. They were mostly hunter-gatherers, but ceramic remains as well as rock art and other archeological evidence indicate that some tribal groups achieved a high level of cultural development, especially in the lower Amazon.

Prelude to the Discovery

Infante Dom Henrique o Navegador (Prince Henry the Navigator) laid the theoretical foundations for Portugal's seafaring exploits. In 1419, he began to attract scientists, astronomers, cartographers and sailors to his remote residence of Sagres (in Southern Portugal) to study navigation. In the same year, an expedition sent out by Prince Henry discovered Madeira Island, and in 1427, Portuguese sailors reached the Azores Islands. In the 1440s, his ships brought the first African slaves to Portugal, thus reviving the slave trade that had not been practiced in Europe during most of the Middle Ages. In 1488, Bartolomeu Dias sailed around the

Cape of Good Hope and in 1497, Vasco da Gama discovered the sea route to the Far East, which gave rise to Portugal's lucrative trade with that region.

In 1494, two years after Columbus' voyage of discovery, Spain and Portugal signed the treaty of Tordesillas, which regulated territorial claims in the western hemisphere between the two nations. According to the agreement, any newly discovered land would be divided into a Portuguese and a Spanish part by drawing an imaginary line from pole to pole, 370 leagues (about 1,770 km/1,100 miles) west of the Cape Verde Islands. The land east of it would belong to Portugal and the land west of it to Spain. This imaginary boundary, which appears on old maps, ran somewhere through central Brazil.

Colonial Brazil
The Discovery
The vast land we know today as Brazil was officially discovered by Europeans on 22 April, 1500. Pedro Álvares Cabral, on a trading expedition to India, had been blown off course in a storm and made a landfall in a quiet bay near today's city of Porto Seguro in the state of Bahia. The discovery of the Terra da Santa Cruz (Land of the Holy Cross), as Cabral named the new land, was reported to the king in such a casual way that some historians suspect that the Portuguese had previous knowledge of land in these latitudes.

Early Explorations
In 1501, the king of Portugal, Manuel I, sent out an expedition with the participation of Italian explorer Amerigo Vespucci to explore the newly discovered land. The expedition sailed along the coast and returned with reports about a lush and beautiful country, ferocious cannibals and a precious red dyewood. Portuguese and French trading ships soon began a lucrative trade with the native Tupinambá people along the coast, who provided the desired logs for shipment to Europe. Red dyewood was commonly known as *pau brasil* (brazilwood) at the time and the name Brasil was soon applied to the new country in general.

Colonisation

In these early years, the Portuguese focused on their lucrative trading expeditions to the Orient, and Brazil received little attention. It was not until 1530 that King João III sent out an expedition to investigate the possibility of permanent settlements in Brazil, fearing that it could fall into foreign hands. In 1532, São Vincente (on the coast near São Paulo) became the first settlement founded by the Portuguese. To encourage colonisation, João III introduced a system of hereditary captaincies, which allowed their owners to commercially exploit their possessions, as long as they saw to the development, settlement and defense of their land holdings. Fifteen such captaincies were established. In 1549, Tomé de Sousa became Brazil's first royal governor and founded the city of Salvador. He was accompanied by Jesuit missionaries who founded several important missions and maintained a strong presence in Brazil until their expulsion in 1759.

Slavery

Early colonial life in Brazil centred around sugar cane plantations established along the coast especially in the captaincies of Pernambuco and Paraíba. To cope with the work load of the expanding plantations, land owners soon depended on slaves imported from Africa. The native Amerindians were considered to be unproductive as slaves because of their susceptibility to infectious diseases and their unsatisfactory performance under forced labour.

Portugal Under Spanish Rule

After king Sebastian of Portugal died in battle in Morocco in 1578, his great uncle cardinal Henrique became king until his death in 1580. Since there was no other legitimate heir, the Spanish king Philip II assumed the Portuguese throne. Thus Portugal and Spain were linked under the Spanish crown from 1580–1640. During this time, the Portuguese began to organise *bandeiras* (flag-bearing expeditions), which explored the interior of Brazil and travelled far beyond the line of Tordesillas into Spanish territories. The expeditions' main goal was to get their hands on anything that could be sold for a profit, from Indian slaves to precious metals. Throughout the 17th and 18th centuries, the *bandeiras* continued to explore overland and navigation routes and expanded their knowledge about Brazil's vast hinterland.

Rival Colonial Powers

The Portuguese were not the only Europeans who took interest in Brazil. The French entered the brazilwood trade soon after Brazil's discovery and founded a colony in Guanabara Bay in 1554. In response, the Portuguese established the nearby settlement of Rio de Janeiro in 1565 and drove out the French two years later. Another French settlement was defeated in 1615. The Dutch also attempted to take hold of Brazil and invaded the captaincy of Pernambuco by conquering the city of Olinda in 1630. They maintained control of a small stretch of coastline and planted sugar cane, until it was ceded back to Portugal in 1654, after losing a battle. In 1680, the Portuguese crown promoted the settlement of Brazil's southern frontier to lay claims to land near the neighbouring Spanish colonies. The region north of the Rio da Prata (River Plate), which is today Uruguay, became an important centre of cattle-raising under Brazilian control.

The Gold Rush

In 1695, a member of a *bandeira* expedition found gold in a riverbed in the interior of today's state of Minas Gerais (meaning General Mines). This discovery gave rise to the first large gold rush in Brazil's history, which depopulated the coastal plantation regions and led to the first large wave of immigration from Portugal to Brazil. Mining activities picked up at a frantic pace, as more and more prospectors scoured the region for deposits of gold and diamonds. During the 18th century, nearly 1,000 tonnes of gold and three million carats of diamonds were mined in Brazil. Since the Portuguese crown charged one fifth in taxes, the colony quickly became Portugal's economic backbone. The large amounts of gold not only filled the coffers of the impoverished court, but also paid for the reconstruction of Lisbon after the devastating 1755 earthquake. The surging need for slave labour in the gold mines led to a vast increase in slave trade, and Rio de Janeiro became an important trade centre both for importing

The monument to the bandeira expeditions in São Paulo.

slaves and for shipping gold to Lisbon. In 1763, the capital of the viceroyalty of Brazil was transferred from Salvador to Rio de Janeiro. But by the late 18th century, gold production began to decline. The gold mining centres fell into decay, and Brazil's interior was deserted once again.

Uprising Against Portugal

In 1789, the first conspiracy against the Portuguese colonial government took place in the gold mining centre of Vila Rica (today's Ouro Preto). Plotted by wealthy citizens and intellectuals, this conspiracy was known as Inconfidência Mineira and was a reaction against Portugal's increasing economic exploitation of Brazil. This uprising was inspired by the ideals of the American Revolution and by French Enlightenment philosophers, but was betrayed before the revolt took place. The group's leader, Joaquim José da Silva Xavier (1746–1792), a young cavalry officer nicknamed Tiradentes (meaning tooth-puller, since he also worked as a dentist), was tried and hanged. The remaining members of the conspiracy were jailed or sent into exile.

The Portuguese Court in Brazil

In 1807, Prince Regent Dom João fled from Napoleon's invasion of Portugal and transferred his entire court to Brazil.

Soon after his arrival in Rio de Janeiro in 1808, colonial life in Brazil began to change. Dom João opened Brazil's ports to allied countries and legalised the manufacturing industry. In 1815, Brazil was promoted from the status of colony to kingdom and became part of the 'Kingdom of Portugal, the Algarve and Brazil.' In the same year, Dom João became King João VI and reluctantly returned to Portugal in 1821, in response to a mounting political crisis that seriously threatened his powers. He left his son Pedro in Brazil as prince regent.

Independence
The Brazilian Monarchy

In 1822, the Portuguese parliament attempted to reduce Brazil's status to that of a colony and requested Dom Pedro's return to Portugal. However, Dom Pedro, following the counsel of his advisors, decided that it was time for the country to stand on its own and proclaimed Brazil's independence on 7 September, 1822. To obtain Portugal's recognition of its independence, Brazil agreed to assume Portugal's debt with Great Britain to the amount of £1.3 million. Dom Pedro became Pedro I, the emperor of Brazil, but his reign was shortlived. The young country was plagued by civil unrest and external conflicts and in 1831, Pedro I was forced to abdicate in favour of his son, Dom Pedro II, who was then only five years old.

Brazil was ruled by regents for nine years until the 14-year-old Dom Pedro II assumed the throne in 1840. He remained Brazil's respected emperor until the end of the monarchy in 1889. During the half century under his rule, Brazil made large strides to become a prosperous and modern nation. The infrastructure was improved, railroads were built and banks were founded. Under the monarchy, Brazil experienced a period of relative peace and stability with only scattered regional unrest. There was only one large international conflict, known as the Paraguayan War. Brazil, Argentina and

In 1850, the Queiróz Law was passed which effectively ended the slave trade from Africa.

Uruguay (the Triple Alliance) became allies in a war against Paraguay from 1864–1870, which was provoked by Brazil's concerns over the region's hegemony. Although Brazil won the conflict, the Paraguayan War was widely unpopular in Brazil and helped raise sentiments against the monarchy.

The Rise of Coffee

Traditionally based on sugar, cotton and mining, Brazil's economy experienced a drastic change during the 19th century, due to increased coffee production. The Paraíba valley, situated in the mountains between Rio de Janeiro and São Paulo became the country's first large coffee growing region. At the end of the 18th century, Brazil began to export coffee. The 'Green Wave', as the rapid coffee expansion was called, spread all over the states of Rio de Janeiro, São Paulo, Minas Gerais and Espírito Santo. In 1867, a railway from São Paulo to the coffee port of Santos was completed, and a network of railways soon linked the various coffee growing regions of the state of São Paulo. These links led to a vast increase in coffee production and export. Coffee surpassed sugar as the main export crop and, by 1890, coffee accounted for 61 per cent of Brazil's total exports.

Abolition of Slavery

Brazil's monarchy was mainly supported by wealthy coffee plantation owners, but starting in the mid 19th century, the Brazilian public began to favour the transition to a republican form of government. The increasingly influential urban bourgeoisie were especially adamant supporters of the republican movement. In 1888, Princess Isabel, the emperor's daughter, acting as regent, signed the Lei Áurea (Golden Law) that finally abolished slavery in Brazil. But by doing so, she acted against the monarchy's remaining supporters who depended on slaves to work in their coffee plantations. In response, the plantation owners withdrew their support. It was now only a matter of time before the republican movement would gain the upper hand.

The Brazilian Republic
End of the Monarchy

On 15 November, 1889, encouraged by widespread public support, the army revolted and demanded Dom Pedro's resignation. The ageing monarch offered no resistance, and after he resigned the royal family went into exile to France. In 1891, the new government drafted a Republican constitution modelled after the United States, which included the division of church and state. A presidential system was established with a bicameral congress and an independent supreme court. The old provinces were transformed into states.

Influenced by the positivistic doctrines of French philosopher Auguste Comte, the new government's ideal was to modernise Brazil. Comte's slogan: 'Order and Progress' was included in Brazil's new flag. Large international loans were obtained and used to build ports, roads, railways, sanitation systems and to modernise the capital of Rio de Janeiro. Starting in the first decades of the 20th century, the large profits from the coffee trade were invested in the development of Brazil's manufacturing industry in São Paulo.

The Canudos Campaign

One of the most serious ideological challenges to the young republic came from a small religious community in the North-east. The messianic religious leader of the group, Antônio Conselheiro (the Counselor) had founded a small settlement known as Canudos, promising his followers a better life. But the community soon faced the disapproval of both the church and the government. Canudos was declared a national enemy because of its rejection of Brazil's new republican principles. The military campaign against the religious community lasted from 1893–1897, and the army suffered several defeats before destroying the settlement after a long siege.

Politics of Coffee With Milk

One of the most noticeable characteristics of the first republic was an excessive federalism that led to increased political

conflicts between states. Brazil's most powerful states took advantage of the constitutional rights to promote their own interests. This period is known as Política de Café Com Leite (Politics of Coffee With Milk), since the two most powerful states, São Paulo (a coffee-based economy) and Minas Gerais (a dairy state) took turns nominating presidential candidates who were then always elected. In 1929, President Washington Luis from São Paulo broke with this tradition when he failed to name a candidate from Minas Gerais as his successor. Leaders from Minas Gerais and the influential state of Rio Grande do Sul protested and nominated Getúlio Vargas, the governor of Rio Grande do Sul, as their own candidate.

The New Republic (1930–1937)

When the candidate from São Paulo, Júlio Prestes, won the presidential election in November 1930, Vargas mobilised the military, marched to Rio de Janeiro and took power. He dissolved the national congress, as well as state and municipal legislatures. He also replaced the state governors with appointed officials, which greatly diminished the power of the states and the old oligarchies that had controlled Brazil since 1889. Vargas instituted a more centralised government and increased the powers of the federal government. Mines, communications and transportation systems were nationalised, and the army assumed a new role as keeper of internal order. During the New Republic era, Vargas had to face serious economic problems caused by the world economic crisis, which led to Brazil's first moratorium on its international debt in 1931. A new constitution was drafted in 1934, giving women the right to vote. In the same year, Vargas was elected president by indirect vote.

The Estado Novo (1937–1945)

In November 1937, before Vargas completed his presidential term and new elections could be held, he declared a state of emergency in response to increased civil unrest and the alleged threat of a communist revolution. Vargas shut down the congress and assumed extraordinary powers to govern by decree. This marked the beginning of Vargas' Estado Novo (New State) dictatorship.

During the Estado Novo, strikes were prohibited and the newly established propaganda ministry censured the press. Opponents of the regime were arrested and tortured. Intellectuals were forced into exile. Vargas focused on expanding the domestic industry to replace expensive imports of manufactured goods with domestic products.

A Glimpse of Democracy

In 1945, political pressure from the army increased in favour of a return to democracy. Vargas agreed to hold presidential elections and General Eurico Gaspar Dutra, Vargas's minister of the army, won. A new democratic constitution was drafted, and Brazil gradually returned to more liberal economic policies with less state intervention. In 1950, Vargas was back on the political stage and won the presidential elections, but from the outset, he was unable to control the country's rising economic problems and mounting civil unrest. When the armed forces officially requested his resignation, Vargas feared a military coup against him and committed suicide.

The Capital of Hope

In 1955, Juscelino Kubitschek was elected president and promised his fellow Brazilians 50 years of progress in five.

The cathedral in Brasília, designed by Oscar Niemeyer.

His goal was high economic growth in the most important industry sectors. Kubitschek established the national automobile industry by creating tax incentives for foreign companies. He also encouraged increased oil production and helped establish Brazil's petrochemical industry. During his administration, Brazil's Gross Domestic Product (GDP) grew an average of seven per cent per year.

President Kubitschek is best-known for the construction of the new capital Brasília. This planned city, designed by urban planner Lúcio Costa and architect Oscar Niemeyer became known as the 'capital of hope', as Brazilians were looking forward to an era of increased prosperity. The new capital was inaugurated in April 1960 after four years of feverish construction. However, instead of a better life for Brazilians, the huge debt incurred by the construction of the new capital brought about a period of recession and high inflation.

Political Turmoil

In 1960, Jânio Quadros won the presidential elections but unexpectedly resigned seven months later. Before Vice President João Goulart, a communist sympathiser, took office, the national congress changed the form of government from a presidential to a parliamentary system to limit the president's power. But the parliamentary system was rejected by voters in a 1963 plebiscite, and Goulart's full presidential powers were restored. Goulart had to deal with a severe economic crisis marked by high inflation, massive strikes and civil unrest. On 31 March, 1964 before the end of his presidential term, the armed forces overthrew Goulart's government and took power.

Military Rule

General Castelo Branco became the first military president. His government sought to stabilise the economy and modernise Brazilian capitalism. To achieve internal stability, they made extensive amendments to the constitution and introduced a series of 'Institutional Acts' that limited civil liberties. Strikes were outlawed, and direct presidential elections were replaced by indirect elections in the congress. When resistance against the military increased and opposition movements gained strength, they reacted by extinguishing political parties. In December 1967, President Artur da Costa e Silva closed down the congress and outlawed direct regional elections. In 1969, Emílio Garrastazu Médici became president. This period is known as the dark years of the military rule, and Brazilians suffered from the severest repression in the history of their country. The media were censured, disregard for human rights was rampant, and political opponents were frequently tortured. At the same time, Brazil's economy grew at one of the highest rates in the world and reached a record high in 1973. Inflation was also contained, and foreign firms began to invest in the rapidly growing economy.

General Geisel, who succeeded Médici as president in 1974, began a gradual restoration of civil liberties. He suspended the censorship of the press and gave political parties access to television and radio. In 1979, President Figueiredo took office. This period was marked by the beginning of a political opening (known as *abertura*) and restoration of full civil rights. A general amnesty for political exiles was enacted in 1979. In 1982, Brazil held the first direct elections for state governors since 1965.

End of Military Rule

Despite an immensely popular campaign for direct presidential elections in 1984, the national congress did not yet approve them. Instead, Tancredo Neves, a candidate of the opposition coalition, was chosen by an electoral college to be the first civilian president in 21 years. When he died shortly before taking office, Vice President José Sarney became president. However, Brazil's transition to democracy was plagued by economic problems. High international interest rates and low prices for Brazil's export commodities caused a severe debt crisis. Inflation reached 233 per cent in 1985 and the economy showed negative growth rates. In 1986, the government declared a moratorium on its foreign debt. In the midst of this extended economic crisis, the congress approved a new civilian constitution in 1988.

After the election of Fernando Collor in 1989 in the first free presidential elections since 1960, the new government gradually opened Brazil's economy to international trade and began to privatise government-owned companies. Collor had promised Brazilians low inflation and economic growth, but he could not keep his promise. His economic stabilisation plans failed, and he was impeached in 1992 on charges of corruption. Vice President Itamar Franco assumed the presidency to complete Collor's presidential term. Several economic stabilisation plans during this period failed, and inflation continued to be high, reaching an astronomical 2,447 per cent in 1993.

On the Way to Stability

In July 1994, Itamar Franco's finance minister, Fernando Henrique Cardoso, a sociologist and intellectual, who had spent many years in exile during the military government, implemented a new economic reform plan to cut inflation and promote economic growth. The new currency, real (BRL), was pegged to the dollar, and inflation was controlled through high interest rates and by freezing wages. Several government reforms were included in the stabilisation programme, among them budget cuts, privatisations and the continued opening of Brazil to foreign markets. As a result of these reforms, inflation dropped and the economy began to show signs of recovery.

The success of this economic plan helped Cardoso win the presidential elections in 1994. President Cardoso continued with his reform plan, kept government spending low, lowered trade tariffs and privatised the majority of government companies, among them telecommunications, railways, highways, ports and several banks. Cardoso was the first elected president since Kubitschek in 1962 to finish a term in office. He was elected for a second term in October 1998, but paralysed by conflicts among his coalition parties, high-level scandals and a severe energy crisis, his second term was marked by a lack of political clout and support to carry out the necessary reforms and programmes he had promised voters.

In 2002, Luiz Inácio Lula da Silva, a man of modest background and founder of the PT-Partido dos Trabalhadores (Brazilian Workers Party), won in the run-off election for president. Despite initial concerns by his opponents, he vowed to uphold Brazil's economic policy and commitment to honouring its foreign debt. Forced to negotiate coalitions with several other parties, Lula's political programmes of improving the lives of the poor were hampered from the start, but some progress was nonetheless achieved, namely his campaign to fight hunger.

After near stagnant economic growth in 2003, the economy began to recover, encouraged by government reforms of the tax and pension systems. The second half of Lula's term was marked on one hand by a pay-off scandal involving his party, and on the other hand by robust economic growth, a stable currency and a large trade and budget surplus.

GOVERNMENT AND POLITICAL SYSTEM
'Cada povo tem o governo que merece.'
(Every nation has the government it deserves.)
—Brazilian saying

Brazil is a federative presidential republic consisting of 26 states and the federal district with the capital Brasília. States are governed by a governor and state deputies (there are no state senators) who are elected and hold office for a term of four years. There are a total of 5,560 municipalities in Brazil, which are political districts that include cities and surrounding rural areas. They are governed by a mayor and the city council, who are also elected once every four years. The federal government is divided into three independent powers consisting of the executive, legislative and judiciary branch.

The Executive Branch

The executive branch is headed by the president of the republic who is both the chief-of-state and head of the government. Both president and vice president are elected by popular vote for a four-year term. The cabinet ministers are appointed by the elected president and report directly to him. A 1997 amendment to the constitution allows the president and vice president to run for a second consecutive term.

The Legislature

The legislature, called Congresso Nacional (National Congress), consists of two chambers, the Senado Federal (Federal Senate) and the Câmara dos Deputados (Chamber of Deputies). The senate has 81 seats (3 for each state and Federal district) and its members are elected for eight years. The Chamber of Deputies has 513 seats which are elected every four years.

The Judiciary

The Judiciary consists of the Supremo Tribunal Federal (Federal Supreme Court), the Superior Tribunal de Justiça (Superior Court of Justice), regional courts and several other courts with different jurisdictions. The Federal Supreme Court has its seat in Brasília and consists of 11 judges, who are appointed for life by the president and approved by the Senate.

The Voting System

Voting is mandatory for all literate citizens between the ages of 18 and 70. It is optional for citizens aged between 16 and

17, senior citizens above 70 and all illiterates regardless of age. In a presidential, gubernatorial or mayoral election, a candidate has to gain the absolute majority of votes to win. If no candidate receives over 50 per cent of the votes, the two candidates with the highest votes compete in a runoff election held 20 days later.

A Multitude of Parties

Since the two-party system of the military government was abandoned in 1979, an excessive number of political parties have emerged, often forcing politicians to negotiate coalitions with smaller opposition parties. Brazil's largest political parties represented in the national congress are the centrist PMDB (Partido do Movimento Democrático Brasileiro, Brazilian Democratic Movement Party), which was the officially approved opposition party during the military regime, the centre right PFL (Partido da Frente Liberal, Liberal Front Party), the centre-left PSDB (Partido da Social-Democracia Brasileiro, Brazilian Social Democracy Party), the right-wing PP (Partido Progressista, Progressive Party), the left-wing PT (Partido dos Trabalhadores, Worker's Party), which is the party of president Lula, the PTB (Partido Trabalhista Brasileiro, Brazilian Labor Party) and the centre-left, PDT (Partido Democrático Trabalhista, Democratic Labor Party).

THE ECONOMY

'O Brasil é uma grande mina de ouro,
que só os brasileiros ainda não descobriram.'
(Brazil is a large gold mine that
only the Brazilians have not yet discovered.)
—Brazilian saying

The Struggle for Economic Stability

After countless reform plans, the introduction of the *plano real* in 1994 put Brazil on a path to more sustained stability and growth. Thanks to the effectiveness of the new stabilisation programme, inflation dropped drastically and reached a 40-year low in 1998. But the strict fiscal and monetary policy came at the price of high interest rates, slow economic growth and growing unemployment, which still continue to affect Brazil in the first decade of the new millennium. Still, Brazil's economy has shown a surprising resilience both against global and internal crises and continues on a relatively stable path.

Foreign Debt

One of Brazil's greatest economic challenges is the country's exorbitant foreign debt, which grew from US$100 billion in 1994 to US$221 billion in 2003. Brazil has the highest debt of any developing nation, ranking second in the world only behind the US. Because of this large debt burden, Brazil remains vulnerable to international crises and dependent on international loans. But thanks to a strict fiscal policy and a growing trade surplus, Brazil has been able to meet its foreign obligations and remains in good standing with international lenders.

Gross Domestic Product (GDP)

Brazil is Latin America's largest economy and ranks among the world's twelve largest economies, with a GDP of US$605 billion in 2004. But due to the country's unequal income distribution, this amounts to a low US$3,400 per capita per year. Brazil's regional distribution of wealth is also very unequal. The wealthy south-eastern and southern states produce 75 per cent of the entire country's GDP. In 2002, industrial production accounted for 38 per cent of the GDP, while the service sector accounted for 54 per cent and agriculture for 8 per cent.

Industry

Until the 1950s, Brazil's economy was mainly based on exports of agricultural products and raw materials. In the past 50 years, however, the manufacturing and service industries have grown rapidly. Today, Brazil's large industrial complex produces a variety of goods such as textiles, shoes, chemicals, cement, tin, steel, airplanes, motor vehicles, machinery and equipment. The state of São Paulo alone is responsible for half of Brazil's industrial output.

An old metaphor about São Paulo's industrial strength still holds true. It was often described as the locomotive of Brazil's economy, pulling a number of empty cars (the other states) behind it.

Agriculture

Agriculture has undergone significant changes during the 20th century. Throughout most of Brazil's history, agriculture was based on monoculture, beginning with cane sugar and then coffee. But in the past few decades, the agricultural sector has diversified significantly. Brazil is still the world's largest producer of coffee and cane sugar, but it is now also among the leading producers of soybeans, kidney beans, corn, cocoa and oranges. Brazil also has the world's second largest cattle herd and is a large producer of beef.

Natural Resources

Brazil has vast natural resources that make it one of the world's wealthiest nations in minerals and ores. There are

The former gold mining town Ouro Preto is today a UNESCO World Heritage Site.

large deposits of bauxite, gold, iron ore, manganese, nickel, phosphates, platinum, potassium, cassiterite, graphite, chrome and uranium, and the country also has large oil and natural gas fields, and produces about half of its oil and gas needs. Brazil also produces a large amount of gems, such as emeralds, aquamarines, amethysts, topazes and diamonds. Timber is also an economically important resource, especially in the Amazon region.

Foreign Investment
As the real (BRL) continues to be relatively stable with single-digit inflation, more and more multinational corporations and investors are attracted by a favourable economic climate and the potential of Brazil's enormous consumer market. Direct foreign investments have risen sharply since the introduction of the real (BRL) in 1994. In 2000, the last year of large-scale privatisations, direct foreign investments amounted to US$33 billion, dropping to US$10 billion in 2003.

Foreign Trade
Since Brazil entered the global market in the 1990s, exports have increased almost twofold. Over 70 per cent of these exports are manufactured goods such as motor vehicles,

electrical and electronic equipment, chemical products, leather products and textiles. Brazil is among the world's largest exporters of coffee, soybeans, cocoa, sugar, orange juice, beef and tobacco. Other agricultural products for export are citrus fruits, wheat, corn, rice, Brazil nuts, cashews and rubber. With the drastic reduction of import tariffs and trade barriers, imports rose dramatically and led to a trade deficit. The devaluation of the Brazilian currency in 1999 helped revert this trend and create a trade surplus, reaching a record high of US$34 billion in 2004.

In 1991, Brazil formed the Southern Common Market (MERCOSUL) with Argentina, Paraguay and Uruguay, a trade agreement that reduces tariffs and promotes the free movement of labour, capital and services. The MERCOSUL accounts for about 10 per cent of Brazil's total exports. The US, countries of the European Union and Japan are Brazil's largest overseas trade partners.

A COLOURFUL BLEND OF FAITHS

'Deus é brasileiro'.
(God is Brazilian.)
—Brazilian expression

Brazilians are a deeply spiritual people with a penchant for the mystical and supernatural. This religious attitude pervades all social groups and is not limited to organised religion alone. Amerindian and African cults, messianic and mystical faiths, Ufology, folk beliefs and superstitions are all expressions of a deep-rooted religious attitude. Most Brazilians believe that supernatural powers exist and that they interfere with their daily lives.

CATHOLICISM

Eighty per cent of Brazil's population are members of the Catholic church. This makes Brazil the world's largest Catholic country. Even though the majority does not actively practice their faith, most have a loose connection to the church through the many festivals and holidays, as well as religious rites such as baptism and marriage.

The Cult of Saints

Pouco padre, pouca missa e muita festa (few priests, few masses, but a lot of feasts) is a common saying that describes the role of the Catholic church in Brazil's history. Due to the country's enormous size and insufficient number of priests, it became the responsibility of *irmandades* (lay brotherhoods and sisterhoods) to care for the spiritual needs of the population. These religious associations united the members of one profession, class or even race, and were responsible for the organisation of religious festivals and processions devoted to their patron saint. This practice gave rise to a widespread cult of saints, to be worshipped as helpers in times of need. Festivals in honour of saints are popular all over the country.

Brazilians find myriad ways to ask a saint for help, and these rituals do not always follow the catechism. Folk beliefs and superstitious practices often play an important role in daily interactions with saints. Most saints have special powers in one or several specific areas of life. São João (St John) and São Pedro (St Peter) are known to help lovers, Santo Antônio (St Anthony) is the helper of women in search of a husband and Nossa Senhora das Dores (Our Lady of Sorrows) protects women in child birth. According to folk belief, saints sometimes need to be forced to help believers. For example, a figure of St Anthony is buried upside down in the ground or submerged in a well until he has helped the maiden in question find a husband.

Personal Expressions of Faith

The most common way of asking a saint for help is to make a vow. If the saint intercedes, the believers pay their vows. The most common vows include prayers, donations to the church, lighting candles, as well as making pilgrimages to distant sanctuaries. Pilgrimages can be made at any time, but they are often planned to coincide with religious festivals. Millions travel to Brazil's major sanctuaries every year to participate in the festivities in honour of the saint they made a promise to. Many carry votive offerings to the site of their pilgrimage. These can be photographs, replicas of healed body parts or other objects to express gratitude to the saint. Special candle holders with hundreds of votive candles can be found at every sanctuary, lit by the faithful in gratitude and devotion.

Several other ways exist to receive help from saints. Outside the church of Nosso Senhor do Bonfim in Salvador, for example, a variety of coloured ribbons are available for sale. They are tied around the wrist with three knots and entitle the bearer to three wishes. When the ribbon naturally wears out and breaks, so the saying goes, one's wishes will come true, but only if the ribbon was received as a gift. These ribbons, known as *fitas*, are a popular souvenir and tourists and pilgrims take them home for friends and family. They are also available in Juazeiro do Norte and other popular pilgrimage sites. Another way for believers to gain three wishes, according to popular tradition, is to visit a church they had never been to before.

Many Brazilians also wear crucifixes or pendants with images of saints for protection against evil and other purposes. A very popular charm, especially in the North-east, is the *escapulário*. It is a pendant with two images of Nossa Senhora do Carmo, one worn in the front and one

Statue of Christ the Redeemer on Corcovado, Rio de Janeiro.

in the back. This amulet is said to protect the bearer and bring salvation.

Liberation Theology

In the 1960s, a new movement known as *teologia da libertação* (liberation theology) began to spread in Latin America in response to the widespread misery of the population. Archbishop Hélder Câmara of Recife was the most outspoken supporter of this movement in Brazil. Liberation theology promoted a radical interpretation of the Gospel and sympathised with the Marxist theory of class struggle. The movement attracted an estimated one to two million followers to its 'ecclesiastic base communities' where people gathered to read and interpret the Bible. The leftist teaching and social Christian agenda however, were opposed by Pope John Paul II, who reduced the power of influential bishops who sympathised with liberation theology. Religious leaders who advocated liberation theology also faced persecution by the military government, which vehemently opposed the movement. Starting in the 1980s, liberation theology began to succumb to its opponents and was further weakened by the rise of Pentecostal and evangelical churches in Brazil.

Charismatic Renewal
In response to liberation theology, the charismatic renewal began to take hold in the Catholic church in the late 1960s. The movement emphasises the acts of the Holy Spirit in the lives of the believers and includes singing and praising as an important element of worship.

Catholic Festivals
Most Catholic holidays are commemorated with processions, masses and celebrations. In addition to the universal Catholic holidays, there are many regional festivals and pilgrimages in honour of local patron saints. Some of them have become known on a national scale and attract millions of believers every year.

Nossa Senhora Aparecida
Brazil's most popular religious festival is celebrated on 12 October, in honour of Nossa Senhora Aparecida (Our Lady Aparecida), Brazil's patron saint. In 1717, the broken ceramic figure of a black Madonna appeared in a fisherman's net in the Paraíba River and the day's catch turned out to be miraculously large. The saint's powers soon became widely known and the sanctuary in the small town of Aparecida do Norte between Rio de Janeiro and São Paulo, is today Brazil's largest pilgrimage site with more than three million visitors every year.

Círio de Nazaré
Among Brazil's largest Catholic festivals is the Círio de Nazaré in Belém. It attracts 1.5 million people and lasts two full

weeks starting on the second Sunday in October. In 1700, the statue of a Madonna was found in a river in the town of Belém in Brazil's northern state of Pará. When miracles began to occur, people recognised the powers of the saint and built a church to honour her. The procession of the statue of Our Lady of Nazaré, the festival's main attraction, has been held every year since 1793. During this event, the image of Our Lady sits on a float connected to a long rope pulled by the pilgrims. They believe that whoever pulls on the rope will have their wishes and prayers fulfilled. The procession takes place at night, and the pilgrims carry torches and large wax candles, known as *círios*.

Padre Cícero

One of the most important contemporary expressions of folk religion is the cult of Padre Cicero Romão Batista (1844–1934), a priest from Juazeiro do Norte in the state of Ceará. It is said that in 1889, the wine during a holy communion held by Padre Cícero turned into blood. The news spread quickly throughout the region, and miracle cures were attributed to him. The alleged miracle was soon discredited by the Catholic church, and Padre Cícero was excommunicated, but he continues to be venerated as a saint-like figure until today.

Figurines of Padre Cicero in Juazeiro do Norte.

Throughout the year, but especially on religious holidays, pilgrims from all over Brazil flock to his tomb and climb the hill where a large statue of the priest stands. An impressive collection of ex-votos attest to the large number of believers who were allegedly helped by Padre Cícero. Other important pilgrimage centres are Bom Jesus da Lapa in the interior of the state of Bahia, Nosso Senhor do Bonfim in Salvador and São Francisco das Chagas in Canindé (state of Ceará).

PROTESTANT AND EVANGELICAL CHURCHES

Throughout Brazil's colonial history, the Catholic church was the one and only official church. It was not until after Brazil's independence that the first Protestant churches were established, among them the Lutheran church, which was introduced by German immigrants in 1823. Other Christian congregations came after the proclamation of the republic and the separation of church and state in 1891. The Assembly of God was introduced by American missionaries around 1910, and is Brazil's oldest and largest Pentecostal sect.

Starting in the 1920s, other protestant churches began to establish themselves in Brazil. Several Pentecostal churches were formed during the 1950s and 1960s, but it was not until the 1980s that evangelical movements became a national phenomenon with a huge following. These churches are especially popular among the poor, who are attracted by a simple theology of hope and change, and a supportive community of believers. The most influential and fastest growing of the new evangelical movements is the Igreja Universal do Reino de Deus (Universal Church of the Kingdom of God). It was founded in 1977 by self-proclaimed Bishop Edir Macedo, a former lottery sales clerk. Today, an estimated 15–20 per cent of Brazil's population attend Protestant and evangelical churches.

SYNCRETISM

Syncretism is a widespread form of religious expression in Brazil and is part of several popular cults. It is a fusion of elements from shamanic beliefs, spiritism, as well as African and Catholic traditions. The degree of fusion of different religious beliefs can vary greatly between the various cults. Candomblé for example, has few Christian elements and is almost purely of African origin. The similarities between Candomblé and Catholicism are mostly limited to the Christian names under which the *orixás* (spirits) are also known. Umbanda on the other hand, is more syncretic and recognises the Candomblé *orixás* and Catholic saints, in addition to elements of Amerindian cults and European spiritistic traditions.

Syncretism in Brazil finds its main expression in popular folk religion, where Catholic saints merge with *orixás* and become powerful deities that are approached in time of need.

Pagador de Promessa

The film *Pagador de Promessa (To Pay Vows*, Anselmo Duarte, 1962), based on a play by Gomes Dias, is a compelling tale about such syncretic folk beliefs. A peasant pays a vow to St Barbara by carrying a life-size cross to a distant sanctuary. When the priest at that church finds out that the man made the promise to St Barbara at a Candomblé ceremony where she is known as Iansã, he refuses to let the peasant enter the church to fulfill his promise. The pilgrim insists that Iansã and St Barbara are identical, and he pledges to pay the vow he made to her. Regarded as a devil-worshipper by the church, a revolutionary by the press, and a troublemaker by the police, the peasant suffers his own stations of the cross in the hands of Brazil's religious and secular authorities.

CANDOMBLÉ

Candomblé is an organised cult that takes its roots in the African spiritistic religions of the Bantu and Yoruba peoples. Since African religions and Catholicism have similarities in their veneration for a supreme being and saints or spirits as intermediaries, African religions were only superficially changed by contact with the Catholic church. Most African gods assumed a second identity under the name of a Catholic saint while maintaining their African characteristics.

Contact with the Spirit World

Candomblé is based on the belief in a supreme being called Olorum, and spirits known as *orixás*. The cult is widespread among the black population of Brazil's North-east, mainly in Bahia, Sergipe and Pernambuco (where it is known as Xangô). Its main component are highly structured and complex feasts with sacred dishes, dances, drumming and sacrificial ceremonies. The objective of Candomblé rituals is to establish contact with the orixás who can help in illness and other needs. The spirits enter the bodies of the worshippers who then fall into a trance. The rituals and ceremonies are held at *terreiros* (Candomblé places of worship) and take place under the spiritual guidance of an elder who can either be a woman (known as *ialorixá* or *mãe de santo*—mother of saint) or a man (known as *babalorixá* or *pai de santo*—father of saint).

The Candomblé Pantheon

The Candomblé pantheon is made up of a large number of *orixás*. The Candomblé of Bahia for example, worships 27 different *orixás*, most of whom have Christian names as well. Each worshipper has one of the *orixás* as a guiding spirit, which they honour by commemorating the *orixá's* festive days, dressing in its favourite colours, and making offerings of its favourite food. Among the most important *orixás* are:

- Exu—The messenger of the gods who also presents the wishes of humans to the *orixás*; the lord of crossroads; erroneously associated with demons or the devil.
- Iansã—The goddess of love and death; also the goddess of storms and the wind; associated with St Barbara; her festival coincides with festivals of St Barbara on 4 December.
- Iemanjá—The goddess of the sea; wife of Oxalá and mother of all *orixás*. Iemanjá is associated with the Holy Virgin.
- Ogum—The god of war, of iron and the sword; the protector of artisans; associated with St George, the dragon slayer or St Anthony.

Dancing Baianas during a procession in Salvador.

- Olorum—The creator of the cosmos; the supreme deity above the *orixás*.
- Omolú—The most feared *orixá*; he rules over health and illness; associated with St Lazarus who rose from the dead.
- Oxalá (also known as Obatalá)—The father of the *orixás* and the personification of heaven; associated with Jesus and Nosso Senhor do Bonfim (Our Lord of the Happy Ending).
- Xangô—The god of fire, lightning and thunder; associated with St Hieronymus, St Peter or St John the Baptist; his festival is celebrated on 30 September.

Candomblé Festivals

Many popular festivals in Brazil are associated with the deities of Candomblé. Among the most popular celebrations of Candomblé, as well as Umbanda, is the Festa de Iemanjá, (Festival of Iemanjá), celebrated on 1 January in Rio de Janeiro. This celebration attracts over a million people to Copacabana beach who make offerings to Iemanjá, the goddess of the sea. A similar festival is celebrated in Salvador on 2 February. The Lavagem do Bonfim (Washing of Bonfim), another popular Candomblé festival, takes place on the second Thursday in January in Salvador. It is a long procession through the city, which ends with the symbolical washing of the steps in front of the church of Nosso Senhor do Bonfim (Our Lord of the Happy Ending). This church, dedicated to the protector of fishermen and sailors, is also a Candomblé sanctuary and is dedicated to Oxalá. There are several other Candomblé festivals, most of which coincide with Catholic holidays.

KARDECISM (SPIRITISM)

Kardecism was founded in France, in the 19th century by a spiritistic medium, Allan Kardec (1804–1869). It is a synthesis of philosophy, science and spiritistic religion, and was well-received in Brazil by the educated classes. It is based on the idea of reincarnation and the ability to communicate with spirits. The seances are simple ceremonies held in dark rooms. No special training or initiation is required of the cult's members. Francisco Cândido Xavier, also known as Chico Xavier, was one of the best-known figures of Brazilian spiritism. Charity is an important element of Kardecism, based on the principle of karma. According to this doctrine, every good or bad action has an influence on an individual's spiritual evolution toward a higher level of existence. Charity is therefore an important element of spiritism and many spiritistic centers have child-care facilities, clinics, food banks or asylums that benefit the population at large. Kardecism has today several million members all over Brazil.

UMBANDA

Umbanda, also known as *magia branca* (white magic), is a spiritistic religion that evolved in the 1920s and 1930s in Rio de Janeiro. It is the most typical of Brazil's syncretic religions, since it combines elements of Catholicism, Kardecism and African religions. The Umbanda pantheon is divided into seven hierarchical lines presided by an *orixá* or Catholic saint. A *congá*, an Umbanda altar is commonly adorned with images of Christian, Amerindian and African deities, revealing the complexity of the religion. Umbanda members dress in white for their ceremonies which take place in a circle and include dance and rhythmic music accompanied by drums. Spiritistic mediums are possessed by their guiding spirits and become their instruments under the guidance of spiritual leaders known (just as in Candomblé) as *pai* or *mãe de santo*. Umbanda leaders counsel their followers to protect them from mystical attacks, help them solve problems of everyday life and identify sources of evil and misfortune.

New Year's Eve is an important celebration for Umbanda members. They build altars along Copacabana beach in Rio de Janeiro in honour of Iemanjá, the African goddess of the sea. Small paper boats containing wishes are floated out to sea. It is believed that if the tide takes the boat out, the wishes will be fulfilled. But if the boat is returned to shore the next day, the wishes will remain unfulfilled.

WITCHCRAFT

In Brazil, *fetiçaria* (witchcraft) contains strong African elements as well as indigenous shamanic influences. It is known under several names such as *magia preta* (black magic), *quimbanda*, or *macumba*. Until only a few generations ago, Afro-Brazilian cults were pejoratively called *macumba* and considered witchcraft by white Brazilians. But neither Candomblé nor Umbanda congregations commonly practice witchcraft. They are oriented toward a positive and benevolent intervention of the spirits, whereas witchcraft is intended to cast spells on people and bring harm to them through certain rituals and animal sacrifices.

SHAMANISM

Pajelança (shamanism) is still widely practiced by Brazil's indigenous tribes today. The *Pajés* (shamans) are also consulted by the population at large, especially in the rural Amazon and other regions with strong indigenous influence. To obtain the requested help, shamans often rely on hallucinogenic substances to enter into a trance and contact the spirit world. Shamans also act as witch doctors as an alternative to modern medicine or when medical help is not available. They give spiritual advice and apply herbs or compresses to extract evil spirits and also to encourage healing.

OTHER RELIGIOUS MOVEMENTS
The Dawn of a New Civilisation

In 1883, the Italian missionary Friar João Bosco had a dream about a promised land where milk and honey would flow, a new civilisation whose capital would be situated near a lake and located between the 15th and 20th degree of southern latitude. When Brasília was built in the late 1950s not far from the location predicted by Dom Bosco, many believed that his prophesy was coming true. Brasília has since gained the spiritual name of 'the capital of the third millennium', and many cults have formed in the vicinity, awaiting the dawn of a new age. Among the better known is the Vale do Amanhecer (Valley of Dawn), founded in 1959 by spiritualist Tia Neiva (Aunt Neiva) and her husband Mario Sassi. They see themselves as descendants of extraterrestrials and believe that a new civilisation will develop in the third millennium. The cult describes itself more as philosophical than religious and combines science with the insights of mediums. Alleged sightings of UFOs in the region have also contributed to the cult's popularity and Ufology has become a widespread popular science.

Brasília's best-known religious centre is the Templo da Boa Vontade (Temple of Goodwill), which was inaugurated in 1989. It houses the headquarters of the Religião do Terceiro Milênio (Religion of the Third Millennium) founded in 1949. The temple's measurements and proportions are based on the number seven, believed to be the number of perfection. On the top of the temple which is a seven-sided pyramid, rests a 21kg (46 lbs) quartz crystal, considered to be the largest in the world. The religion is a union of oriental mysticism and occidental pragmatism, and is based on universal love and an ecumenical spirit. It promotes the unification of all religions and combines, according to founder Alziro Zarur, 'all of science, all of philosophy, all of politics, and all of morality ... '

The Use of Ayahuasca

There are several religious and spiritual movements that use a hallucinogenic tea made from a vine known as *ayahuasca* (vine of the soul), which is also used in indigenous religious ceremonies. The tea is ingested during ceremonies and helps believers gain clarity and spiritual insights on their path to becoming better human beings.

The oldest of these movements is the cult of Santo Daime, founded by Raimundo Irineu Serra (also known as Mestre Irineu) in the Amazon state of Acre in the 1930s. A similar movement, now popular all over Brazil, is the União do Vegetal (UDV), founded by Mestre Gabriel in 1961. It was not until 1986 that Ayahuasca was legalised in Brazil for religious and ceremonial purposes.

> Religious groups such as Jehovah's Witnesses, the Church of Jesus Christ of Latter-day Saints (Mormons), the Seventh Day Adventists, and the Moon Sect are also active in Brazil.

Mythology

Folk beliefs and mythologies have dwelled in the Brazilian imagination for centuries. Some of them still survive today in isolated rural areas, where the influence of television and the global consumer culture are less noticeable, and where people lead simple lives that have remained unchanged for decades or even centuries. Although Portuguese and Catholic traditions have greatly influenced Brazilian folklore, many myths can be traced to indigenous and African origins.

The forest spirit, Curupira, is one of Brazil's best-known mythological figures from Tupi-Guarani mythology. He is a small man-like creature with backward-turned feet. Curupira protects the forest animals and lures hunters deep into the forest until they are lost.

Caipora, another forest spirit, is also part of Tupi-Guarani myths. The name means 'forest dweller' and its appearance varies with different regional folk traditions. It is generally described as a one-legged woman or man, often riding a wild boar.

Matitaperê, also known as Matintaperera, Saci-pererê and by several other names, is another popular creature of Brazilian folklore. It is described as a small one-legged black boy with a pipe who follows people at night and plays pranks on them.

Iara is a female forest creature from Tupi-Guarani mythology. Iara, who is also known as *boiaçu* (big snake), was originally a water snake, but under the influence of European mythology, has evolved into a mermaid over time. Iara lives in rivers and lakes and she is also referred to as *mãe d'água* (mother of the water).

Boiúna or Cobra Grande (large snake) is the most feared of all of Brazil's mythical creatures. It is a big snake who lives in the depths of the rivers. The snake is said to be able to transform itself into a riverboat with its eyes beaming like the spotlights on a ship. The myth of the Cobra Grande is very popular in the Amazon, where it is said that the gigantic snake scares and kills fishermen.

Another animal thought to have magical powers is the *boto* (river dolphin). Native tribes likened the dolphins to humans and the playful mammals were therefore never extensively hunted. According to mythology, dolphins are endowed with superior sexual powers. Male dolphins are said to appear to women in the form of attractive young men to seduce them while they are bathing. Many illegitimate children along the rivers in the Amazon are said to be the children of the *boto*. Folk medicine in the Amazon has made use of body parts of dolphins as aphrodisiacs, as well as medicines and charms.

Negrinho do Pastoreio, the 'little black guy of the pasture,' is a popular mythological figure from Southern Brazil. Negrinho was the slave of a rancher and a dedicated devotee of Our Lady. One night, the horses he was in charge of, ran away. He lit a candle and went in search of them. Wherever wax dropped on the ground, a light lit up until the entire countryside was lit as if it were morning, which made the horses return quickly. It is believed that those who have lost something can ask Negrinho to help find the item by lighting a candle in front of an image of Our Lady.

Superstitions

Superstitions are a common element in the lives of a people steeped in mysticism and folk beliefs. The most common superstitions regard situations that must be avoided to avert bad luck. Among these are walking under a ladder, breaking a mirror or getting up with the left foot. A black cat crossing the street brings bad luck. Leaving a bag on the ground keeps money away. Opening an umbrella inside the house brings rain or bad luck.

Some other actions have positive consequences: Drinking from someone's cup reveals the other person's thoughts. Telling a lie with fingers crossed won't count as a sin in the eyes of God. An itching hand announces money or good news. Knocking on wood keeps evil away. A broom behind the door keeps unwelcome visitors away. A butterfly landing on someone brings good luck.

THE BRAZILIANS

CHAPTER 3

PHOTOS

'We Brazilians are an extremely homogenous people in cultural terms. Our regional differences are mere variations on a basic cultural theme, the result of a fusion of Western and Portuguese with African and Amerindian traditions.'
—President Fernando Henrique Cardoso,
inaugural address, 1 January 1995

A MELTING POT OF RACES

One of the most fascinating aspects about Brazil is the racial blend of its people. From the bustling streets of São Paulo to the languid villages of the interior, Brazilians display myriad shades of skin colour and ethnic traces. While most nations colonised by Europeans are characterised by the racial separation of their citizens, Brazil is a country where the opposite has happened. During the 500 years since its discovery, Indians, Europeans and Africans have come to form a complex racial melting pot. The first Portuguese settlers took native wives, giving rise to a new race—the mestizos. Later, the mulattoes, descendants of Portuguese settlers and African slaves, became part of Brazil's growing racial blend. With the abolition of slavery in 1888, race distinctions have become more and more blurred. Where once Brazilians were mainly white and black, they are today increasingly brown. It is not uncommon even for apparently white Brazilians to have a mix of European, African and indigenous ancestors.

Mário de Andrade in his novel *Macunaíma* (1928), provides a great metaphor for Brazil's racial mix. Macunaíma, the protagonist, is a 'hero without any character', a trickster figure borrowed from native Amazonian mythology. In the novel, he is described as an Indian of black colour who turns white when he takes a bath in a pool. Macunaíma is therefore Indian, African and European, and the novel comically reflects on the issue of national and cultural identity of a people with different racial backgrounds.

A Wealth of Regional Types

Brazil's immense size, the geographic isolation of its regions, and the large number of immigrant groups have led to the formation of distinct regional populations with unique traditions. The Caboclos of the Amazon paddle in dugout canoes as did their native ancestors, dark-skinned Baianos practice African religions and southern Brazilians organise German-style beer fests. Regionally, one also finds traces of Japanese, Lebanese and Jewish foods and traditions. Yet, these cultural characteristics are today regarded as different customs of Brazilians and not of specific ethnic groups.

Canoes are a common mode of transportation in the Amazon.

Gaúchos

Brazil's southernmost state, Rio Grande do Sul, is home to the Gaúchos, the descendants of Portuguese and Spanish settlers and Guarani Indians. The Gaúchos once hunted wild cattle and developed a unique South American cowboy culture. They adopted the region around Rio da Prata (River Plate) as their homeland, which is now part of Brazil, Uruguay and Argentina. The *chimarrão*, a beverage made from the maté herb, served in a gourd with a silver straw, is the traditional trademark of the Gaúchos. Today, this tea is also enjoyed in southern Brazil by the descendants of more recent German and Italian immigrants, just as the term Gaúcho is now used for the inhabitants of Rio Grande do Sul in general. The mountain range of the Serra Gaúcha in Rio Grande do Sul is home to the descendants of Italian immigrants who cultivated Brazil's first vineyards. German traditions are also kept alive in Brazil's south, especially in Santa Catarina. This state is not only home to towns with German names, but also to a lively tradition of Germanic cuisine and festivals.

Paulistas and Paulistanos

The Paulistas, the inhabitants of the state of São Paulo, are a very dynamic and entrepreneurial people. Through the slave trade, mining expeditions and coffee plantations, the Paulistas have made São Paulo Brazil's wealthiest state and are proud of their region's prosperity. With similar pride, the Paulistanos, inhabitants of the city of São Paulo, think of their city as the economic and cultural centre of South America. São Paulo is doubtlessly Brazil's most cosmopolitan city with descendants of all immigrant groups.

Cariocas

The Cariocas, inhabitants of Rio de Janeiro, consider the *cidade maravilhosa* (marvellous city) as they call it, not only the most beautiful city in the world, but also the most important one in Brazil. Cariocas are known to have a very laid-back and easy-going lifestyle, as a result of their many beaches. Every weekend, thousands of residents head for the beaches for a day of fun and relaxation. The Cariocas vehemently deny São Paulo's claim to be Brazil's most important city and this has led to a permanent rivalry between the two cities.

Mineiros

The Mineiros are the inhabitants of Minas Gerais, a state in the interior north of Rio de Janeiro. They are hard-working people who play a vital role in Brazil's politics and economy. Brazil's much revered president, Juscelino Kubitschek, was mayor of Belo Horizonte, the capital of Minas Gerais, before being elected president in 1955 and building the new capital. The Mineiros are more serious and reserved than the easy-going Brazilians of the coast. Carlos Drummond de Andrade, one of Brazil's most accomplished poets, is considered a typical Mineiro with his dry humour and somewhat restrained language. He was born in Itabira, a large centre of iron ore mining. As he writes in one of his poems:

'A few years I lived in Itabira.
Mainly, I was born in Itabira.
That's why I am sad, proud: of iron.
Ninety per cent iron in our souls.'

Baianos

The state of Bahia is the centre of Afro-Brazilian culture, and the Baianos practice traditions that go back to distant African origins. Among them is the Bahian cuisine, Candomblé (a religion of African origin) and *capoeira* (a dance fight developed by slaves). Some of these traditions have spread all over Brazil and have contributed to the assimilation of Afro-Brazilian culture into the Brazilian mainstream. Baianos have the reputation that they love festivals more than anything else in the world. Indeed it is difficult to spend a day in Bahia without coming across a festival, parade or some other celebration. Thus the fun-loving characters of Bahian writer Jorge Amado are not as exaggerated as one might suspect. Where else, if not in Bahia, could Amado's character Quincas Berro d'Água spend an entire night partying with his friends, without them noticing that he was dead?

Sertanejos

The Sertanejos are the inhabitants of Brazil's impoverished and drought-stricken backlands—the *sertão*. They are a tough people, mostly of European or mixed European and African descent, who have learned to carve out a meager living from the arid land. In the literary works of writers such as Graciliano Ramos and João Guimarães Rosa, the Sertanejos emerge as an exploited and abused people who are nonetheless able to maintain a glimpse of hope in their never-ending struggle for a better life. The Sertanejos still keep alive rich folk art traditions and folklore infused with a mysticism typical of a people who have always looked to heaven to bring them rain.

Brazilian literature of the 20th century has adopted the Sertanejos' struggle against drought and poverty as a recurring theme, and Brazil's most remarkable works of fiction take place in this barren landscape.

Caboclos

The term *caboclo* literally means 'copper-coloured' and refers to acculturated Indians or mestizos of Portuguese and Indian descent who live mainly in the Amazon region. They lead simple lives of subsistence farming, fishing and extractivism

A thatched roof hut of the Caboclos.

along the rivers of the Amazon. Isolated in a vast region where rivers are the only means of communication, the Caboclos keep alive traditions, customs and mythologies that go back to the time of their native ancestors.

THE BRAZILIAN SOUL

Being a people of several cultures and races, Brazilians have inherited a little bit of the characteristics of each of their ancestors. They share the extrovertedness and love of rhythm of their African forefathers, show traces of mysticism from their Indian ancestors, and have inherited a Portuguese melancholy that perhaps originated in a deep longing for the distant mother country across the ocean.

Saudade

Saudade is probably the most significant and typical expression of the Brazilian soul, a combination of longing and desire, mixed with nostalgia and melancholy. *Saudade* is the desire for something or someone who is far away or is unattainable. Brazilians have *saudades* when they live abroad and get homesick, when they are separated from a loved one, or when they recall good old times. But *saudade* is not merely an emotional response to a situation or memory. It is a state of mind that Brazilians seek and thrive on. *Saudade* has not only inspired poets and musicians for centuries, but it also provides Brazilians with a pinch of melancholy in their daily lives. The traditional folk song *Luar do Sertão* expresses *saudade* this way:

> 'Oh, what saudade for the moonlight
> in my homeland there in the mountains,
> brightening the dry leaves on the ground.
> The dark moonlight here in the city
> does not give me that same saudade
> as the moonlight back there in the sertão.'

This song is as much about the longing for the distant home, as it is about the longing for the sentiment of *saudade*, which the moonlight in the city does not inspire.

Hope

Another sentiment that lies buried deep in the Brazilian soul is hope. My first Portuguese professor, a Jesuit priest from Recife, taught us an important saying early on in class: *a esperança é a última que morre*—hope is the last to die. For Brazilians, hope is strongly related to religious sentiments. *Se Deus quiser* (God willing) is an often-used phrase that implies hope, but it is also an expression of the lack of control over what the future may bring. *Esperança*, the Portuguese word for hope, is a blend of fatalism, expectation and faith, and has a strong mystical connotation. In one of the best-known Brazilian short stories of the 20th century, *The Third Bank of the River*, João Guimarães Rosa developed perhaps the most significant metaphor for the Brazilian attitude of hope. The story is about a man whose father had disappeared in a canoe on the river when he was still a child. All his life, the man hopes for his father's return and puts food out for him by the river bank every night. The man's unbending hope is like a 'third river bank', a mystical dimension that exists beyond the physical realm (the two known river banks) of our lives.

Although Brazilians often live in the hope of something that has yet to happen, they are also joyful and light-hearted enough to enjoy the present as much as possible. The ability to celebrate and have a good time despite severe hardship, is a long-practiced and deep-rooted Brazilian attitude. This doesn't necessarily make Brazilians hedonists; it just shows that they have developed an inner wisdom that lets them balance the good and not so good things in life, that even in a bad year, there is always Carnaval to look forward to.

Expressions of the Brazilian Soul

The art form that best expresses the complexities of the Brazilian soul is undoubtedly music. Music combines *saudade*, sadness and hope, but also joy and happiness, and intensifies these emotions. Poet and diplomat Vinicius de Moraes best described the necessary ingredients for good Brazilian music in his *Samba da Benção*:

'It is better to be happy than to be sad.
Joy is the best thing there is:
It is like a light inside our hearts.
But to play a samba with beauty,
You need a little bit of sadness.
Otherwise you won't play the samba right'.

For most Brazilians, music is more than just listening to a tune. It accompanies them everyday in everything they do. Music helps them celebrate life, but it also helps them overcome lost love. It gives them hope and consolation, and inspires happiness. Song lyrics are frequently quoted in conversation and lend their wisdom to a variety of daily situations. Music is essentially a social art form and fits well into the cultural framework of an outgoing people. It brings them together to listen and dance, to play, sing, socialise and have a good time.

Drawing from a long and rich tradition of rhythms and song writing, Brazilian music has achieved a complexity that is unrivalled among folk music traditions. Nowhere else can a song performed to the heated poly-rhythm of African drums inspire both joy of life and sadness, surprise with sophisticated atonal chord sequences, and invite with a simple harmonious melody, all at the same time. The complexity and diversity of Brazilian music is perhaps the most accomplished expression of a national soul of many origins.

BRAZILIAN REALITIES

'If at the end of my mandate all Brazilians are
able to enjoy breakfast, lunch, and dinner,
I will have achieved the mission of my life.'
–President Luiz Inácio Lula da Silva,
Inaugural address, 1 January, 2003

The First Inhabitants

First admired as the inhabitants of an earthly paradise, later missionised by Jesuits, and hunted by slave traders, Brazil's Indians have suffered from centuries of abuse. The first efforts to protect them only took place during the First Republic

(1889–1930). In 1910, Cândido Rondon, an army marshal, founded the Serviço de Proteção do Índio, SPI, (Indian Protection Service) after contact with native tribes during several Amazon expeditions. The SPI considered Indian tribes to be under the tutelage of the state, and the main goal was to speed up the tribes' acculturation and adaptation to Brazilian culture. But this turned out to be a mixed blessing for many tribal groups. They were often completely wiped out by diseases brought by Brazilians, overrun by settlers and prospectors, or they simply merged with Brazilian society and ceased to exist as a cultural and tribal entity. In the 1960s, the increasingly corrupt SPI was replaced by FUNAI or Fundação Nacional do Índio (National Indian Foundation), which is still the official government Indian agency today. FUNAI's main goal has been to pacify newly contacted tribes, to open land to development and mineral exploitation.

The Native People

Brazil's Indians are the only racial group that does not share the same culture or language with the rest of the population. They belong to an estimated 227 different tribes with 175 languages and lead an existence apart from the rest of the country. At the time of the Portuguese discovery, there were an estimated five million indigenous people in Brazil.

The fate of Brazil's Indians gradually began to change with the new constitution of 1988. For the first time, the Brazilian government recognised the Indians' right to their land, culture and language. The constitution also gave indigenous tribes the right to represent their own interests, and there are about 280 indigenous institutions that deal with a variety of tribal issues and lobby for the Indians' interests in Brasília. In 1996, a new law took effect that allowed legal challenges against demarcated reservation territory, if someone could prove a legal claim to the land. One of the most disputed issues with regard to the reservations has been the right to mineral exploration. Since the land of indigenous reservations is the property of the Brazilian state, exploratory rights also remain

In April 2000, Brazil's Indians organised protests and demonstrations in line with the 500th anniversary of Brazil's discovery. According to them, Brazil's discovery was really an invasion that has led to 500 years of genocide, forced labour and exploitation of the indigenous population.

with the federal government. This has led to numerous mining concessions on reservations, which has led to conflicts with several tribes.

In addition to legal disputes, Indian reservations also suffer illegal invasions from gold diggers, land grabbers and mining companies. In 2004, newly discovered diamond fields on Indian reservations in the Amazon led to serious stand-offs and clashes between the local tribes and invading miners. These events show that despite ample legislation and goodwill on the part of the federal government, the rights of Brazil's indigenous peoples are far from guaranteed.

The Hard Reality of Life

'O rico acorda tarde, já começa a rezingar
O pobre acorda cedo, já começa a trabalhar.'
(The rich wakes up late and starts complaining right away.
The poor wakes up early and starts working right away.)
—Song lyrics from Maria Moita,
Carlos Lyra and Vinicius de Moraes

Even though Brazil's economy is among the world's tenth largest, a well-developed industry and a wealth of natural resources, the standard of living is quite precarious. Brazil is one of the countries with the highest inequality of income distribution in the world. This division of Brazilian society has not changed since colonial times, when wealth and power were concentrated in the hands of a few.

Making Ends Meet

Brazilians are a hardworking people. Most of them have learned early on in life to deal with the *dura realidade da vida* (hard reality of life), which they call the never-ending struggle to make ends meet. Vulnerable to the slightest economic downturn, Brazil's poorer half has got used to its uncertain status over the decades. Although the 'tax of the poor,' as rampant inflation is called, has been controlled since the introduction of the real (BRL), the real income of Brazil's average wage-earners has not significantly increased. They still have little extra money for consumer goods, travel or entertainment. In order to maintain a minimum standard of living, people often work several jobs and every family member has to contribute to the household income. The automobile, so commonplace in the wealthy industrialised countries, is still a luxury that only the middle and upper classes can afford. Imported cars are only for the wealthy.

Living in Poverty

'For the common people to survive the conditions they live in, isn't that a miracle, and one of the greatest?'
—Jorge Amado, *O Sumiço da Santa*
(The War of the Saints)

Poverty is an ever-present element of Brazilian society. More than a third of the population is considered poor by Brazilian standards. They do not have enough money to satisfy daily necessities, and healthcare and education are a luxury. The

causes of the widespread poverty are complex and primarily linked to a social elitism prevalent since colonial times. Brazilian society has always favoured the rich and simply does not provide adequate opportunities for the poor to improve their lives and achieve a higher standard of living. Although Brazil's expenditures on social programmes have increased since the mid-1990s, statistics have shown that they mainly benefit the middle and upper classes. While upward social mobility is possible and does happen, most of Brazil's poor only have a slim chance of moving out of the shantytowns that sprawl the outskirts of every major city. Rare examples such as football players become the heroes of the impoverished masses, personifying hope for a better life.

Informal Economy

The informal economy plays a vital role in the survival of Brazil's poor. The streets of Brazil's large cities are crowded with *camelôs* (street vendors), who sell anything from lottery tickets and snacks to pocket calculators, stereos and clothing. Street vendors are a barometer of the national economy

A street vendor with a selection of natural remedies from Brazil's wealth of medicinal plants.

since their number increases during periods of economic crisis and recession. The informal economy is not limited to street vendors, but also includes service workers and skilled labourers, or just about anyone who is out of work and needs to support a family. In Brazil's six largest metropolitan areas, the percentage of workers in the informal sector has risen, meaning that more than half of Brazil's economically active people do not pay taxes, or make contributions to social security. While this constitutes an enormous loss in revenues for the government, informal economic activities improve the lives of millions of Brazilians and are an indispensable alternative to widespread urban unemployment.

The Fate of Children

Due to poverty, children are often sent to work by their parents, to help make ends meet. Although federal laws prohibit the employment of children, and school attendance is mandatory until age 15, working children are a common sight in most cities. They sell snacks, sweets and refreshments, and young boys polish shoes, and work as parking attendants. But thanks to government programmes, the percentage of children attending school has increased. It is now more common to see children selling snacks after school hours, as opposed to working all day long. While organised child labour is rare in cities, many children in rural areas perform the hard labour of adults. They load furnaces to make charcoal for the pig iron industry and work on orange plantations and sugar cane fields. It is estimated that there are over five million working children and adolescents (aged 5–17) in Brazil.

Still worse is the situation of children who have been abandoned by their parents because they can no longer support them. These street kids live in small gangs and usually get by with stealing and foraging. In the early 1990s, the shooting of homeless children by death squads caused such a widespread public outrage that several social programmes, often funded by international organisations, were implemented to help these children by offering them room, board and an education. The movie *Pixote, a lei do mais fraco* (*Pixote*, by Hector Babenco, 1981) passionately portrays the reality of several street children in São Paulo, who live off petty crime and drug dealing, and sniff glue for brief moments of bliss.

Taking a Chance with Luck

Since upward social mobility is difficult in a country that has always favoured the rich and powerful, most Brazilians believe that it is easier to strike it rich by playing any of the many games of chance. Lottery ticket vendors crowd the streets in every Brazilian city, selling tickets for the federal and state lotteries as well as tickets for sports pools. The government operates over 6,000 lottery booths throughout the country, which sell tickets for all types of lotteries. TV game shows with audience participation and big prizes are also immensely popular.

One of the most popular lotteries is the *Jogo do Bicho*, the Animal Game. Though outlawed since 1941, it is still played regularly by many Brazilians, especially in Rio de Janeiro. The game works like a lottery, but uses animal symbols instead of numbers. It was invented in 1892 by a zoo owner in Rio de Janeiro, to attract more visitors to his zoo. Today, the illegal lottery is estimated to bring in more than US$1 billion per year in bets. The *bicheiros* (bookmakers) are known to make large contributions to Rio de Janeiro's samba schools and have become important patrons of Brazil's greatest Carnaval celebration.

Surviving in Rural Brazil

'They would arrive at a distant land and would forget the caatinga with its low mountains, rocks, dry rivers, thorns, vultures, dying animals and dying people.'
—Graciliano Ramos, *Vidas Secas* ('Barren Lives') 1938

Brazil is characterised not only by the extreme contrast between rich and poor, but also between urban and rural areas. While the urban middle class has a lifestyle that resembles that of developed countries, life in rural Brazil is marked by poverty and underdevelopment. Road conditions are precarious, public transportation is sparse, schools are far away, access to healthcare is difficult and unemployment is rampant. Many impoverished families live off subsistence farming without opportunities to improve their lives. Human development indicators such as education, literacy, infant mortality and life expectancy are all significantly inferior compared to Brazil's cities.

Cycles of Migration

Throughout Brazil's recorded history, the North-east has been affected by recurring droughts. They are mainly affect the semiarid *sertão*, where small farmers often have no other choice but to abandon their land and move to a city. Since 1994, more than 450,000 families of small farmers have abandoned their land and moved to the cities. *Retirantes* (drought refugees) have long since become part of north-eastern folklore and have also made their way into the works of writers and artists. Cândido Portinari's painting *Os Retirantes* is perhaps the most moving visual representation of a family escaping the drought. The painting is of emaciated, ghostlike figures, rendered in Portinari's expressionistic style in pale earth tones, as if the painting itself had been bleached by the relentless sun of the *sertão*.

The widespread misery of small farmers in Brazil's north-east is not only related to drought cycles. It is also the result of structures of land ownership and power inherited from the past. *Coroneis* (large landowners) have dominated local politics for a long time and often control vast tracts of land. Their exploitation of landless rural workers and ruthless tactics of land acquisition have left many with no other choice than to leave their homeland.

New Frontiers

In response to severe droughts in the North-east in the 1960s, military president Médici decided to create a new focus of migration and to open up a vast pioneer front in the Amazon. With the slogan 'a land without people for people without land', the government created the Program of National Integration (PIN). Its main goal was the construction of the

Transamazon Highway from Brazil's north-east coast to the distant border with Peru, which began in 1970. In the years that followed, thousands of north-eastern families were settled along the new motorway that cut through the pristine Amazon rain forest. But without the government support promised and infrastructure needed for settlement, many migrants did not stay and abandoned their land.

Another pioneer front was opened in 1979 in Rondônia, a state in the southern Amazon. The news about free land attracted nearly one million settlers during the 1980s, but poor soil quality and lacking government assistance soon complicated the lives of settlers. Many ended up selling their small properties and went to work as sharecroppers and peasants on the region's increasing number of large ranches. Rondônia is today largely deforested and covered with vast cattle ranches that belong to wealthy land owners.

The Movement of the Landless

Although the Brazilian constitution provides for an agrarian reform to disown and redistribute land 'that does not serve its social function,' Brazil continues to have an extremely elitist land distribution. About one per cent of landowners own 45 per cent of Brazil's agricultural land, and much of this land is used for extensive cattle grazing, or is not utilised at all. In contrast, the number of landless peasants is estimated to be about 12 million. Since its foundation in 1984, the Movimento dos Trabalhadores Rurais sem Terra, MST (Rural Landless Workers' Movement) has been engaged in the struggle to improve the fate of landless peasants. It is a non-profit organisation supported by union leaders, leftist politicians and lawyers, who have been lobbying for a sweeping land reform to redistribute unused land to landless families of rural workers and to receive government start-up assistance. The organisation maintains constant political pressure on the government with protests, demonstrations and road blocks. Occupation of unused land is also a common strategy and the bus caravans of the MST are feared by landowners throughout rural Brazil. Unfortunately, peaceful squatting operations have often resulted in fierce retaliation by landowners who defend their land with armies of gunmen. Excessive police violence and killings have also occurred during the eviction of squatters.

URBAN CHAOS

'A Favela é o quarto de despejo de uma cidade. Nós, os
pobres, somos os trastes velhos.'
(The favela is the lumber room of a city.
We, the poor, are the old junk.)
—Carolina Maria de Jesus, author of
O Quarto de Despejo ('Child of the Dark'), 1960

After decades of rapid and unplanned growth, Brazil's large urban centres have become unmanageable behemoths. Traffic is at a near standstill, air and noise pollution have reached critical levels, and increased urban crime has lowered the quality of life. The cities also suffer from an ageing infrastructure, high unemployment, lack of affordable housing, and sprawling growth that adds ever more *favelas* (shantytowns) on the outskirts without adding roads or services.

Favelas

One of the most noticeable aspects of Brazil's urban centres are its *favelas*. They first emerged toward the end of the 19th century, when rural migrants began to arrive in Rio de Janeiro and built huts on the unoccupied slopes of the city's mountains. Today, *favelas* are a widespread urban phenomenon that attests to the large income discrepancy among Brazil's urban population. Twenty years ago, about one third of the population of Brazil's largest cities lived in *favelas*. Today, half of them live in these clandestine housing developments.

> *Favelas* occupy unused land on hillsides, riverbanks, marshes, motorway median strips, and wherever else there may be room to build a shack.

While some of the *favelas* such as Rocinha in Rio de Janeiro have existed for decades and boast brick houses and a decent infrastructure, more recent squatter communities consist of shacks built with salvaged materials and have no plumbing, sewage system or electricity. After decades of

Shantytowns spring up in cities wherever there is unused land.

trying to demolish these shantytowns, city administrations have realised that *favelas* can no longer be ignored and have begun to make basic infrastructure available. Some *favelas* now have rubbish disposal, a sewage system and also receive water and electricity from the city. But life remains difficult for millions of impoverished residents all over Brazil. Drug lords often reign sovereign in these communities, especially in Rio de Janeiro, and violent crime is rampant. Inadequate sanitary conditions favour the outbreak of infectious diseases, and *favelas* have neither hospitals, kindergartens, schools, police stations or other basic government services.

Urbanisation

Since the mid 20th century, millions of migrants have arrived in the cities from the impoverished states of the North-east, in search of a better life. Today, about 82 per cent of Brazil's population lives in cities. Rio de Janeiro had 1.1 million inhabitants in 1920 and is today a mega-city of 6 million people. São Paulo had 579,000 inhabitants in 1920, but today it is Brazil's largest city with over 10.7 million people. Even Brazil's great planned cities such as Belo Horizonte and Brasília, which were designed as models of order, progress and urban development, have long since outgrown their orderly planned proportions. *Favelas* cover the hillsides on the outskirts of Belo Horizonte and in Brasília, *favelas* and satellite cities have sprung up around the *plano piloto*, the city's original design.

Homelessness

Those who don't have the means to rent a hut in a *favela* or build a shack, end up living on the streets. These are often recently arrived migrants, lured to the cities by the promise of a better life. However, they soon find themselves worse off than they were before and live off begging, selling aluminium cans and rummaging through rubbish.

Model Cities

Against all current trends, Brazil's southern cities have managed to keep their infrastructure up-to-date with their growth and maintain a level of organisation, cleanliness and quality of life that is comparable to cities in developed countries. Of these, Curitiba is especially known to be one of Brazil's most livable cities. It has an excellent public transportation system, large parks, pedestrian zones and social programmes for poor citizens. When asked where they would like to live, most Brazilians mention Curitiba, or one of the other pleasant and orderly cities, such as Florianópolis and Porto Alegre.

A pedestrian mall in Curitiba, Brazil's most liveable city.

HUMAN RIGHTS

'Brazil is a democracy. But what I see here is a wretched,
sad situation where there is no justice.'
—Asma Jahangir, United Nations Human Rights Envoy,
during her visit to Brazil in 2003

Decades of dictatorship and military regime in the 20th century gave rise to an authoritarian and violent society, where civil order was based on intimidation and threat. Unfortunately, some of these practices still survive in the present democratic society. The above quoted Human Rights Envoy suggested that it was time for the Brazilian government to get to work and improve the nation's human rights record. Brazil's main problem with enforcing human rights is that it is often the representatives of law and order who commit these crimes. Hundreds of crime suspects are killed by police every year before they ever have a trial. Beatings, threats, intimidation and abuse are also widely practiced by police to extract confessions from detained suspects. Prisoners are tortured and abused, and death in custody as a result of police violence is common knowledge.

Brazil's prison system is notorious for its disregard for human rights. The overcrowded and unsanitary conditions are cause for regular riots, hostage taking and breakouts. Police often retaliate with excessive force, torture and killings. Violence is also used to deal with political and social unrest. Clashes between police and squatters have resulted in numerous casualties throughout the 1990s. *Grupos de exterminio* (death squads) are known to operate in several states, often with the participation or toleration of the police. These hit squads work for influential local figures and are involved in drug running and other illegal activities. They also carry out assassinations of undesirable elements such as political activists, as was the case with several local leaders of the MST and of indigenous tribes, who were killed because they fought for their rights.

Faced with the difficult situation of daily human rights

Torture was recently added to the penal code as a crime, which should make it easier to prosecute police violence against suspects and convicts.

violations, the government has taken steps to improve the situation and established a National Human Rights Program and National Human Rights Bureau. Very gradually, the widespread 'institutionalised impunity' of police is beginning to be challenged as well. Brazilian citizens have also developed a higher awareness of human rights violations and have founded human rights groups to fight for more justice.

Racial harmony

Brazilian society gives the impression of a harmonious conglomerate of races where people with different skin colours coexist peacefully, and where racial conflict is not an issue. Brazilian social historian Gilberto Freyre called his country a 'racial democracy', where all citizens had equal opportunities regardless of skin colour. But a closer look at Brazil reveals that this is not the case, and that equality of all races is still far from accomplished. Although there is no open conflict between Brazil's various ethnic groups, there is a noticeable class distinction between the white elite and middle class, and a predominantly dark-skinned poorer half of the population.

A new magazine, *Raça (Race)*, is geared toward the emerging black middle class and is the only magazine in Brazil that regularly features blacks on its cover page.

While it is rare to find racist attitudes among Brazilians, the daily realities of many black and brown-coloured Brazilians shows that social discrimination exists, and that they continue to be economically and socially disadvantaged. The infant mortality rate among them is higher, life expectancy is lower and black men are more likely to be arrested as crime suspects. The socioeconomic disadvantage is also reflected in housing, health, education, income and standard of living. While white Brazilians live in middle-class neighbourhoods, most dark-skinned Brazilians live in *favelas*. The main obstacle for dark skinned Brazilians to more equal opportunities is the lack of education. As a result, many work in low-paying service jobs. The vicious circle continues when it becomes necessary for their children to quit school early to help support the family.

Despite these difficulties, many mulattoes and blacks have been able to better their lives, get a university education, earn a higher income and move to a better part of town. Though it is still rare to see a black Brazilian in a business suit, it is more common now than ever before. Black Brazilians are also beginning to appear on the national political scene as federal deputies and mayors. World-famous soccer star Pelé became Brazil's first black cabinet minister when President Fernando Henrique Cardoso nominated him Minister of Sports in 1995.

THE WOMAN'S WORLD

'O lugar de mulher é em casa.'
(The woman's place is in the home.)
—Old Brazilian saying

Although women have long been engaged in the struggle to expand their 'place' in the world beyond the domestic sphere and achieve the same rights as men, the above quotation is still a widely held view in Brazil's patriarchal society. It was

not until 1932 that President Getúlio Vargas passed a law granting women the right to vote, thus giving women a small role in public life. Since then, the role of women in Brazilian society has undergone gradual changes. Despite traditional patriarchal attitudes, women have made small but significant steps toward achieving equal rights.

Women at Work

Brazilian women today make significant contributions to both family income and the economy at large. They have entered the workplace in large numbers and account for 42 per cent of Brazil's entire work force. The 1988 constitution prohibits gender-based discrimination with regard to employment and salaries, but this law is rarely enforced. The salary discrepancy between women and men still remains high. The average income of employed women is one third less than that of men. Women are also traditionally concentrated in a small number of occupations, such as primary school teachers, secretaries, telephone operators, nurses and receptionists. These are the lowest paying jobs in Brazil.

Despite these difficulties in the employment market, women do hold a variety of professional occupations today, even though still in relatively small numbers. They are

Women in Bahia at their daily work place.

lawyers, judges and doctors and hold important positions in the government. In 1995, a quota system for elections was passed by the national congress, requiring that at least one third of the candidates of each political party be women. In October 2000, the first woman was appointed to the Federal Supreme Court. Brazilians also elected several woman as state governors and mayors of important cities.

Housewives and Mothers

In addition to becoming an indispensable part of the work force, the domestic role of Brazilian women has also changed in the past few decades. Until 1962, women needed their husband's approval to seek employment and depended on them as the sole breadwinner. Today, women are the head of the household in an increasing number of Brazilian families. Women have also taken a different approach to family planning and birth control, which has contributed to a drop in population growth. A large percentage of Brazilian women now use birth control, and the average number of life births per woman of reproductive age has dropped. Although abortion is illegal except in cases of rape and where the pregnancy poses serious health risks to the mother, an estimated one million abortions are performed every year.

Women's Police Stations

Another serious issue that affects Brazilian women is widespread domestic violence, which has only surfaced as a topic of discussion in recent years. It was not until 1991, that the Brazilian supreme court outlawed the 'defense of honour' argument as a justification for wife murder. In 1985, as a response to increased violence against women, the city of São Paulo established an experimental *delegacia da mulher* (women's police station). It was run only by women police officers who were responsible for investigating crimes against women, mainly abuse and domestic violence. Due to the success of this experiment, over 200 women's police stations were set up all over Brazil and half of them are in São Paulo alone.

'When people ask me why I keep wanting to go
to Brazil, part of the answer is that it's because
the country is so vast and so raw and sometimes
so monstrously beautiful; but it is mostly because
I find it easy to get along with the people.'
—John dos Passos, *Brazil on the Move*

FAMILY LIFE
Family Ties

The family is the central focus in the lives of most Brazilians. Loyalty and commitment to one's family often come before personal interests, and many important decisions are made with the greater good of the family in mind. Families are usually close-knit, providing a network of social contacts, assistance, and, of course, gossip. It is common to find three generations living under one roof. Brazilian families are traditionally quite large, but this is gradually changing. The number of children per family is not nearly as high today as it was only a generation ago. An important factor that keeps several generations living together are economic considerations. Rent is expensive and neither the old nor the young can easily afford to live by themselves. Young people often live with their parents or relatives until they get married or can afford an apartment with a partner.

Since the mid 20th century, widespread internal migration has significantly affected the traditional family structure, as millions left their homes in the impoverished North-east to seek employment in the big urban centres of South-eastern Brazil.

The internationally acclaimed Brazilian film *Central do Brasil (Central Station,* Walter Salles, 1998) is a tale about a family separated by economic hardship. In the film, a young boy in Rio de Janeiro teams up with a retired school teacher after his mother's death, to look for his father. It is a film that relates to thousands of separated families.

Marriage

Traditionally, Brazilians get married young and have children early. Nowadays, an increasing number go to university and postpone marriage until they are financially more secure. There are also many young Brazilians who live together, but do not get married, and many decide not to have children, or not have them right away. These attitudes are predominantly found among the urban middle class. However, for a large number of Brazilians, an early marriage and children are still the main goals in life.

Engagement

In Brazil, exchanging engagement rings is a common practice and a couple may even throw an engagement party. Before the wedding day, female relatives and friends of the bride will organise a kind of bridal shower, called *chá de panela* or *chá de cozinha*, where the bride receives kitchen and household items. The bridegroom, on the other hand, gets together with his male friends who take him out to a bar or strip club for the *despedida de solteiro* (bachelor's farewell party).

The Wedding

A wedding is always reason for a great feast, regardless of social class or region. Most couples have both a civilian and a religious wedding ceremony. Following the ceremony, guests are invited to a lively reception, which includes a lot of food and drink, as well as music and dancing lasting until the wee hours. Several traditions common in other Western cultures are also found here, such as the white wedding cake, the first dance of the married couple, and the throwing of the bridal bouquet. The *viagem de núpcias* or *lua de mel* (honeymoon) is also popular, although such a trip depends on family income. The practice of cutting the bridegroom's tie during the reception comes in handy as pieces of the tie are sold to the guests for a nominal amount, to help pay for the feast or raise money for the honeymoon.

The Household

The husband is usually the head of the household. He represents his family and is in charge of making the big decisions outside the domestic sphere.

The wife's role is not only limited to keeping the house clean. She is also responsible for the home's atmosphere, decoration and furnishing, and takes great pride in her domestic powers.

Traditionally, he is the principal breadwinner and is responsible for the material comforts of his family. But in an increasing number of families today, the wives also go out to work to help make ends meet. This is often a mixed blessing for Brazilian men, who see it as a threat to their traditional patriarchal role as head of the family.

Taking care of the household is the exclusive responsibility of the wife, whether she works outside or not. Husbands rarely assist with these tasks and see it as their privilege to come home from work and enjoy an evening of leisure. Hospitality is also the domain of the *dona*. Depending on the status of the visitors and the occasion of the visit, she provides for them in the appropriate manner. She sometimes stays in the background and just ensures that food and drink are plentiful. In a typical middle-class family, the *dona de casa* (housewife) is not alone in her efforts. There is usually also the *empregada*, a maid who helps with all domestic chores such as laundry, cooking and cleaning.

Divorce and Separation

While divorce was legalised in 1979, Brazil's divorce rate is significantly lower than that of most industrialised countries. However, this doesn't necessarily mean that Brazilians have happier marriages. It may just indicate that people have stronger reasons to stay together, whether economic, social or personal. Religious values also come into play in a country that is traditionally Catholic, and with large Protestant and evangelical congregations.

Children

The birth of a child is an important event in every Brazilian family, and it is always a reason to celebrate. Baptism is the first important ritual in the life of a Brazilian child, and the parents will ask friends, a business partner or even a boss to become the child's godparents. This is an obligation that lasts into the child's adulthood and includes giving birthday presents and providing help with the upbringing, education and other important issues in the child's life. Within the Catholic tradition, the rites of the First Communion and the Confirmation are also important events in the child's coming of age. There may be celebrations and godparents are expected to give presents.

Child Rearing

The daily task of child-rearing is usually left to the mother and/or nanny. Although fathers have an affectionate relationship with their children, they have no essential role in their daily upbringing. Children are an integral part of family life, and they accompany adults on most social events and visits. They are generally brought up with few restrictions, and strict discipline is rarely observed. The parent-child relationship is based more on affection and warmth than on authority. One of the most noticeable qualities about Brazilians is how tolerant they are toward children, both their own and those of others. On a flight from Los Angeles to São Paulo, I had a memorable experience of how Brazilians deal with children. There were several Brazilian families on the flight among those of other nationalities. The Brazilian children were the only ones allowed by their parents to run up and down the aisles, scream and play hide-and-seek between the seats. While the other passengers reacted with consternation, the Brazilian passengers enjoyed watching the children play. It wasn't long before the children calmed down and spent the remaining hours of the flight exhausted and in deep slumber.

Disparate Childhoods

Social factors determine a child's life early on, depending on family income and neighbourhood. It is a contrast to watch the well-dressed children of middle-class families on their Sunday outings to the shopping centres, while outside on the street, children from *favelas* (shantytowns) sell knick-

Fishing is a popular pastime among boys.

knacks to help support the family. The children of the upper class attend piano lessons, private English classes and spend their vacations in the US or Europe, whereas children of poor families play football on dirt lots with unshapely balls. In the countryside, children of peasant families usually help in the fields and with domestic chores, but they also have more opportunities for play than their counterparts in urban *favelas*. They are often seen splashing around in ponds and rivers, their favourite playgrounds.

The Third Age

Ageing in Brazil often means living with family members who can care for their elderly. Old folk's homes are only considered as a last option, since Brazilians have close family ties and a sincere respect and love for their ageing relatives. When retirees live by themselves, they usually cannot get by on the meager government pension and struggle to make ends meet. In the film *Central do Brasil* (*Central Station* by Walter Salles, 1998), retired school teacher, Dora, supplements her pension by writing letters for illiterate passers-by at Rio de Janeiro's central train station. Similarly, many retirees sell lottery tickets on the streets or engage in other activities of the informal sector, which also provide social contact in addition to extra income. Socially active and outgoing all their lives,

most retirees continue to socialise with friends and family as long as their health allows. Every neighbourhood has its informal gathering places such as a park or bar where the elderly meet to chat, and play chess, cards or dominoes.

Death and Dying

Brazil has a youthful and life-affirming culture, and ageing and dying are unpopular topics. Since Brazilians have close family ties, the death of a relative is an especially sad event. Catholic rites usually accompany the ill or dying. A priest is called for the anointing of the sick, and to pray for their recovery and salvation. A wake is commonly held for one day. Candles are lit and placed around the bed or coffin, and relatives take turns keeping vigil. The funeral is held the day after the wake, and the extended family is usually present. As a tribute to the deceased, a eulogy may be read. On Dia de Finados (All Soul's Day) on 2 November, people bring flowers to the graves of their deceased relatives and pray for their souls. The class distinctions of Brazilian society continue all the way to the grave. While the upper classes maintain family tombs or graves in well-kept private cemeteries, public cemeteries are often run-down, neglected and resemble a bone depository rather than a place where the dead can rest in peace.

FRIENDSHIP
'Amizade é como o vinho, quanto mais velha, melhor'.
(Friendship is like wine, the older the better.)
—Brazilian saying

Brazilians enjoy themselves most in the company of others. Family, friends and the community at large are an integral part of their lives, providing companionship, assistance and simply good times. Although they are quick to call someone a friend, it is only close friends who are treated as family. Such friends share the intimacies of family life and are invited to parties, dinners and family outings. But in a country where little is accomplished unless one knows the right person, friendship also means doing each other favours in business and politics, which, in some cases, can go as far as bending rules and circumventing laws to help a friend out or, reciprocate a favour.

LOVE AND SEXUALITY
'Fundamental é mesmo o amor. É impossível ser feliz sozinho'.
(It is love that is fundamental.
It is impossible to be happy alone.)
—from the song *Vou te contar* ('Wave'), Antônio Carlos Jobim

Since Brazilians are a social and outgoing people, it is easy to make contact with the opposite sex. Traditionally, it is considered the man's role to make the first move and express interest in a woman. This attitude is changing however, and it is today quite acceptable for a woman to initiate contact with a man she finds interesting. Educated urban women often have more liberal sexual attitudes than their rural counterparts. They don't intend to marry the first man they date and often have several relationships before settling with one partner. They also have easier access to birth control methods and are more knowledgeable about them. A stereotype that exists abroad about Brazilian women is that they are promiscuous and have a strong sexual appetite. This cliche has developed from the images of near-naked women during Carnaval, which is a time where accepted behaviours are reversed, and has little to do with how women act toward men during the rest of the year.

In a patriarchal society like Brazil, men doubtlessly enjoy more sexual freedom than women. Until a few decades ago, brides were expected to be virgins, while it was accepted for men to gain sexual experiences before marriage. This societal tolerance toward men's sexual behaviour also extends to extramarital relationships, which are not uncommon. Well-to-do middle-aged men often find a young lover whom they support financially. Extramarital relationships of wives are not nearly so well tolerated. A wife cheating on her husband will most likely be divorced, while the wife is expected to forgive her adulterous husband and accept him back into the family.

Who Brazilians choose to date is, to a certain degree, influenced by status considerations. Dating usually takes place between people of the same social class. The middle class is less status-oriented, and relationships occur more frequently across lines of skin colour and economic and social status. Rarely will a member of the upper class date someone of the lower class. Women in Brazil are, to a certain degree, status symbols for their boyfriends and husbands, and skin colour and social background can be important considerations. Brazil's beautiful mulatas may be desired lovers for the sons of the upper crust, but these women rarely become their girlfriends or wives.

GAYS AND LESBIANS

Brazilians are fairly tolerant of alternative lifestyles, including sexual orientation, but there are great regional variances. In general, gays and lesbians are much more accepted in large cities, as small towns and rural areas tend to be more conservative. Brazil's large cities usually have numerous gay nightclubs, and many host an annual gay pride parade. There is also a thriving tranvestite culture in major urban areas, which becomes most noticeable during Carnaval, when tranvestites take to the streets in large, glamorous parades. Rio de Janeiro is known as a popular travel destination for gays from all over the world.

But amid wide-spread tolerance in urban areas and some regional gay-friendly legislation, there is also considerable prejudice and discrimination. An underlying current in much of Brazilian society is the country's tradition of male prowess. Although Brazilian machismo is softer than in other Latin American countries, there is still a prevalence of homophobia and despise for homosexuals. The violence against gays in Brazil is a problem that is widely recognised by Human Rights organisations, and the situation has shown no signs of improvement in recent years.

NATIONAL PASSIONS

Of all things dear to Brazilians, Carnaval and football are among their favourites. There are no other public events in Brazil that inspire more joy and enthusiasm. Love for football and Carnaval is almost synonymous with being Brazilian, and these two national passions are the most significant collective expressions of a unified national identity.

Carnaval

Carnaval, which is Portuguese for carnival or Shrovetide, is a time when Brazil is turned upside down, when social conventions are lifted and even reversed, and when the entire country explodes in non-stop merry-making. Derived from the Catholic tradition of pre-Lenten revelry and spiced up with African rhythms, Carnaval is an essential element of Brazilian culture and uniquely reflects the fusion of European and African influences. There are a number of regional Carnaval traditions, but the underlying idea is the same: to have a good time and to drink, flirt, listen to loud music and dance, dance, dance, until the sun comes up the next morning. During the four days of Carnaval, all economic activities come to a standstill, and the streets of Brazil are filled with groups of musicians, dancers and parades. In Rio de Janeiro where Carnaval has become a gigantic spectator event, people engage in heated discussions about which of Rio's glamorous samba schools will win the first prize in the highly competitive Carnaval parades. This topic also dominates the media for weeks and puts politics on the back pages of the newspapers.

The Brazilian Carnaval is a great democratic feast where class distinctions disappear, and the poor take on identities of the rich and/or famous. For four days, the *folia*, the crazy revelry of Carnaval, replaces the otherwise hard reality of life. Daily worries are forgotten, and everybody is allowed to escape into their own fantasy world. Maids become queens, men become women, women get undressed, and everyone is as wealthy and powerful as they want to be. The lyrics of *A Felicidade*, by Vinicius de Moraes, from the film *Orfeu Negro* (*Black Orpheus*, Marcel Camus, 1958) summarises the meaning of Carnaval for many Brazilians:

'The happiness of the poor is the great illusion of Carnaval. People work for an entire year for one dream-like moment, to dress up as king, pirate or gardener, only for everything to end on Ash Wednesday'.

Ironically, it is the rich and famous who end up impersonating themselves: during Rio de Janeiro's glitzy Carnaval parades, actors, TV and football stars make appearances with various samba schools, but they are never more than just themselves, as if their successful personae disqualified them from joining the same game of disguise and make-belief as everyone else.

The historic town of Olinda prides itself on its traditional Carnaval celebration.

Football

While Carnaval is a seasonal event, a short and intense frenzy of four days, football games are a reason for parties all year round. Introduced to Brazil from England in 1894, *futebol* (football) has become a national sport that unites all Brazilians in their passion for their team. As with Carnaval, all economic activity stops when the national team has a game. Streets are empty, and people gather around television sets in offices, bars and even on pavements. In recent years, large television projection screens have been set up in Brazil's large cities so football fans can watch the national team in a crowded atmosphere not unlike that of a football stadium.

But if during a national football game, an oppressive silence begins to spread in bars and living rooms across the country, this usually means that the Brazilian team is losing. Scoring or missing a goal can determine the ecstasy or frustration of the entire country, a frightening power and responsibility for the Brazilian teams. If the Brazilian team wins, the whole country goes into a frenzy of parades, fireworks, drinking and partying all night long. Brazilians say that when the national football team brings home trophies, their politicians' inadequacies are more easily forgotten. A victory of the Brazilian team during an election year can also boost the popularity of the government, regardless of its performance. Considering the popularity of football, it is not surprising that one of Brazil's most beloved national heroes, Edson Arantes do Nascimento, known as Pelé, is a former football star. He played in three consecutive World Cup tournaments and helped his team win three World Cup titles. This is a feat that the Brazilians, a people who have learned to thrive on short blissful moments, can never forget.

Football is not only the most popular spectator sport, it is also played by all males aged three and up, from the steaming rain forest of the Amazon, to the dirt lots of São Paulo's shantytowns. Even Indian tribes have taken up football, since this team sport fits well into

When the Brazilian team scores a goal, the TV or radio announcer lets out a high-pitched "Go-o-o-a-a-a l" for as long as his breath allows. At the same time, screams and cheers resonate throughout the country and fireworks are lit everywhere.

their communal way of life. Football is a game that builds friendship and community spirit, as it is easy to play and no costly equipment is required. All over Brazil, Sunday afternoon is a popular time for a *pelada*, a casual game of football with friends.

SOCIALISING WITH BRAZILIANS

Brazilians are an outgoing people, and regardless of your Portuguese skills, you will soon make contacts, and have opportunities to spend time with Brazilians. Although most Brazilians are casual and do not observe a very strict etiquette, it is a good idea to familiarise yourself with the basic rules of courtesy and conduct. That way you appear as knowledgeable and respectful of their customs, and you will not give the impression of being an ignorant newcomer.

Greetings

A firm and friendly handshake is the traditional greeting when arriving and departing. Brazilians practise good eye contact in greeting and conversation. When shaking hands, they use common terms such as *"Oi"* ("Hi"), *"Bom dia"* ("Good morning") or *"Boa tarde"* ("Good afternoon"). These greetings are often followed by phrases such as *"Tudo bom?"* ("Everything is fine?"), to which the other person responds with *"Tudo bem!"* ("Everything is fine!").

When greeting someone, women offer their hand or they may offer their cheek for a kiss depending on the intimacy and the situation. Kisses are light and are usually given on both cheeks by both men and women. Male friends shake hands in greeting and pat each other on the shoulder. When introduced to someone, they shake hands and say *"É um prazer"* ("It is a pleasure"). Among women, an embrace and kiss is more common than a handshake. People usually take leave of each other with a casual *"Tchau"* (from the Italian *"Ciao"*), *"Até mais"* ("See you later"), or by wishing each other *"Boa noite"* ("Good night"). New acquaintances usually say *"Foi um prazer conhecé-lo"* ("It was a pleasure meeting you"), to which the other person may respond *"O prazer foi meu!"* ("The pleasure was all mine!").

Forms of Address

When addressing an adult, it is customary to call them *senhor* (Sir/Mr) or *senhora* (Lady/Ms). Brazilians usually address each other by their first names soon after they have been introduced. When using a title such as *doutor* (masc.) or *doutora* (fem.) (doctor), first names, rather than last names follow. Women are often called *Dona* followed by the first name. As a general guideline, use the formal address for people you don't know and for those older than you. In Portuguese, the polite form is expressed in the third person singular. "Would you like a coffee?" is politely expressed as *"O senhor/a senhora quer um cafezinho?"* ("The Sir/Lady would like a coffee?"). To formally address a group, it is customary to use *senhores* (gentlemen), *senhoras* (ladies), or *senhoras e senhores* (ladies and gentlemen). The informal address *você* (and more rarely *tu*) is used among young people and those who know each other. *Você* is also appropriate for casual social contacts in bars, on the street or the beach. If you intend to express respect however, it is best to use *senhor* and *senhora*.

A Puzzle of Names

Following Portuguese traditions, every person has two last names. If José Fagundes Pessoa marries Maria Carvalho Castelo, the wife's name changes to Maria Carvalho Pessoa and their children's last names will be Carvalho Pessoa as well.

The most common first names are Biblical names such as João, José, Ana, Maria, or other traditional European names such as Henrique, Isabel, Fernando or Antônio. There are also many first names that are uniquely Brazilian, such as Aldemar, Valdecir, Jurandir and Itamar. It is quite common to name children after the last names of popular or historical figures, and English last names such as Washington, Wilson and Emerson are used as first names in Brazil.

Nicknames

It is perhaps due to the long and complicated Portuguese names, that Brazilians frequently use *apelidos* (nicknames) to address each other. Nicknames are mostly used among family and friends, but Brazilians invent nicknames for everybody, including bosses or public figures such as actors, politicians, and even the president. Some nicknames are just short forms of first names, such as Zé (José) or Chico (Francisco), but most are based on easily noticeable personal characteristics. In Rio de Janeiro, somebody from Brazil's south could be nicknamed Gaúcho, and in Rio Grande do Sul, somebody from Rio de Janeiro could be nicknamed Carioca. Other nicknames refer to physical traits such as Gordinho (the fat one) or Careca (the bald one). Romário, one of Brazil's best-known football players during the 1990s, is nicknamed Baixinho (little short one) with reference to his height.

In Conversation

Brazilians love conversation and be it at a bank, bar or bus, you will notice that people easily get into conversations with each other. Casual conversations usually start out with general topics. Favourite topics among men are football, politics and the state of affairs in their country. Brazilians are very critical of their government, and current events from society and politics are frequently discussed. You should however be careful with expressing negative opinions about Brazil, since Brazilians are sensitive to criticism, especially from foreigners.

Women in general talk more about their families, homes and children. *Telenovelas* (television soap operas), which are watched by the majority of Brazilians, are also a favourite conversation topic among women, who seem to be especially drawn to the melodramatic stories of love, betrayal and redemption.

Since few foreigners speak Portuguese, Brazilians are excited when someone actually tries to speak their language. They are also interested in finding out what brings foreigners to their country and what they think of Brazil. However, they will usually contain their curiosity out of courtesy and only throw in an occasional question. Brazilians never ask strangers about their personal lives nor do they expect to be asked personal questions about their family, work or private lives. In this aspect, Brazilians draw a line between acquaintances with whom they discuss general topics and friends with whom they share information about their personal lives.

Jokes

Brazilians are good-humoured, and jokes are a common element of conversation. Brazilian jokes can cover any topic, but they are often about current events in politics and sports. Another category of jokes is about the inhabitants of certain regions in Brazil and their alleged laughable behaviours or attitudes. Among men, jokes with sexual content are also quite popular. They are often shared in bars over a few beers.

Body Contact

Brazilians are very comfortable with their bodies, and have few inhibitions about physical contact. This is reflected in the way they behave, move and touch each other. They stand very close in conversation, pat each other on the shoulder and touch each other's arms, especially when emphasising a point, or simply as a gesture of friendship. Brazilians display emotions freely, even in public. Hugging and kissing are very common and people of all ages walk on the streets, arm in arm or holding hands.

A HOSPITABLE PEOPLE

'We were received with a hospitality hardly to be equaled, I think, out of Brazil, for it asks neither who you are nor whence you come, but opens its doors to every wayfarer.'
—Louis Agassiz and Elizabeth Cabot Cary Agassiz,
A Journey in Brazil, 1879

Brazilians are not only a friendly and outgoing people, they are also very hospitable. A Brazilian home always has a door open for friends and relatives, who often drop by unannounced. The most common gesture of hospitality is to offer a visitor a *cafezinho*. You will find this custom in wealthy homes in São Paulo, middle-class apartments in Rio de Janeiro and simple huts in the interior. It is also customary to offer food if someone unexpected arrives at a meal time.

Brazilian hospitality goes far beyond the sharing of a meal or a cup of coffee. A visitor is often taken into the family and treated like a family member. Staying with a Brazilian family means sharing their daily lives and being invited to all their activities, from a Sunday football match to a visit to the ice cream parlour, or an outing to the shopping centre. This book would not have been possible without the many Brazilians who opened their doors and invited me to share their lives.

Visiting a Brazilian Home

Brazilians are generally very informal, and the etiquette for a home visit is casual and relaxed. While most urban households have intercom systems, it is still customary for visitors in rural areas to announce their arrival by clapping their hands since few houses have doorbells. When entering a Brazilian home, it is not necessary to take your shoes off. The *sala de visita* or living room is intended for social gatherings and visits, and is usually located in the front of the house where shoes are not an issue. While Brazilians are hospitable and keep their homes accessible, they distinguish between private and common areas. You will not be given a tour of the house, allowed to view the bedrooms and areas of the home that are considered private.

Dinner Parties

Being invited to eat at a Brazilian home is a great opportunity to experience Brazilian hospitality. Although a meal at a more modest home will have simpler fare, Brazilian hospitality knows no class distinctions. It is as much a pleasure to eat with poorer hosts in a simple wooden hut, as it is with a middle-class family in a high-rise apartment.

Dining etiquette at Brazilian homes is very casual and informal, although good table manners are considered a sign of good education and social status. It is best to tell your host in advance what foods you don't eat to avoid disappointment and embarrassment for both parties. For a dinner invitation, it is common for the guest to bring dessert or a beverage, which is usually arranged with the host beforehand.

Nobody arrives on time for a dinner party. Arriving half an hour to one hour late is customary. Hosts do not expect their guests at the hour specified in the invitation and will usually serve dinner late. Guests are welcomed with an alcoholic beverage such as beer or wine, which continue to be served during and after the meal. Soft drinks and fruit juices are also usually available. An empty glass is an invitation for the host to pour more, and unless you want a refill, let your host know. The lady of the house will make the call for dinner, upon which the dinner guests will approach the table. There is usually no seating order, but guests may wait until they are assigned a seat by the host. Unless you are invited into the kitchen or asked to deliver food items for a dinner party, the kitchen is considered a working area for the maid and the *dona de casa* (housewife) and guests do not usually go into the kitchen to investigate.

A dinner invitation is primarily a social event, and people don't usually show up just for the food and then leave soon after. A dinner invitation includes time for conversation and socialising before, during and after the meal, and guest don't usually leave before dessert and coffee have been served.

Brindes (toasts) are popular when there is a special occasion to be celebrated, such as a birthday, an anniversary or the welcoming of a close friend. Toasts are sometimes humourous and can be used in jest depending on the situation. In a merry round of friends, you may come across such toasts as *que nossas mulheres não fiquem viúvas* (that our wives may not become widows). You will probably hear several others of these humourous toasts at social gatherings.

Parties

Brazilians love to celebrate, and it is not difficult for them to come up with an excuse for a *festa* (a party). Parties at home tend to be informal, and there is usually no strictly observed party etiquette. Dressing is usually casual and the occasion will tell if more formal clothing is required. The host usually introduces the guests to each other, and at smaller gatherings, it is common for all guests to shake hands. Young people may merely acknowledge each other with a casual *"Oi or tudo bom?"* instead of shaking hands. It is customary at smaller gatherings to say goodbye to everyone before leaving. Alcoholic beverages are popular, especially beer and wine. Mixed drinks such as *batidas* and *caipirinha* are also common. *Salgadinhos* (savoury pastries) and *tiragostos* (cocktail snacks) are popular party snacks.

Sarau

The *sarau* is an organised cultural event, usually held at someone's home. It is a private party and is best described as a domestic variety show with literary or poetry readings, music, theatre skits and dance. It is an informal way for people to get together and enjoy each other's creative efforts. A *sarau* may be a semi-public event where not only invited guests, but also their families and friends are welcome.

Inviting Brazilians home

If you invite Brazilian friends to your home, keep in mind that they are used to being hosted the Brazilian way. Offering them a *cafezinho* will doubtlessly make them feel more at home. Although they will feel more at ease with food and drink they know, they will also be intrigued if you present them with dishes or beverages from your home country. However, it is a good idea to offer a familiar food choice as well, so your guests are not obliged to eat an unfamiliar dish. If you organise a dinner party, remember that nobody will arrive on time so don't plan on serving dinner early. Offer the arriving guests an alcoholic beverage, which will put everyone in a good mood and get the party going.

The Extended Living Room

Although the privacy of their homes is important, Brazilians also enjoy being in public while at home. Especially in small towns, it is common for people to sit in their front yards or out on the street and exchange town gossip with passers-by. Even though Brazil's cities are no longer as safe as they used to be, the old Brazilian custom of moving out onto the street at night has survived in some urban neighbourhoods. When I lived in Rio de Janeiro's Copacabana district, my

Family photos and saints are important wall decorations in Brazilian homes.

residential street became a public living room at night. People set up their folding chairs on the pavement in front of their apartment building to chat, play cards and have a few beers with neighbours.

The Third Place

Public gathering places away from home play an important role in the daily lives of Brazilians, since socialising is among everybody's favourite activities. You will notice that Brazilians undertake few leisure activities alone. For most of them, leisure time means time shared with friends and/or family. There are a great many ways in which Brazilians get together in public, and each region has its own unique activities and locations for socialising. In addition to neighbourhood taverns and outdoor bars, town squares, especially in small towns, are very popular and attract people of all ages. It is not uncommon to see young couples on a bench kissing, next to seniors enjoying an evening chat. Brazil's warm climate encourages people to be outside year-round, especially after dark. Staying up late is very common, since people enjoy the pleasant evening temperatures and are more active then. At night and at weekends, Brazil's cities revert to a different pace as leisure and social activities take over the streets that are dominated by the hustle and bustle of the working world during the day. Even on São Paulo's Avenida Paulista, Brazil's busy banking centre, bar owners put folding tables and chairs out on the sidewalk in the evening, where people can enjoy beers and conversation in a much more relaxed atmosphere than during the day. At weekends, some cities close traffic lanes on major avenues for pedestrians, roller skaters and cyclists. All along Brazil's coast, beaches are favourite gathering places both during the day and at night.

Socialising with the Opposite Sex

Brazilians engage in a variety of activities to spend time with the opposite sex. Each town has its own well-known meeting places for young people called *pontos de encontro* (meeting points). Teenagers hang out at squares and streets, meet in parks or enjoy a soft drink or ice cream at a *lanchonete* or snack bar. The most popular places to meet are of course bars and dance clubs. These are the places where young Brazilians go to meet friends and a potential girlfriend or boyfriend. *Paquerar* (flirting) seems to be the young's favourite night-time activity. Those who have formed a couple enjoy going to the cinema or a restaurant, watching the sunset or taking a walk on the beach. Since most young people live with their parents, a couple may even go to a motel, a Brazilian love hotel, to enjoy some privacy. Don't be surprised if Brazilians talk about sex by using words usually associated with eating. Sex is strongly associated with food terms in Brazilian culture, and people commonly use words such as *comer* (to eat), *gostoso* (tasty), and several others to describe sexual activities.

OPINIONS
Brazilians about Themselves

Brazilians consider their country the most progressive and wealthy South American nation, but they suffer from a slight inferiority complex when talking about Europe or North

America. In comparison, Brazil is nothing but a backward third-world nation for them and they often consider things Brazilian to be second-rate. For many, it is more important to read the latest translated novels by John Grisham and Sidney Sheldon than to explore what Brazilian authors are writing. Similarly, imported consumer goods are considered better and often become status symbols. European art exhibits attract immense crowds, as if the act of seeing an Auguste Rodin sculpture would magically transport them to what they consider a higher cultural plane.

When talking about their country, Brazilians are embarrassed by the cyclical political and economic turmoil. They resent that while Brazil is an immensely rich country, much of the wealth is lost and ends up in the hands of a few corrupt politicians and officials. There is a well-known story about Brazil that I have been told many times in various different versions. It is the story of the creation of Brazil: 'When God created Brazil, He made it a big, rich and beautiful country with wonderful beaches, mountains, lush forests, pristine rivers, large reserves of gold, diamonds, metals, minerals, timber, and petroleum. And unlike other countries, God did not provide for volcanic eruptions, earthquakes, landslides, or floods. St Peter, when he saw how much God had given to Brazil in comparison to other places, asked: "Why did you make this country so rich and not put any natural disasters there like everywhere else?" And God answered: "Just wait and see the kind of people I will put there."'

Brazilians about Foreigners

What Brazilians think of foreigners depends on a variety of factors. As few travel abroad, their knowledge of foreign countries is based on second-hand experience and what they see on television. This is especially true in regions with few foreign visitors where Hollywood movies, Coca-Cola and Walt Disney characters are the only contacts with foreign culture. In a remote village in the Amazon, both my Brazilian girlfriend and I were thought to be French, because the only other foreigner in town was a French priest.

Gringos

The term *gringo* is universally applied to foreigners of European descent, and is rarely used in a pejorative way. Brazilians are very respectful of foreigners and rarely call a foreigner *gringo* in public. Based on their observations, Brazilians have developed their own general stereotypes about *gringos*. They consider them serious people who can't dance well and don't know how to have a good time unlike Brazilians.

In cities like Rio de Janeiro, the locals make jokes about European women who are less recognised by their pale skin than by the old-fashioned bathing suits they wear. It has also become known in Rio de Janeiro, that foreign men, especially Europeans, love mulatas, and during Carnaval, exotic beauties from all over the city flock to the tourist areas in search of good-looking *gringos*.

Brazil's Neighbours

While Brazilians exhibit curiosity and interest in Europeans and North Americans, this is not usually the case with their South American neighbours. Near the border, especially with Bolivia and Paraguay, there is a noticeable contempt and disrespect toward their neighbours.

Many Brazilians consider themselves superior to the citizens of these poorer countries who often come to Brazil to smuggle merchandise and take on jobs that Brazilians don't want to undertake.

Indians

The attitude of Brazilians toward native tribes is ambiguous and varies from region to region. While urban Brazilians talk about the natives as 'our Indians' who need protection and help, the opposite opinion prevails in areas near Indian reservations. The natives are envied for their land and for the government money they receive. 'A lot of land for few Indians' has become a slogan in pioneer settlement regions to argue that the reservations are too big, while settlers struggle to secure a small piece of land for themselves.

ATTITUDES
Privacy

Since many Brazilians live in large families and living quarters are often small, they are not very demanding with regard to privacy. Bedrooms are commonly shared by siblings, and visiting friends or relatives sometimes take over the entire house and make themselves at home. Within one family, possessions are often considered communal as opposed to personal and are often shared by everyone. This may apply to anything from clothing and CDs to vehicles.

Nudity

Brazilians have a somewhat ambiguous attitude toward nudity. Most men welcome female nudity, but at the same time they have high moral expectations of their own wives and girlfriends. It is okay for a beautiful woman to dance practically naked during Carnaval as long as she is someone else's wife. And while the erotic performances are tolerated for a few days of revelry, Brazilian laws are much stricter the rest of the year. Bikinis and bathing suits worn by Brazilian women are as small as one can make them, but topless

or nude bathing is illegal. In January 2000, a woman was arrested in Rio de Janeiro for topless sunbathing. In response to the hypocritical attitude shown by the city (naked women are applauded during Carnaval in February, but are not allowed on the beach in January), Rio's beaches were crowded with topless women. Faced with this embarrassing situation, the mayor dropped the charges and decided that it was best not to enforce the city's decency code as strictly.

Waiting in Line

Waiting in line is one of the most common experiences of life in Brazil. I remember a visit to São Paulo's Ibirapuera shopping centre. First, I waited in line at the cashier to pay for an espresso, only to wait in line at the counter to get the drink. Afterwards I waited in line at the elevator to get to my car, after which I waited in line to pay for parking, only to wait in line ... You get the idea. Brazil's inefficient bureaucracy and low standards of customer service pervade every aspect of life and there is simply no way of avoiding it. It is even worse at banks, post offices or government agencies where people work at a snail's pace and waiting in line for at least an hour is common.

When queueing, the phrase 'first come, first serve' is only valid as long as the person who came later doesn't think that he/she is more important than the other people in line, and as long as the person at the end of the line doesn't know someone who can assist with jumping the line. *Doutor fulano* (doctor so-and-so) for example may cut in front because the bank director is a patient. Likewise *coronel sicrano* (colonel so-and-so, probably just a retired sergeant) is served first at the petrol station because of his long service to the country. It is these hidden dynamics that not only determine who is next in line but also who gets ahead in Brazilian society.

Perception of Time
'In Brazil it may safely be assumed that things will always be a little behind time.'
—Louis Agassiz and Elizabeth Cabot Cary Agassiz,
A Journey in Brazil, 1879

If you live in Brazil for some time, you will soon notice that time and timeliness are very flexible concepts. Arriving one hour late at a social event is common, and when a party is scheduled for 10:00 pm, people will start arriving only at 11:00 pm. Brazil's public life makes an effort to be punctual, but television seems to be the country's only institution that is reliably on time. Although performances, movie theatres, airplanes and buses are officially committed to their schedules, there are usually slight delays. But whenever a plane is held up or a bus late, Brazilians accept these twists of fate with a graceful attitude and good humour since they can't do anything about it. If nothing else, these delays are an ideal opportunity for a chat with other passengers.

Respect and Courtesy

While etiquette prohibits Brazilians from being outrightly rude in public, they are not particularly courteous either. Respect is an attitude that is not extended to just every *fulano* (so-and-so) on the street. Brazilians walk ahead of you in lines, shove you when getting on the bus, and will cut you off when driving, apparently oblivious of your existence. This attitude, common in the anonymous public space, is contrasted with the respect and courtesy extended to people of one's own social circle. You will also notice that people in service professions such as waiters, porters, concierges and maids are regarded as servants and are treated without much respect. They are addressed as *moço* (boy) or *moça* (girl) regardless of age, and waiters are called to the table by whistling.

Avoiding Conflict

Although Brazilians are an outgoing and expressive people, they avoid attracting attention by speaking up or arguing in public. Displays of anger, verbal arguments or complaints in public are rare. Brazilians often prefer a casual, jovial and indirect

Brazilians are very agreeable, docile and even submissive in everyday situations. Open conflict is avoided and people often seek indirect and non-confrontational solutions. Endowed with a good sense of humour, it is easier for them to joke about a difficult situation than to discuss it up front. Brazilians rarely say 'no' directly. It is more polite to make up an excuse to get out of an unpleasant situation.

expression of their opinions and feelings and rarely address a desired topic of discussion directly or immediately. They usually begin with a casual topic and gradually shift the conversation to what they really want to talk about.

Cursing

Brazilians rarely curse in public, since this is considered a sign of low social status and a lack of education. Many curse words include references to male body parts. If curses are used, they are never blasphemous since Brazilians have a high respect for religion. Exclamations such as *"Nossa Senhora!"* (Our Lady!) or *"Meu Deus!"* (My God!) are merely expressions of surprise or disbelief.

Noise

Although Brazilians are not usually loud in public, they love loud music. Music is equivalent to fun and loud music is a way of letting everyone know that you are having a good time. This can be especially entertaining or challenging if you live in a large apartment building, where you will hear the loud music of all your neighbours. Wherever people get together, there is music. It is not unusual to find three outdoor bars next to each other, all with the volume of their sound systems set on high and playing different tunes. I remember the massive

Wherever Brazilians gather, there is music.

loud speakers set up on the deck of river boats in the Amazon to provide passengers with lively music on extended trips. I had been looking forward to a quiet voyage with only the sounds of the water and the wind! While excessive loud music can be annoying at times, this kind of public noise is upbeat and cheerful and people always have a good time. Similarly, many Brazilians enjoy whistling or singing in public as an expression of their good mood.

Machismo

'Quero uma mulher que saiba lavar e cozinhar
Que de manhã cedo me acorde na hora de trabalhar.'
(I want a woman that knows how to do laundry and
cook and who wakes me early in the morning
when I have to go to work.)
—from the samba *Emília*,
Wilson Batista and Haroldo Lobo, 1940

Brazil is traditionally a highly patriarchal society, and machismo is still a common attitude among men. Men are used to being in power and control, both in public and private life. Many Brazilian men still see themselves as the protectors and providers of their female companions, and women are sometimes regarded as possessions to which men have exclusive rights. Brazilian men can be very jealous of their women, especially when it comes to other men. Wife murder in defense of honour was only outlawed by the supreme court in 1991.

Independent women and those who speak up and take initiative are not held in high regard by men. They call them *mulher chamosa* (commanding woman) or *mulher mandona* (bossy woman). A popular proverb: '*Em casa que mulher manda, até o galo canta fino*' ('In a house where a woman rules, even the rooster crows quietly'), exemplifies men's sentiment about dominant women. With many women having jobs and being less available and interested in serving their husbands, many Brazilian men quietly resent that their wives are no longer an 'Amélia', a popular stereotype of a docile woman who does everything for her man.

Personal Appearance
'Boa aparência é carta de apresentação.'
('Good appearance is a letter of introduction'.)
—Brazilian saying

Brazilians are status conscious, and personal appearance is important regardless of social class and income. Hence clothing and demeanor all indicate the status of the person you are talking to. Someone in a business suit will doubtlessly receive better treatment than someone dressed in shorts and a T-shirt. When they can afford it, urban Brazilians are very fashion-conscious with a penchant for European fashions, especially French and Italian. Brazil's warm climate has a great influence on clothes and fashion.

Women dress especially well and often wear the latest styles. Partly because of the heat, most women wear only light make-up during the day. More accentuated make-up is sometimes used for social evening activities or formal events.

Natural breathable fibres such as light linen, cotton and silks are very popular. Stylish clothing and especially clothes with recognisable brand names known as *roupa de grife*, are important status symbols.

Everyday Attire
Whether at work or in public, people always dress neatly even if simply. Sloppy appearance is a sign of low status and suggests that the person cannot afford to be well-groomed or buy new clothes. Jeans or slacks and T-shirts are very popular with both men and women for everyday activities. Low-cut dresses or tops are not commonly worn to work, but are popular at weekends or at night. Brazilian men rarely wear shorts during the week and some government offices do not admit men in shorts or sleeveless tops. When I arrived in Rio de Janeiro, I had to go to the Ministry of Foreign Affairs to get an additional stamp for my visa. After a long and difficult trip due to a strike of bus drivers that paralysed the city that day, I arrived at the stately building, only to be sent away because I was wearing shorts.

Clean shoes are also an important status symbol, and *engraxantes* (shoeshine boys) in every city ensure that Brazil's business people walk around in shiny shoes. Tennis shoes are considered casual and may not be allowed in some nightclubs and fancy restaurants. Rubber thongs are popular on the beach and for leisure activities, but are otherwise a sign of low social status. Brazilians don't wear socks with sandals, which they consider unstylish and a trademark of *gringos*.

Leisure Time Appearance

Shorts, tank tops, miniskirts, sandals and thongs are very popular at weekends. For dinner parties, men often wear slacks with short sleeved shirts and women may wear low-cut dresses or skirts with a matching top. Similar attire is worn for going out to a restaurant or nightclub. In general, Brazilians only dress formally for special evening events such as a concert or banquet. Women usually wear cocktail dresses or long gowns, and men put on dark suits.

At the beach, Brazilian bikinis are well-known for the fact that they are very tiny and leave little to the imagination. The so-called *fio dental* (dental floss) is especially popular, as it leaves the slightest tan marks. Another popular item is the *canga* (sarong), which come in a variety of sizes, colours, and fabrics. Women wrap them around their waist over the bikini or bathing suit on their way to or from the beach.

ARRIVING AND SETTLING DOWN

CHAPTER 5

'Be careful in Brazil, because that country
increases in everyone the spirit of ambition
and the relaxation of virtues.'
–Marquis de Pombal, Portuguese War and
Foreign Affairs Minister from 1750–1777,
in a letter to his newly arrived brother in Brazil.

ENTRY REQUIREMENTS
Tourist Visas

Brazil employs a reciprocal policy with regard to tourist visas. That means if your home country requires a visa for Brazilian tourists, Brazil also requires a visa for citizens of your country. The same applies for visa fees. Citizens of the US, Australia and Canada need to obtain a tourist visa and pay reciprocal visa fees, whereas citizens of Western Europe can enter Brazil without visas or fees, and simply fill out a visitor card. All visitors must have an onward or return ticket to document the temporary nature of their visit. In order to enter Brazil, foreigners must carry a passport that is valid for at least 180 days. Tourists are allowed to stay for up to 90 days, but they can extend their stay for another 90 days by applying for *prorrogação* (an extension) at the *polícia federal* (federal police) for a small fee. Tourists are only allowed to stay in Brazil for a total of 180 days in any 12-month period regardless of the calendar year. Tourists are not allowed to engage in any paid activity in Brazil.

Temporary Visas

There are seven types of *visto temporário* (temporary visas). They include visas for researchers, business people, athletes, journalists, missionaries, as well as student and work visas. A student visa is issued to foreigners who intend to study at a Brazilian institution at the undergraduate, graduate, postgraduate or technical levels. Those on a student visa are not allowed to work. A work visa is only granted to those who have an employment contract with a Brazilian company or who perform volunteer work. This visa is valid for up to two years and can be renewed for another two years. Obtaining a work visa for Brazil can be a lengthy process and may take several months.

Permanent Visas

A *visto permanente* (permanent visa) which is a visa granting permanent residency in Brazil is difficult to obtain. It is usually granted to foreign employees who have lived in Brazil for three years (mainly company executives, researchers and scientists), foreign family members (such as a spouse, parent or child) and retirees with pension funds transferred to Brazil (of at least US$2,000 per month). A permanent visa may also be granted to those who make personal investments in Brazil, or who are the director of a religious or social service organisation.

All visas must be obtained at a Brazilian embassy or consulate before entering Brazil. Your first arrival in Brazil must take place within 90 days from the date your visa is

Other Requirements

- A yellow fever vaccination certificate is required for anyone who has travelled to the following countries within 90 days of arrival in Brazil: Bolivia, Colombia, Ecuador, French Guyana, Peru, Venezuela and several African countries.
- International visitors under 18 years of age must be accompanied by their parents or legal guardians, or carry a written permission that is signed by both parents. Contact the nearest Brazilian consulate for detailed instructions.
- If travelling to Brazil with a small child, make sure to bring the child's birth certificate.

issued. It is not possible to get a visa at the airport when you arrive. If you enter as a tourist and are offered a job, you will have to leave the country first to obtain the appropriate visa from the Brazilian consulate in your home country.

Customs Regulations

Visitors are allowed to bring certain personal items that are exempt from import duties. These include clothing and common electronic equipment such as a camera or CD player, as well as items for personal use. New merchandise is exempt from duties up to a value of US$500 when arriving by airplane, and US$300 when arriving on land or by sea. In addition, visitors entering Brazil are allowed to buy an additional US$500 worth of goods at airport duty-free shops upon arrival. Foreigners who temporarily or permanently move to Brazil should enquire at a Brazilian consulate about the importation of household goods, personal belongings and professional equipment. They may have to submit an itemised list of all household items they would like to bring, to a Brazilian consulate for approval.

Possession of illegal drugs such as marijuana and cocaine is a serious offence in Brazil. You should stay away from them and never try to take an illegal substance out of or into the country. Brazil is a major corridor for cocaine trafficking from Bolivia and Columbia, and the federal police is on the alert. It is prohibited to export live animals, animal skins and furs, uncut precious stones, fossils, indigenous artifacts made with bird feathers, and other products made from endangered animals. Taking pets or plants with you to Brazil is a somewhat bureaucratic process. Any pet you bring needs a health certificate from a veterinarian, which needs to be approved by a Brazilian consulate. A recent rabies vaccination may also be required on top of other routine vaccinations. It is best to check with a Brazilian consulate about the detailed requirements and procedures that are necessary to take your pet into Brazil. Bringing pets other than dogs, cats or birds requires the prior approval of the Brazilian Ministry of Agriculture. Plants require a phytosanitary certificate issued by a competent authority in your country.

WHAT TO BRING TO BRAZIL

If you plan to bring a lot of belongings for an extended stay in Brazil, be aware that there are import restrictions depending on your type of visa. Keep in mind that Brazil is a large consumer market with a strong manufacturing sector. You can buy almost anything in Brazil that you might need on an extended stay or assignment. Most household items, furniture, appliances and electronic goods manufactured in Brazil are comparable in quality and price to those in developed countries. On the other hand, camera equipment and some computer accessories are imported and are more expensive. Computer software is also mainly available in Portuguese, and the selection may not be as wide as in your home country.

Tips Regarding Electronics

When bringing television equipment or video tapes, keep in mind that Brazilian television uses the PAL-M system, which is not compatible with the North American NTSC system or any other system. Most video tapes in Brazil use the NTSC system however, and to deal with this confusion of different systems, most Brazilian VCRs are dual-system units and work both with PAL-M and NTSC tapes.

DVDs in Brazil are available for PAL and NTSC, and most Brazilian DVD players work with both systems.

Electric current in Brazil varies from state to state. You should find out about the voltage of the city you will be living in, in order to determine if it is worth bringing electrical equipment from home. Most Brazilian appliances and electrical equipment have adjustable voltage and work everywhere in Brazil.

Although Brazilian clothing shops and boutiques offer a wide variety of clothing and accessories, some items may be difficult to find. Should you require Gore-Tex-lined hiking boots or a breathable extra-light rain jacket, purchase them at home and bring them with you. If you pursue any special interests, sports or hobbies, you should keep in mind that speciality shops and equipment may be hard to find, especially outside major urban areas. Many bookshops carry English books, but the selection is small. If you enjoy reading and have room in your luggage, stock up on a supply of books. English books in Brazil cost much more than in English-speaking countries.

DOCUMENTATION AND OTHER FORMALITIES
National Registry of Foreigners
All foreigners with a visa granting temporary residence (such as a work or student visa), are required to register with the federal police within 30 days of their arrival for finger printing, and to get their Registro Nacional de Estrangeiro, RNE (alien registration card). You will need an application form, your passport, passport-size photographs, proof of payment of the processing fee, and several other documents. It is best to enquire at the Brazilian consulate for a detailed list of required items. The RNE is your official Brazilian identification card, which you are required to carry at all times. You are allowed to carry a notarised copy and keep the original in a safe place.

Tax Identification Card

If you will be working and paying taxes in Brazil, you also need to get a tax identification card—the CPF (Cadastro de Pessoas Físicas). The CPF is not only used to withhold taxes, but is also necessary to open a bank account, finance a purchase or take out a loan.

Driver's License
To drive in Brazil, you need an international or inter-American driving permit issued by an automobile association in your country. For the international permit to be valid, you need to carry your home country's driver's license with you as well. If you have a residency visa, you can get a Brazilian driver's license at the local DETRAN (Traffic Department) without taking a test. You need your valid license from your home

country, your alien registration card (RNE) and your passport. Foreigners with a temporary residency visa have to renew their Brazilian driver's license every six months.

Notarising your Signature

For your visa requirements or other important legal documents, it might be necessary to have your signature notarised. This is done at a *cartório* (notary's office), which can be found in the commercial centres of every city. Your signature is registered with the *cartório* (with a valid identification) and your document then receives a seal attesting to the authenticity of your signature. Your signature card remains on file at the *cartório* for future authentication.

Authentication of Documents

For many legal procedures, it is necessary to submit authenticated copies of original documents. Many Brazilians carry only authenticated copies of their tax identification card or identification cards and keep the originals in a safe place. To have a document authenticated, you need to go to a *cartório* (notary public) and ask for an *autenticação de documento* (document authentication). A photocopy of your document then receives the notary's seal and signature to attest to its authenticity. With this procedure, the copies have the same legal validity as the original.

Registering with your Consulate

To facilitate assistance in case of problems (such as a stolen passport), it is recommended that you register with your consulate after your arrival in Brazil. It is also a good idea to have your passport authenticated by a notary public. That way you can carry the copy and leave the original in a safe place. It you lose your passport, report the incident to your consulate as soon as you can.

FINDING A HOME
Where to Look

Unless your employer in Brazil has arranged housing for you, this daunting task will be left to you. The easiest way to find an apartment is via word of mouth. People in the expatriate community, co-workers or co-students can be immensely helpful when looking for housing. They may know someone who has a rental available, or they may at least be able to refer you to a reputable rental agency. It is also a good idea to explore neighbourhoods that you are interested in, since apartments for rent are sometimes advertised with a sign in the window saying *aluga-se apartamento*. Your next best choice is to locate a rental agency, which can be found through the classifieds or yellow pages. Such an agency can provide you with a list of housing that suits your needs with regard to size, cost and location. Another option is checking the classifieds in newspapers (look under *imóveis*—real estate) for rentals. This is a more difficult and time-consuming method of apartment search, since you will have to speak Portuguese to contact landlords and make appointments.

Furnished Housing

If you plan to spend less than a year in Brazil, it might be a good idea to rent a furnished apartment complete with furniture and appliances. Look under *imóveis mobiliados* (furnished property) in the classifieds, or under flats or *apartamentos para temporada*. It can take months to have a telephone line installed, so you should try to find an apartment that comes with a telephone.

> If you are going to stay for longer, it is probably best to rent an empty apartment, and furnish it according to your own tastes. In this case, you will have to buy your own appliances, cabinets, wardrobes and light fixtures.

Lavanderias automáticas (laundromats) are not common in Brazilian cities, since most middle-class households have washing machines.

The Rental Contract

Make sure you enquire about fees, commissions, deposits, the length of the rental agreement, and penalties that may apply if you move out early. The commissions vary between real estate agencies, but they are usually based on a

If you plan to purchase a car in Brazil, make sure you enquire about parking at your new residence. It is unsafe to leave your car parked overnight on the street in most large cities. All newer apartment buildings have an underground garage or walled-in ground-level parking. The garage entrance is usually monitored by camera.

percentage of the rent. The rental agreement has to be signed by the tenant, the landlord, and a *fiador* (guarantor) who is someone who owns property or a company. In most cases, your employer will act as guarantor. Rent is paid in advance and one month's rent is usually paid as a security deposit when the lease is signed. In addition to the rent, tenants are also responsible for paying the municipal property tax (IPTU), and the shared expenses of condominiums and apartment buildings.

Security

With urban crime on the rise in most large urban centres, Brazil's middle and upper class have got used to living behind bars and high fences. Security systems such as burglar alarms are usually in place in houses or ground-floor apartments. If you plan to live in a house in a large city, it is advisable to enquire about a neighbourhood association with its own private security. High walls and large dogs are some additional security measures used by many home owners to increase their safety. Most apartment buildings have an intercom system linked to the doorbell, or they have 24-hour security where a concierge at the entrance announces visitors by telephone. Surveillance cameras and security guards are also quite common.

What to Expect from your Home

The largest area in any Brazilian home or apartment, is the *sala de visita* or living room. This is usually found toward the front of the house, while the bedrooms are in the back. If you rent a large apartment, there will be a maid's room with bathroom attached to the kitchen. The laundry or service area is usually close to the kitchen, often with a balcony with laundry lines. Due to the warm climate, most Brazilian apartments and houses do not have hot water heaters. Instead, electric water heaters are built into the shower heads.

Make sure the unit is functional, since it is easy to get an electric shock from old shower heads with faulty switches or connections. Faucets in the kitchen and bathroom generally only have cold water. Since the plumbing and sewage systems in many cities are old-fashioned, toilet tissue is not thrown into the toilet bowl, but is deposited in a waste basket next to it. Fans and air conditioning units are indispensable during the hot summer months. When you move into an apartment, you will probably notice a rectangular opening on the outside bedroom walls. This is for the air conditioning, and you will have to purchase a unit that fits the opening. Apartments rarely provide for air conditioning in the living and dining areas, and central air conditioning is rare. In most apartments, you will find hammock hooks mounted in the corners of rooms. Known as *redes*, hammocks are a unique and practical furniture item, since they can be put up and taken down in seconds, and are great for relaxation at any time of the day.

UTILITIES IN YOUR HOME
Electricity
Brazil is largely dependent on hydroelectric power. Blackouts are common both in cities and rural areas. To protect your sensitive electronic equipment, it is best to use surge protectors. Most computers in Brazil are connected to an uninterrupted power supply (UPS) to avoid the loss of information in the event of a power failure.

To have electricity turned on in your newly-rented apartment or home, call the local power company. Electric current in Brazil is not standardised, and most electric appliances and electronic equipment in Brazil have adjustable voltage. Rio de Janeiro and São Paulo have 110 or 120 volts AC, 60 hertz, whereas Belo Horizonte has 127 volts 60 hertz. Recife, Brasília, Salvador, and many other cities have 220 volts, 60 hertz. Fortaleza has a current of 240 volts. Both round pin and flat prongs are in use, and two-way adapters are commonly available. If you bring electric equipment, enquire about transformers to convert the local current to the voltage needed for your equipment.

Water

The water supply and plumbing are reasonably reliable in the cities, and running water is available in every neighbourhood except in the *favelas*. Tap water is not recommended for drinking. It is best to use water filters which are available in a variety of styles. Some filters attach directly to the faucet and can be turned on when you want to filter the water. A more widely used form of filter is a big ceramic pot where tap water trickles through ceramic filter elements. It is also common to have large bottles of purified water delivered to you.

Gas

Gas is the preferred energy source for cooking, but gas lines in homes or apartments are rare and only available in some cities and neighbourhoods. Most households have large bottles of butane gas delivered to their homes, which are easily connected to the stove.

Domestic Help

Although you will find that the standard of living of Brazil's middle class is not as high as in North America or Western Europe, there is one luxury that even the lower middle class can afford: the services of a maid. Having an *empregada doméstica* (domestic maid) is seen as a status symbol in Brazil, because it relieves the lady of the house of the heavy domestic work. Since an increasing number of Brazilian women work outside the home, the help of an *empregada* is often indispensable in a large household.

If you decide to get a maid, you should ask friends or co-workers for a recommendation, since it is not always easy to find reliable domestic help. Word-of-mouth usually works better than pursuing the more official way through classified advertisements or employment agencies. Once you decide on a candidate, make sure that her employment status is legal. To properly employ a maid, you must sign her work card, the Carteira de Trabalho e Previdência Social (CTPS), which entitles her to social security benefits.

While you should not pay your maid more than what she would get elsewhere, you should make sure that she is compensated according to her experience and skills. An experienced maid should receive several times the legal minimum wage. Ask your neighbours, friends or co-workers how much you should pay. It is also important to talk about your expectations when you first hire a maid so she knows what to expect. Each employer wants things done differently, and you cannot assume your new maid knows how to iron and cook your way.

WHERE TO LIVE

Every city offers both centrally located neighbourhoods with apartment high-rises, as well as quiet residential areas with homes which are usually on the outskirts. When considering a location, keep in mind the distance to shopping areas, school and work. Commuting time is an important factor when looking for an apartment in a Brazilian city. Make sure you enquire about public transportation, especially if you don't have a vehicle. Also keep in mind the noise factor. Is the apartment on a busy street with city buses going by day and night? Is the location safe, or is it close to a *favela* with drug wars and police raids? The following list suggests a few attractive and livable neighbourhoods in Brazil's largest cities.

Belo Horizonte

Belo Horizonte is a hilly city surrounded by mountains. As a planned city, it enjoys many tree-lined avenues, among them the Avenida Afonso Pena, the city's main commercial street. Belo Horizonte is among Brazil's most livable urban centres. It has many parks and a good public transportation system including a suburban railway. With the exception of the exclusive suburb Pampulha, north of the centre, the majority of middle and upper class neighbourhoods are in the city's south zone. Among them are Cidade Jardim, Santo Antônio, Cruzeiro and Mangabeiras.

Curitiba

Curitiba has a pleasant subtropical climate and is considered one of Brazil's most livable cities. There are parks and gardens everywhere, and the public transportation system is considered the most efficient in Brazil. In addition to the extensive green areas within the city, there are several nature parks in the vicinity, and beautiful beaches along the nearby coast. Living in the centre here is not as noisy as in other cities, and there is easy access to all amenities. Not too far from the centre are the pleasant districts of Santa Felicidade (the old Italian quarter), Batel, Champagna and Jardim Botánico. A little further out are the quiet suburban districts of Bigorrilho and Portão.

Recife

Recife is among the North-east's most important trade centres in a beautiful location on the coast. Central neighbourhoods such as Boa Vista can be noisy, but they are within walking distance of the centre. Further north of the centre are middle class districts such as Espinheiro, Aflitos, Tamarineira and Casa Forte. Located east of the centre along the beach is the affluent district of Boa Viagem.

Rio de Janeiro

Rio is doubtlessly among Brazil's most beautiful cities. Unfortunately, urban problems such as a deteriorating

Despite its modernity, Rio de Janeiro still has a number of historic buildings, such as this 18th century church in the Glória neighbourhood.

infrastructure, violence and crime have taken away the city's once marvellous quality of life. Close to the centre are the pleasant districts of Flamengo and Botafogo located near Guanabara bay. The Zona Sul (South Zone) is the preferred district for the middle class. Gávea, Leblon and Ipanema are somewhat exclusive, but Copacabana is a regular middle class neighbourhood. Since the subway finally arrived in Copacabana, it is much easier and faster to get to the city center. Further south along the coast, are the upscale suburbs of São Conrado and Barra da Tijuca, with modern high-rise apartments.

The city skyline of São Paulo.

Salvador

Salvador is the North-east's largest city and most important economic centre. The city's main attraction is its cultural life and Afro-Brazilian traditions. There are several attractive neighbourhoods not far south of the city centre, all of them along or near the coast. Among them are Barra, Graça, Vitória and Canela. Further west are nice suburban neighbourhoods such as Brotas, Horta Florestal and Itaigara. There are also pleasant beach districts further west, such as Itapuã and Ipitanga.

São Paulo

São Paulo is Brazil's largest city, a dense urban conglomerate with little room for breathing. Living in São Paulo is noisy and traffic congestion is bad. Consider these factors seriously when looking for housing. The Zona Sul is the middle and upper class residential area which stretches across the south-western and southern part of the city. Among the districts closest to the city centre are Alto de Pinheiros, Jardim Paulista, Itaim Bibi and Moema, whereas the upscale residential districts Morumbi and Santo Amaro are on the south-western outskirts. Each of these neighbourhoods has its own commercial districts and shopping centres.

EXPERIENCING CULTURE SHOCK

'A stranger cannot of course expect the habits
of the people to be changed to suit his convenience ... '
—Louis Agassiz and Elizabeth Cabot Cary Agassiz,
A Journey in Brazil, 1879

First Adjustments

Spending time in Brazil is a wonderful opportunity to get to know a different people and another way of life. But leaving home for an extended period of time is also a considerable challenge to our own cultural beliefs. Once the excitement and novelty wear off, newcomers find themselves in an unfamiliar country whose culture they know little about, and whose language they don't understand. Overwhelmed with these sudden changes, foreigners often react with homesickness, stress and anxiety. While this confrontation with an unfamiliar way of life is an inevitable part of living abroad, there is a lot that can be done to minimise its effects and make your stay more pleasant.

Getting Informed

One of the most important steps you can take to prepare yourself for your stay is to learn about the culture, language and customs before you go. Most common mishaps and misunderstandings can be avoided by carefully gathering information about your destination. This book is intended to save you a lot of research by providing essential information about living in Brazil all in one volume. If you need to deepen your knowledge in some areas of special interest, check out the Resource Guide for a list of recommended reading and websites that provide a plethora of other useful information.

Dealing with Unfamiliarities

How well you handle unfamiliar situations depends a lot on your attitude. An open mind, curiosity, and patience are your best survival tools. Don't expect things to work and people to act the way you are used to, since Brazilian customs and etiquette are probably quite different from those of your home country. But the more you approach unfamiliar situations with flexibility and a willingness to learn, the easier the transition will be. If you convince yourself that your new experiences are enriching and interesting, as opposed to strange and threatening, you will be able to maintain a more positive outlook, and adapt more quickly.

Beginner's Mistakes

Another important attitude is to take everything lightly and with a sense of humour. The ability to laugh about your own mishaps is a very powerful remedy against discouragement and homesickness. Most daily problems you encounter are little more than embarrassments, and there is no need to lose your sleep over them. Trust that you will figure everything out in time, and allow yourself to make the inevitable beginner's mistakes. Living in a foreign culture is a little bit like becoming a child again. Everything has to be relearned, from pronouncing words, to using the telephone and polite conversation. For several months during my first stay in Brazil, I mispronounced the number three in Portuguese, and whenever I ordered three of anything, the vendor would ask "Ten?" This was very frustrating, since I did not know what I was doing wrong, but at the same time it was also very funny because I could always count on being offered 10 when ordering three.

Meeting People

Newly-arrived foreigners are often affected by isolation and loneliness, especially when they come to Brazil alone. This can make for a difficult beginning, and it is no surprise that expatriates often flock together to avoid culture shock, loneliness and the Portuguese language barrier. That's why it is important to be part of a social environment such as a school, work place or host family to have regular contact with the locals. Meeting people is difficult at first because of the language, but there is no better remedy against culture shock than making Brazilian friends. They help you get an insider's view of Brazil, and pretty soon you will gain a better understanding of the people and the culture. It was not until a few months after my first arrival in Brazil, that I began to feel more at home and at ease, mainly because I was starting to make Brazilian friends.

Don't Be Intimidated

An Englishman married to a Brazilian told me that when he first moved to Brazil, he felt threatened by the temperamental way in which Brazilians speak. Used to the different communication style in his country, Brazilians gave him the impression that they were always arguing and yelling at each other because of their vivid gestures, raised voices and the unfamiliar intonation of the language.

Patience is important when first spending time with Brazilians. You may not understand everything they say and their body language and gestures may be indecipherable. But with time, your language skills will improve, and you will get used to their different demeanor and ways of expressing themselves.

Seeking Familiarities

Keeping in touch with people from your own country can be especially important during your first few months in Brazil. You will be able to compare your experiences and find ways to assimilate the new impressions as meaningful learning experiences. A mistake many foreigners make however, is to escape altogether to an expatriate community. While they may make numerous friends from their home country, they end up having little interaction with the locals. Reading your favourite author, watching a movie in English and listening to music you enjoy will also help ease the transition to a different culture, and is a welcome change to an otherwise unfamiliar environment.

Making Sense

Culture shock is as much an experience of the senses as it is an experience of cultural values and behaviours. Trying to make sense of all the different sights, sounds, smells and tastes is one of the biggest challenges to newcomers. Brazil's tropical climate for example, requires a big adjustment for those coming from temperate climate zones. Coastal cities such as Rio de Janeiro, Salvador and Recife are hot and humid, while Brasília on the central plateau is hot and dry. This may require a change in lifestyle, since it is too hot for many activities during the day. Hence people here are more active at night and usually stay up late to take advantage of the cooler temperatures.

Although some Brazilian food may be similar to what is served in your home country, the flavours and ingredients inevitably vary. I remember seeing pastries at a *lanchonete*, which resembled a pastry from my home country that is filled with nuts. As such, I didn't bother asking what the filling was, especially since I spoke little Portuguese then. But when I took the first bite, I discovered that it was filled

Noise

Noise is an important factor that newcomers will have to get used to. Brazil's cities are densely populated, and residential buildings are often built close together. Not only can you hear all your neighbours going about their daily activities when you open the windows, but there will also be the sound of traffic and other unexpected noises from above and below your apartment. Brazilians in general don't treasure silence, and the cities are therefore just a bit noisier than their counterparts in Europe or North America.

with a hot dog! Fortunately, Brazilian cuisine is interesting and varied enough so that most will usually find something they like. This requires a period of trial and error however, which is not always pleasant. What can help reduce food shock is to indulge in familiar dishes once or twice a week at an ethnic restaurant of your liking, a pizzeria or fast-food restaurant. If you prepare your own food, it is worthwhile to find a local gourmet or delicatessen market that sells imported food, so you can enjoy your favourite cheese, wine or chocolate once in a while.

Among the most unpleasant sights for foreigners are the rampant poverty, unsightly shantytowns, street children, beggars and a good many other societal ills common in Brazil. Dealing with all these issues on a daily basis is a difficult challenge for many newcomers. It is impossible to ignore them, but it is also impossible to do much about them. If you buy sweets from a child, there will be 20 more children selling you the same thing that day, and they will be sent out again the next day instead of going to school. A good approach to the obvious misery on Brazil's streets might be to help a little bit everyday. Giving a street child half of your sandwich, or a beggar a few coins won't change society, but it will help them on that day.

Bringing Your Children

Children may be especially vulnerable to the cultural changes around them, and you should pay special attention to their well-being during the transition to a new environment. Maintaining some of their favourite routines from home may help them adapt more easily to the new environment. This can be in the form of toys, games or other activities they enjoy. Making new friends is also important and having contact with English-speaking children will ease the language shock they would otherwise suffer. It is important to talk to your children about all the changes that await them in Brazil, including school, language and weather, as well as food, a new home and safety rules.

Personal Safety

What foreigners find most difficult to get used to is the high crime rate in Brazil's cities. Living with the constant threat of assault is not easy for many who may be used to safety in their home country. It is not only highly inconvenient to lose your credit cards, money and identification cards, but there is also a chance that you could get hurt. Stories about violent muggings are only all too common in the news.

Blending In

Since most foreigners stand out as being from somewhere else because of the way they dress, speak, or look, they are more easily targeted for petty crime. This is especially true in tourist centres such as Rio de Janeiro, Salvador and Recife. In order to lessen such risks, it is important to learn how to blend in. Less conspicuousness means less danger. Since foreigners are often recognised by the different clothes they wear, it is a good idea to buy Brazilian clothes to blend in better with the crowd. Avoid wearing flashy clothing, expensive watches, and jewellery on your day-to-day activities in public. In Rio de Janeiro, street kids were routinely eyeing my brand-name running shoes, so I quickly switched them for locally produced sandals, since I didn't want to lose them at knifepoint.

Do as the Locals Do

Where once only tourists were targets of muggings, Brazilians are nowadays as much if not more at risk. Assaults on cars and even public buses have become common, and have created an urban climate of fear, especially in Rio de Janeiro and São Paulo. Brazilians make considerable adaptations to their lives in order to reduce the risk and impact of being robbed or assaulted. You can learn a lot by watching them and following their example. When driving in large cities in their cars, most Brazilians keep the doors locked and windows up. Many drivers have two wallets in their cars, one with their documents and money, and one with some change to hand over in case of an assault. Small fanny packs worn in the front instead of wallets in back pockets are a common way for Brazilians to carry money, keys and documents. When travelling in a public bus, or walking on a crowded street, many people hold their bags or briefcases in front of them.

What to Watch out For

As long as you take common precautions, you can significantly reduce the risk of becoming a victim of crime. To avoid potentially dangerous situations, it is essential to be alert and cautious, especially when unfamiliar with a city. Newcomers should take special precautions when walking around, until they have been initiated by a local who knows which neighbourhoods and streets to avoid. Dark streets with little traffic invite muggings. Unless you know the area well, you should avoid walking or waiting for the bus on deserted streets, after dark. Late at night, taxis are a safer alternative to buses. As a rule, *favelas* are always off-limits to foreigners. Not even Brazilians go there unless they are invited or live there.

City centres, beaches, and tourist areas are often frequented by pickpockets, and you should always keep an eye on your belongings. Be especially careful in crowded places and on buses, trains and boats. Never carry anything on you that you cannot afford to lose. If you need to carry your documents, keep them in a money belt under your clothing. Instead of carrying original documents, bring authenticated copies. Carrying your wallet in your back pocket only invites pickpockets. It is best to carry as little money as possible, and only keep a few notes in your front pocket. If you are ever mugged, don't resist even if the assailants are just kids. Remain calm and don't attract attention as it will only startle the assailants, and put you in danger. Keep in mind that they are armed and may not

hesitate to hurt you. Hand over your money and leave the scene as quickly as possible.

EVERYDAY LIFE
Banking and Money

> 'Mais vale um amigo na praça, do
> que muito dinheiro no banco.'
> (It is better to have a friend in the town square,
> than a lot of money in the bank.)
> —Brazilian proverb

Since the currency reform in 1994, Brazil's currency has been the real (BRL), pronounced "*hey-OW,*" which has turned out to be Brazil's most stable currency in decades. The currency is issued by the central bank in denominations of 1, 2, 5, 10, 20, 50 and 100 reais (the plural form of real, pronounced "*hey-AH-ees*"). One real (BRL) consists of 100 centavos, and there are coins of 1, 5, 10, 25 and 50 centavos.

Foreign Exchange

Although there are three different exchange rates to the US dollar that are published daily in the newspapers (the *dólar comercial*, the *dólar paralelo*, and the *dólar turismo*), only the *dólar turismo* rate is used for foreign exchange transactions at banks and exchange houses. The real (BRL) was slightly stronger than the US dollar after its introduction in 1994, but it has dropped to less than half of its original value since then. At the end of 2005, the exchange rate of the real (BRL) was between BRL2.10 and BRL2.20 to the US dollar, with minor fluctuations. There is currently no black market exchange in Brazil, and with the exception of large hotels, businesses usually do not exchange foreign currency. When changing money, the bank or exchange house will issue a receipt, which you will need, to change reais back to the currency of origin when you leave Brazil. The best place to change foreign currency in Brazil is a *casa de câmbio* (exchange house). The exchange rates are usually better than at banks, the service is faster, and exchange houses don't charge a commission. Exchange houses are open late on weekdays and even on Saturdays. The drawback is that they are mainly found in tourist centres or large cities such as São Paulo, Rio de Janeiro and Salvador. In some cities, travel agencies also operate as exchange houses, and most of them offer better rates than banks as well.

Opening hours at banks are usually from Monday to Friday, 10:00 am–4:30 pm, but foreign exchange is usually only handled until early afternoon. Expect a long wait for exchange transactions. While several European currencies can be exchanged in Brazil, the most widely accepted foreign currency is the US dollar. Banco do Brasil is the most common bank, and can be found in almost every Brazilian town. Unfortunately, the bank charges a commission for exchanging traveller's cheques and for exchanging cash. Several other banks also routinely handle foreign exchange transactions, among them Bank of Boston, Citibank, Banespa and Itaú. Some require a minimum amount to exchange traveller's checks. It is best to ask and compare rates before exchanging money.

Although traveller's cheques are not as easy to exchange as cash and the exchange rate is lower, it is the safest way to carry money. To take advantage of the protection traveller's cheques offer, write down the serial numbers of your cheques, and keep the purchase receipt separate. Also note the international contact number or phone number in Brazil, so you know where to call, should your cheques be lost or stolen. The most commonly accepted traveller's cheques are American Express and VISA. To exchange money in remote areas and small towns, it is best to have US dollars, either in the form of traveller's cheques or cash.

Credit Cards, Debit Cards and ATMs

VISA, Mastercard, American Express and Diners Club credit cards are widely accepted in Brazil. Debit cards with the VISA or Mastercard symbol can be used in the same way as credit cards. You can use them to pay at hotels, shopping centres and better restaurants and shops. Keep in mind that many smaller merchants do not accept credit cards, or that they may offer discounts for paying with cash or by cheque.

Money Transfers

If you need money sent to you, most banks will receive money wires and process them within a few working days. All you need is the routing number of the bank where you would like to receive the funds. Money wired to Brazil is paid out in Brazilian currency at the turismo rate.

In addition to making purchases, you can also use your credit or debit card for cash advances and withdrawals at bank machines. *Caixa electrónico* or *caixa automático* (ATMs) are very common and can be found at bank branches, on commercial streets, shopping centres, bus terminals, airports and petrol stations. To use an international credit card, find an ATM that displays either the VISA/Plus or Maestro/Cirrus symbol. All other ATMs only work with Brazilian credit cards. Many ATMs at Bradesco, Banco do Brasil, BBV (Banco Bilbao Vizquaya) and Citibank display the VISA/Plus logo. Maestro/Cirrus ATMs are available at Citibank, Banco HSBC, Banco Itaú, Unibanco and Banco 24 Horas, a nationwide ATM network. If an ATM does not accept your credit or debit card, it is best to go to a teller inside the bank to complete the cash withdrawal. Money withdrawn from a credit or debit card is exchanged at that day's turismo exchange rate. It is only possible to withdraw Brazilian currency from ATMs.

Bank Accounts

To open a bank account, foreigners need a Brazilian identification card (RNE) and an income tax identification card (CPF), which they can only get if they have a residency visa (temporary or permanent). The most common form of bank account in Brazil is the *conta corrente*, a basic account accessed through ATMs. Another popular account is the *cheque especial*, a current account (checking account) with overdraft protection, which includes a *talão de cheque* (chequebook) and a bank card. Paying by cheque is a very common mode of payment.

A drawback to banking in Brazil are the high interest rates. In the case of the *cheque especial*, the overdrawn amount is charged a monthly interest rate of around 10 per cent, which amounts to 120 per cent per year. Brazilian credit card companies charge similar interest rates of around 150 per cent per year. Interest rates of Bank loans for durable goods range from 30 per cent per year for a new car to 51 per cent per year for home appliances. There is also a tax for financial transactions, the CPMF (Contribuição por Movimentação Financeira), which is 0.38 per cent of the amount of all transfers, cheques and automatic debits.

Paying your Bills

In Brazil, bills are not paid by sending a cheque in the post. Utility bills such as that for water, electricity, gas and telephone come with a *boleto bancário* (bank payment slip) and are paid in person at a bank, post office or government lottery office. This explains why banks and post offices are so crowded in the first days of every month. But an increasing number of people pay their bills through the Internet, or at ATMs using their bank cards with the *código de barras* (bar code) on the payment forms. For regular monthly bills, *débito em conta* (automatic payments) from a current account (checking account) are also a popular and time-saving way of paying bills. Tax returns are also filed at banks, but an increasing number of Brazilians submit their tax forms and payments through the Internet.

DRIVING IN BRAZIL
Legal Requirements
To legally drive a car in Brazil, you need a valid driver's license, a *certificado de registro de veículo* (vehicle registration certificate), a receipt to certify the payment of the *imposto sobre a propriedade de veículos automotores* or IPVA (motor vehicle tax), which is issued by the traffic department (DETRAN) of the state you live in, and proof of the *seguro obrigatório* or DPVAT (compulsory insurance). *(For information on how to get a Brazilian driver's license, see Driver's License under* 'Documentation and Other Formalities' *earlier in this chapter).*

Rules of the Road
Brazilians drive on the right-hand side of the road. Seatbelts are mandatory and police can stop and fine you for not using one. The speed limit on highways is 80 kmph (50 mph) in urban areas, and 110 kmph (68 mph) in the countryside. Speed limits of residential, commercial and main through streets vary from 30–60 kmph (19–37 mph). Radar traps at intersections and speeding zones are becoming increasingly common, especially since statistics have shown that they have significantly reduced traffic fatalities over the past few years. If you are involved in an accident, call the police (190), have them write a report and assist you where necessary.

Getting Your Bearings
Brazil's large cities are impenetrable concrete jungles without the help of a map. While landmarks such as Pão de Açucar (Sugar Loaf Mountain) in Rio de Janeiro provide some visual orientation, São Paulo is an endless sea of skyscrapers without any distinguishable landmarks. Before you get behind the wheel, get the best available map, study it and get your bearings. Brazilian drivers have little patience for

a newcomer who is in the wrong turning lane and blocks traffic. As you begin to explore your new surrounds, it is a good idea to write down the addresses of places you discover. This makes it a lot easier to find that great boutique, bakery or bar again at a later time.

Road Conditions

Road conditions vary greatly from region to region. Divided motorways are rare and only exist in the South and South-east, which are the only regions where roads are reasonably well-maintained. With the privatisation of federal motorways in 1994 in the state of São Paulo, the maintenance and condition of some national motorways have improved, but tolls have also increased. In much of the rest of the country roads are marked with potholes, and driving can be especially dangerous for someone unfamiliar with the roads. Only about 10 per cent of the roads are paved and three quarters of the federal roads (with the prefix BR-), which act as the main connections between different cities and states, are in need of repair. Due to the poor road conditions and poor vehicle maintenance Brazil has a very high accident rate.

Driving Hazards

The most important rule you need to learn when driving in Brazil is that there are no rules, or at least that rules are only rough guidelines. Drivers don't respect red lights, change lanes abruptly, and only observe lane markers when there is oncoming traffic. Speed limits, so it seems, are for cowards. It is thus not surprising that Brazil's rate of fatal traffic accidents is four times higher than in the US, France or Japan. In addition to erratic driving habits and potholes, you also need to watch out for speed bumps that are set up within city limits on many motorways and roads. Sometimes there are signs but no speed bumps, and at other times there are speed bumps but no warning signs, which usually results in a last-minute slamming on the breaks to avoid damaging your car. Speed bumps are officially called *lombada*, but people commonly call them *quebra-molas* (suspension breakers).

Assaults on cars have become quite common in large cities, and motorists usually keep their windows up and their doors locked when driving. Security bars and car alarm systems are also standard items in many cars to discourage theft and break-ins.

Parking

Finding a parking space is a serious challenge in Brazil's large cities. Street kids and the unemployed have made a new profession out of the parking problem: the *flanelinha* (dust cloth boy), who helps you manoeuvre into and out of a tight parking spot, and watches your car while it is parked. When you return to your car, he expects a tip. Sometimes he may even dust off your car with a flannel cloth, known as the *flanela*, which gave the profession its name.

Long Distance Travel

Long distance travel is not for passenger cars as they are small and not comfortable enough for long hours of driving. The high cost of petrol also makes it more economical to take a bus for long-distance travel. Brazil's overland routes between state capitals and large cities are mainly the domain of flatbed trucks and buses. Because of the constant truck traffic, road services are frequent and can be found even on remote routes. *Postos de gasolina* (petrol stations) usually have a service station or garage, and a restaurant attached to them. To fix a flat tyre, look for a *borracharia* (tyre repair shop) sign along the road.

Buying a Car

Buying and registering a car can be a lengthy process and is only feasible for foreigners with a residency visa who are planning to stay in Brazil for a long time. Brazilian cars are in general simpler and cheaper than their European or North American counterparts. The most common

Volkswagon, Fiat, Ford, General Motors, Mercedes, Toyota and several other multinational companies produce cars in a number of different categories and price ranges. Most of the cars imported from Japan, US and Europe are more expensive mainly due to high import tariffs.

type of car in Brazil is the *carro popular*, a small and affordable car, offered in a variety of models by several manufacturers. Most of these basic car models are also available with an engine that runs on ethyl alcohol produced from sugar cane. Alcohol-powered cars were Brazil's answer to the world oil crisis of the 1970s, and their popularity had faded until recently. Record-high oil prices in recent years, however, have revived the demand for alcohol-powered and mixed fuel cars. New technologies now allow these new 'flex-fuel' (flexible fuel) cars to run on any combination of petrol, alcohol and natural gas at their highest efficiency, which has made the new automobiles very popular in Brazil. At the same time Brazil is becoming less dependent on oil imports.

Car Rental

Car rental is expensive, but you may be able to find a cheap weekend special in some locations. Always ask if there is a discount available. Make sure you know what costs are included in the rental price, and if and what kind of insurance is included. Since petrol is expensive and distances are enormous, a rental car is not recommended for extensive travel in Brazil, but is best for weekend trips and brief explorations in the vicinity. In addition to several large international car rental agencies such as Avis and Hertz, there are also a number of reputable Brazilian companies such as Interlocadora, Localiza, Nobre and Unidas. To rent a car in Brazil, you need to be 21 years of age, have had a valid driver's license for at least two years and possess a credit card. You also need an inter-American or international driver's license, issued by an automobile association in your home country.

LAW ENFORCEMENT

One of the first things that foreign visitors notice about Brazil is the high visibility of police. Brazil has several different police units, all with a different jurisdiction.

Federal Police

The most powerful police unit is the federal police. It controls air, sea and border traffic, and is responsible for maintaining national security. It also cooperates with local police in cases of federal crimes, such as drug trafficking and smuggling, and is responsible for immigration and border procedures. The immigration officials who stamp passports and check visas, are federal police officers.

Motorway Police

The Polícia Rodoviária Federal, the federal motorway police, is another federal police division. It is responsible for patrolling federal motorways and maintaining road safety outside the cities. The motorway police maintains checkpoints and stations along federal roads.

Military and Civil Police

On the state level, there are two police forces, the military and civil police. Since there are no municipal police departments in Brazil, the state military and civil police are divided into precincts, called *batalhões*, which have jurisdiction over a certain geographical area or city district. The Polícia Militar (military police), is a paramilitary unit of the army. Commonly known as PM, it is responsible for maintaining law and order through street patrols. Police booths at street corners usually belong to the PM. They are heavily armed and can function as part of the armed forces if needed.

The Polícia Civil (civil police) maintains *delegacias* (police stations) in Brazil's cities and is responsible for investigating crimes. All crimes are reported to the civil police, but unless you need a statement for your insurance company, reporting theft, robbery or a mugging is rarely helpful since the stolen items will most likely never be recovered. You will spend several hours at the police station, possibly face language difficulties, and waste a lot of time. If you decide to go through with the procedure of reporting a crime, ask for a *boletim de ocorrência* (police report). Brazil's *delegacias da mulher* (women police stations), where women can go to report domestic violence, are part of the civil police.

Popular tourist destinations such as Rio de Janeiro and Salvador have established another police unit, the *Polícia do Turista* (tourist police), to provide a safe environment for the many foreign visitors, especially during popular festivals such as Carnaval.

Drug Offenses

As a general guideline, it is best to stay away from illegal drugs, since penalties are stiff, and Brazilian prisons are notorious for their disregard for human rights.

Although illegal drugs such as *maconha* (marijuana), and to a lesser degree, *cocaína* (cocaine) are commonly used, the police has little tolerance for them and takes every drug offence very seriously. In large cities, the police are engaged in a literal war against drug traffickers, which often leads to police raids and shootouts in *favelas*, mostly in Rio de Janeiro.

Police Violence and Corruption

The Brazilian police has a bad reputation, which is unfortunately not undeserved. Although there are many honest and hard-working police officers, Brazilian policemen have been involved in organised crime, drug running, money laundering, the sale of weapons and many other serious and often violent crimes. Since police officers often enjoy virtual impunity, it has been nearly impossible to prosecute these offenders. Part of the problem is the low salaries of policemen, which makes them vulnerable to bribery and corruption as a means of increasing their income.

However, most foreigners will rarely be confronted with the shady aspects of Brazil's law enforcement. While there is no reason for foreigners to seek police contact, there is also no reason to be worried in case of police controls. Foreigners are generally treated with respect and left alone. The best way to stay out of trouble, is to make sure that your identification papers are in order, and always carry them with you. If you are involved in a situation that might lead to extortion, be careful what you say. Keep in mind that police officers almost always have the law on their side. Remain polite and don't offer money directly. You might be accused of bribery. The best you can do is to ask if there is a way out of the situation. If money is suggested, you may then give the police officer the requested *propina* (payoff) and get out of the situation quickly.

SHOPPING

'Buy today, and only pay after Carnaval.'
—Sign in shop window in São Paulo

Shopping in Brazil is at first a considerable communication challenge for foreigners, but it is also a great opportunity to improve your language skills and explore Brazilian culture. If you are a newcomer, it is best to bring along a detailed phrase book for your shopping trips to help you with the names of food items and merchandise.

Shop Hours

Most retail shops are open from 9:00 am–6:00 pm, Monday to Friday, and 9:00 am–1:00 pm on Saturday. Some supermarkets, chemists, pharmacies and bakeries close as late as 10:00 pm, and are also open on Sundays. Shopping centres usually open seven days a week until about 10:00 pm.

Groceries

Your happiness with food shopping will greatly depend on how much you are willing and able to adapt to a Brazilian menu, since many of your favourite food items may not be available in Brazil. Whole grain bread, for example, is very hard to find, and the common varieties of cheeses and cold cuts may taste different from what you are used to. Some fruits and vegetables from temperate climatic zones are not available, or are more expensive. On the other hand, you will have the world's best selection of tropical fruits, and if you are willing to substitute peaches with mangos, cherries with *acerola*, and blueberries with *jaboticaba*, you are on your way to adapting to life in Brazil.

Farmers' Markets

The weekly *feira livre* (outdoor farmers' market) is a popular event in most towns and city neighbourhoods. Many

Brazilians wait for market day to buy fresh fruit and produce. For foreigners, these markets are a great opportunity to learn about the enormous wealth of Brazil's agricultural products. The sheer variety of colours, shapes and smells is overwhelming at first, but with time you will know what most things are, and you will be able to pick out the best fruits and vegetables. In addition to outdoor markets, many cities have a *mercado municipal* (municipal market) held in a market hall. It offers the same wide variety of produce in addition to fish, meat, delicatessen and speciality foods, all under one roof.

Supermarkets

Supermercados (supermarkets) can be found in most neighbourhoods in Brazil's large cities. Like those in other western countries, most supermarkets also sell household items and fresh baked goods in addition to groceries. Multinational companies dominate the processed food market, and products by Quaker, Knorr, Maggi, Kraft, Nestlé, and other giants of the food sector are very common. The largest supermarket chains are Pão de Açucar, Carrefour, and Bompreço.

A typical street market in north-eastern Brazil.

Bakeries

Padarias (bakeries) are popular and can be found in almost every neighbourhood. The most popular bread items are *pãozinhos* (white rolls), also known as *pão francês* (french roll), and *pão de forma* (white loaf), which are sold oven-warm. Most bakeries have extended opening hours, and also operate as *lanchonetes* and *lojas de conveniência* (convenience shops).

Craft Fairs

Many cities have regular *feira de arte e artesanato* (arts and crafts fair), that are usually held at weekends. Depending on where you live, there may be interesting regional handicrafts for sale. Artisans in Minas Gerais specialise in gemstone jewellery and soapstone sculptures. Ceramics and leather goods such as sandals, bags and hats are popular craft items in the North-east. The state of Ceará is known for its beautiful cotton hammocks. Ask at the local visitor information centre if your city has such a fair. In São Paulo, the most popular craft fair is in Embu, about 28 km (17 miles) south-west of the centre. In Rio de Janeiro, there is a weekly arts and crafts fair in Ipanema (Feira de Ipanema). Salvador has a permanent handicraft fair at the Mercado Modelo. In Recife, it is at the Casa da Cultura, and Belo Horizonte holds a weekly crafts fair on Sundays, on the city's main thoroughfare, the Avenida Afonso Pena. One of the North-east's largest fairs is in Caruaru, Pernambuco, where wholesalers offer the region's best arts and crafts.

Retail Shops

In the old commercial districts of Brazil's cities, small family-owned retail shops are still the most common form of retail business. Chain shops and large national department stores can also be found in city centres, but they are now often located in shopping centres. Large commercial buildings in city centres have multi-storey shopping centres known as *galerias*, with a variety of retailers and an environment not unlike a shopping centre. Shopping at a small retail shop in Brazil can be an interesting experience. You may have to direct yourself to a salesperson behind a counter to place your order. The person will then get your item and write you a sales slip, which you will need to take to the cashier to pay. Then you return with the sales receipt to the salesperson who helped you. The salesperson will then wrap the purchased item in paper and hand it to you.

Shopping Centres

In Brazil's large cities, 'shoppings' (shopping centres) are gradually replacing old-fashioned commercial districts as the preferred shopping environment of the middle class. These centres offer greater convenience with parking garages and ATM machines, and offer a clean and safe shopping environment with security guards on patrol. Shopping centres are also located in more affluent districts, and often have exclusive boutiques, as well as trendy chain shops, restaurants, movie theatres and video arcades.

Street Vendors

Brazil's informal commerce is a big business, and it is possible to buy almost anything from *camelôs* (street vendors). Except where expressively prohibited by the city government, there will be small booths on pavements, pedestrian overpasses

A coconut vendor on a beach in Bahia.

and squares in most cities. Much of the merchandise is contraband, and prices are usually much lower than in retail shops, which makes pavement shopping popular with the working class. Most of the items are second-rate, but many Brazilians don't have the choice to buy higher quality and more expensive items. Sometimes it is also more the convenience it offers, than price that makes people buy from *camelôs*. Instead of entering an office supply shop to buy envelopes, people can get the same item from a *camelô* in front of the post office. Telephone cards, bus tickets, pens and some daily necessities are items that people regularly buy from *camelôs*.

Bargaining

Bargaining is quite popular, especially at markets and fairs. It is also common for Brazilians to ask for discounts at retail shops where prices are marked. After a little bit of haggling, salespeople will often lower the price. Brazilians don't just bargain out of need, they also do it for fun and for the social interaction.

> For most, shopping is not just limited to purchasing goods. It is also a ritual that includes social interaction and conversation. It is amusing to listen to the rhetorical arguments that evolve from trying to get a CD for a few reais less.

Buying on Credit

Since the buying power of the average Brazilian is weak and credit cards charge horrendous interest rates, businesses offer direct consumer credit, which allows the customer to purchase an item and pay in monthly instalments. Since inflation has been mostly at single digit figures since 1995, many shops offer up to six instalments without charging interest. Anything from appliances to international vacations and plastic surgery is paid this way, making it easy for people to buy more expensive consumer goods without the high interest rates of credit cards, or overdraft current accounts (checking accounts).

Tipping

Dar uma gorjeta (tipping) is not widely practiced, but there are several situations when a small tip is appropriate. Most restaurants add a 10 per cent service charge to the bill, but you can leave a little extra for good service. At businesses where service is not included in the bill (as in the case of beauty parlours, hair dressers and barbers), a 10–15 per cent tip is the general rule. Porters at hotels, bus terminals and airports should be tipped for every bag they carry. Attendants at public restrooms should be given a few centavos. Taxi drivers are not tipped, but it is common to round up the fare. When parking on the street, it is customary to give the *flanelinha* (self-declared parking attendant) a tip for 'watching' your car.

POSTAL SERVICE

Every town and city district has at least one post office. Look for the yellow and blue Correios (postal service) sign. Most post offices are open from 8:00 am–6:00 pm from Monday to Friday and on Saturday until noon. Lines at post offices can be long especially at the beginning of the month when people pay their bills. The postal service in Brazil is not known for its speed or reliability. In addition to conventional mail, you can also send domestic and international express mail (SEDEX), as well as registered and insured mail. Most larger post offices have facilities to send both domestic and international faxes. You can also buy boxes and envelopes at post offices. Aerogrammes are available for cheap international postage. Brazilian envelopes come without adhesive because the flaps would seal easily given the high humidity. There are usually small glue bottles at post office counters to seal envelopes. If you are interested in philately, most large post offices have separate counters, where you can buy colourful stamps featuring Brazilian fauna, flora and more.

For international mail, you have to use special airmail envelopes, which have yellow and green stripes along the edge, and have *via aérea* (by airmail) printed on them. To send a package overseas, you have to fill out a customs form. International parcel rates are high even when shipped by surface mail. In addition to the postal service, several private companies such as UPS, Federal Express and DHL Worldwide, also provide international express mail services to and from a large number of Brazilian cities.

PUBLIC TRANSPORTATION
Since many Brazilians can't afford to own a car, public transportation is well developed throughout the country.

Taxis
Taxis are a common and inexpensive form of transportation, that is both faster and safer than taking a bus. There are two types of taxis. One is the *taxi comum* (common taxi), which you can find at a taxi stand or hail from the street by waving your hand. The other is the radio taxi, which you need to call by phone to arrange for pickup. They are more reputable, but the fare is also higher.

Until recently, conversion charts were used to convert the meter reading to the actual fare. Currently, the fare corresponds to the amount shown on the meter. Tipping is not customary, but the fare is usually rounded up. Sometimes drivers may try to get a higher fare from foreigners, especially in tourist centres. Make sure that the meter is turned on when you get into the taxi. To avoid being taken on an especially long route to your destination, you can arrange a flat fee with the driver, who then turns his meter off. In smaller towns *mototaxis* (motorcycle taxis) are very popular. They are much cheaper than regular taxis and take you around town for a fixed fare.

City Buses
Public buses are cheap and run frequently from about 5:00am until midnight. Many cities also have night routes with reduced schedules. Since traffic in most cities is dense, expect bus travel to be slow. In large cities, there are also express routes that directly connect distant suburbs to the city centres for a higher fare.

Municipal buses have conductors who collect the fare, and give change for small notes. Most bus routes have numbers, and the destination is written on the front of the bus. Buses get very crowded during rush hour. It is a

> To decipher the maze of bus routes in Rio de Janeiro and São Paulo, I wrote down the numbers and destinations of the buses I was taking to figure out the best and fastest routes. This list saved me a lot of time and confusion, and helped me avoid taking the wrong bus twice.

good idea to write down your destination, so you can show it to the conductor or driver, if you don't speak the language well. Some detailed city maps also include bus routes, which can be very helpful for newcomers.

Shared Transportation

As an alternative to slow city buses, privately operated vans and minibuses have conquered a large clientele in the past few years. This type of informal urban transportation, known as *lotação*, now operates in many large cities, and is often the only public transportation in *favelas*. The vehicles are usually as crowded as regular buses, but they don't stop as often, and travel much faster. The fare is usually just slightly higher than the city bus.

Subways

The *metrô* (subway) is the most efficient means of urban transportation. Unfortunately only a few Brazilian cities have a subway or urban rail system, namely São Paulo, Rio de Janeiro, Belo Horizonte, Brasília, Recife, Porto Alegre and Salvador (under construction). Unfortunately, there are not nearly enough lines to cope with the increasing number of passengers, but new lines have been planned and will be introduced in time. Most subways operate from 5:00 am to midnight. The subway in Rio de Janeiro is closed on Sundays.

Long-Distance Buses

Intercity buses are a reliable, comfortable and cheap means of long-distance travel. Depending on the destination, departures are regular and frequent, and generally on time. Keep in mind that distances are enormous in Brazil. What looks like a short distance on a map, may take an overnight bus ride. For long-distance travel, it is best to purchase your ticket a day or two in advance, especially during school vacation from December–February. Seats are usually reserved, and if you buy your ticket early, you can pick your seat. Most buses for long-distance travel have a toilet in the back, so it is a good idea to get a seat toward the middle or front of the bus. Many travel agencies in city centres sell long-distance bus tickets, so it is not always necessary to purchase your ticket at the distant bus terminal. *Leitos* (sleeper buses) operate on overnight routes between Rio de Janeiro, São Paulo, Belo Horizonte, Brasília and several other destinations. They have comfortable reclining seats with plenty of legroom, and passengers arrive well-rested at their destination. Tickets are more expensive than for conventional buses, but the trip is much more comfortable. *Executivo* (executive) buses are also available on several routes between large cities. They provide more direct and faster service, have more legroom, and provide refreshments and video entertainment.

Railways

Brazil has a very sparsely developed railway system mainly used to transport cargo such as grains and ore. Passenger transportation accounts for only a very small portion of the total revenue. Both Rio de Janeiro and São Paulo have a large net of suburban passenger trains that service the metropolitan areas, but passenger railway service between Brazilian cities is rare and infrequent. There is a railway from São Paulo to the interior of the state and to Rio de Janeiro, and there are international routes to Bolivia, Uruguay and Argentina. Short passenger trains are in operation on a few other routes, mainly as tourist attractions.

Air Travel

Due to Brazil's enormous size, air travel is the only means of transportation that connects all parts of the country within a day's travel. All cities have airports with daily flights to Brazil's major urban centres or state capitals. But since domestic flights are expensive, they only account for a small percentage of all passenger travel in Brazil. Varig and TAM are Brazil's largest airlines, offering both international and domestic flights. Rio-Sul and Gol provide domestic service only, and there are also several regional airlines. A departure tax of US$36 is charged for every passenger leaving Brazil on an international flight.

Passenger boats are a common means of transportation in the Amazon.

Boat Travel

Brazil has about 50,000 km (31,000 miles) of navigable inland waterways. Most of them are in the Amazon region, which is still largely inaccessible by land. Since roads frequently wash out during the heavy rains, river navigation is the region's most important and reliable means of ground transportation. Both cargo and passenger boats frequently travel up and down the Amazon river and its major tributaries. Boat cabins are small and stuffy, and most passengers prefer to pay less and sleep in a hammock on a covered deck. Food is included in the fare, but it is very basic (rice, beans and some meat). It is best to bring fruit and snack food for the trip. Since there is absolutely nothing to do, most passengers just relax in their hammocks, and watch the scenery go by.

TELECOMMUNICATIONS

The government-owned telecommunications company, Telebrás, was privatised in 1998. Since then, Brazil has experienced the ups and downs of the private telephone market. So far, the improvements have not been implemented at the desired pace, and reliability, expansion, and customer service all remain below government expectations.

Public Telephones

Telefones públicos (public telephones) can be found everywhere and are easily recognised by their coloured plastic shells, which gave them their popular name *orelhão* (big ear). Most public phones can be used for local, long-distance, and international calls. They are operated by a magnetic *cartão telefônico* (telephone card), which is available at newsstands, *lanchonetes* and from street vendors. When making an international call, make sure that you buy a telephone card with at least 100 units, otherwise your call will be very short. You can also make phone calls and send a fax, telex, or telegramme from a *posto telefônico* (telephone office). In large cities, you will find one in every district, and smaller towns have at least one near the city centre. Telephone offices usually have phone books of all Brazilian states.

Faxes

A *fax* (fax) can be sent from main post offices, telephone offices and large hotels. Some copy shops also offer fax services. Since international faxes are charged at the regular rates of international phone calls, they are quite expensive, especially during business hours.

Mobile Phones

Brazil's *telefone celular* (cellular telephone) market has exploded in recent years. In 1998, a prepaid mobile telephone system was introduced, which has become very popular, since expenses can be more easily controlled. With this system, customers purchase a telephone credit card with a desired value, which allows them to make calls on their mobile phone until the value runs out.

Residential Telephones

Since the privatisation of Telebrás in 1998, the number of telephone lines has increased. Before the privatisation, it could take years before a telephone line was available, and residential lines were traded on the black market for large sums. Today, it usually takes several months to have a line installed, and the installation costs are reasonable.

A telephone booth inspired by the local fauna.

For residential lines, there is a small monthly service fee plus charges for local and long-distance calls. To have a residential telephone line installed in your home, you will need your residency documents, as well as proof of income and address.

If you plan to use a computer modem with your telephone line, keep in mind that most telephone wall jacks are large rectangular sockets designed for four large prongs. Fortunately, telephone cords that plug into these wall jacks usually have the standard American telephone plug (US RJ-11) on the other end, which fits most international telephones, fax machines or computer modems, that you may have brought with you. If your modem does not recognise the local dial tone, set the modem on your computer to ignore it.

Long-Distance Calls

Of Brazil's 12 large telecommunication service providers, only Embratel and Intelig handle international and long-distance calls to all locations in Brazil. All other telephone companies only connect to numbers within their service areas, which can include several states. To make a long-distance call within Brazil, you need to dial the national prefix 0 plus the number of the service provider of your choice (Embratel 21 or Intelig 23 in most cases), plus the area code and the phone number. Regardless of which telecommunications company or telephone you use, reduced rates for domestic and international long-distance calls are usually in effect on weekends and in the evenings. The area codes for Brazilian cities are listed in every telephone directory.

City Codes

The most important city codes are:

- Belém   91
- Belo Horizonte   31
- Brasília   61
- Campinas   19
- Curitiba   41
- Fortaleza   85
- Porto Alegre   51
- Recife   81
- Rio de Janeiro   21
- Salvador   71
- São Paulo   11
- Vitória   27

For international calls, dial the international prefix 00, plus the service provider access code (21 or 23), followed by the country code, area code and phone number.

Collect Calls

You can make a *ligação a cobrar* (collect call) from any telephone in Brazil. For local collect calls from a public phone, dial 90-90 before the phone number. For long distance collect calls from a private or public phone, dial 90 before the national prefix (0), provider access number (21 or 23), area code and phone number. This will connect you to a recording, where you will be asked for your name and where you are calling from. If the recipient accepts the charges, the call is put through.

EDUCATION IN BRAZIL
'Cada escola que se abre é uma cadeia que se fecha.'
(For every school that opens there is a prison that closes.)
—Brazilian saying

Illiteracy
Throughout Brazil's history, education has been a privilege of the elite. The public school system for the common people has been far from adequate, which has led to high illiteracy levels. Brazil has only recently made progress in the fight against illiteracy, mainly thanks to government funded adult literacy campaigns. In 2004, Brazil's overall illiteracy rate was 10.5 per cent. The North-east has the highest rate of illiteracy, and the South and South-east have the lowest. In addition, almost a third of Brazil's population are considered functionally illiterate, which means that they attended school for less than four years, and only have very basic reading and writing skills.

The Education System
An education reform in 1996 has restructured Brazil's education system. There are now two levels of education: *educação básica* (basic education) and *educação superior* (higher education). Basic education includes nurseries, preschools, the *ensino fundamental* (primary school level), with eight years of instruction from ages seven to 15, and the *ensino médio* (secondary school level), with three years of instruction until age 18.

The school year runs from February to the beginning of December, with a month of vacation in July. School attendance is mandatory at the primary level. School attendance has improved significantly in recent years, thanks to a government programme that provides a monthly stipend for low-income parents to keep their children in school.

Higher education is provided by a number of universities both public and private, offering *graduação* or *bacharel* (bachelor's degree), *pós-graduação* (master's degree) and *doutorado* (doctorate degree). Eighty per cent of Brazils institutions of higher learning are private universities with high tuition fees, whereas the government-funded public universities are free. This leads to fierce competition among students to pass the entrance exams for free university access, and shuts many low-income students out of higher education.

International Schools

If you come to Brazil with your children, you have to decide whether you want to send them to a private school to be instructed in English, or a Brazilian school to be instructed in Portuguese. Younger children generally adapt more easily to a different language of instruction than those who have already attended an English-speaking school for several years.

Every major Brazilian city has at least one international school. Most of them follow the British or American educational system, but some offer an international high school diploma, that is recognised worldwide. Many international schools offer education from kindergarten all the way through secondary school, making it easy for expatriate families to provide for an English-speaking educational environment of their children at an early age. Cost is an important factor to consider when deciding where to send your children. Public schools are free and most Brazilian private schools are much cheaper than international schools. (*See the Resource Guide section at the back of the book for a list of international schools in Brazil*).

STAYING HEALTHY

'Pouca saúde e muita saúva, os males do Brasil são.'
(Bad health and a lot of ants are the ills of Brazil.)
—Mário de Andrade, Macunaíma, 1928

Before You Go

Brazil's predominantly tropical climate favours a number of diseases uncommon in temperate zones, but as long as you take a few common-sense precautions, it is relatively easy

I'M GOING TO BRAZIL AND I'VE ALREADY GOT ALL THE ILLNESSES AND DISEASES!

HYPOCHONDRIACS ANONYMOUS

to stay in good health. The best way to prepare yourself medically for a trip, is to arrive in good health. Seeing a doctor in a foreign country can be a challenge because of the language barrier, and the uncertainty that comes with seeking medical help abroad. See your doctor or a travel clinic at least one month before your departure, to determine what boosters or immunisations you will need. In addition to the standard immunisations such as tetanus-diphtheria (Td), MMR (Measles, Mumps, Rubella) and polio, many foreigners also get a typhoid and yellow fever immunisation. Since Hepatitis A is a food-borne disease, it may be a good idea to get an immunisation as well. Bring an international immunisation record with listed health conditions and allergies, which can help you get the right medical treatment, if necessary. If you take prescription medication, either bring a supply large enough to last you for your stay, or see a local doctor soon after your arrival to get a similar prescription. If you wear glasses or contact lenses, bring a spare pair, or write down the prescription to be able to get a replacement easily. You should also consider bringing your favourite brands of non-prescription medications, since you might not be able to find them in Brazil.

Water and Food Precautions

Although water from municipal water supplies is treated, you should avoid drinking unfiltered tap water. Filters for home use are readily available, and natural mineral water is sold everywhere. Home delivery of large bottles of drinking water is also available. Avoid ice cubes, unless you know that they are made from purified water. In rural Brazil, intestinal parasites are widespread due to impure drinking water. You might want to bring water purification tablets, or a portable water filter, in case you travel to areas where no purified water is available. If you drink unfiltered water in rural areas, you should get tested for worms after you return home.

Numerous diseases and germs are food-borne, and you should check your eating habits to determine if you are at risk. It is important to adapt your sanitary practises to the tropics where germs are more abundant. Wash your hands often and always before you eat. Avoid touching food with unclean hands. Hygiene standards in most Brazilian restaurants are high, and food safety at restaurants is not a serious concern. You should be more careful with street vendors, road-side food stalls and *lanchonetes*. Pick an establishment with a high turnover, which is the best assurance that the food is safe. In rural Brazil, sanitation is not always up to standard, and the chances of catching a food-borne disease are greater. If you eat raw fruits or vegetables, make sure they are peeled, or washed in purified water. Be careful with seafood, especially shellfish, and with lightly cooked meat dishes. Food should be cooked thoroughly and served hot. Avoid unpasteurised dairy products.

Dealing with the Heat

If you arrive in Brazil from a temperate climatic zone, be prepared to make adjustments to the heat. Give your body time to adjust to the different climate, and drink a lot of water. Use sunglasses, sunscreen, as well as a hat to protect yourself from the effects of the tropical sun. On Brazil's north-east coast for example, white skin can only resist the tropical sun for about half an hour before burning. It is best to use a sunscreen lotion with sun protection factor 30 or above.

Stock up on sunscreen from your home country, since it is expensive in Brazil. Wear light and light-coloured clothing, and remember to drink a lot. *Água de coco* (the juice of green coconuts) is a great natural rehydration drink.

Insects

Despite Mário de Andrade's wise words quoted above, the ills of Brazil are not so much the voracious leaf-cutter ants, as a number of other small insects, which transmit serious diseases. The best protection against mosquitoes and sandflies is appropriate clothing that covers as much of your body as possible. Most insects that transmit diseases are active at dusk and dawn, and it is especially important to use insect repellent during these times. If possible, sleep in a room with insect screens on the windows, or use bed netting.

Common Diseases
Traveller's Diarrhoea

Travellers' *diarréia* (diarrhoea) is common among foreigners who are just getting used to the different bacteria contained in tropical foods. However travellers' diarrhoea usually subsides by itself after a few days. If the condition persists longer than a few days or worsens, you should see a doctor. General symptoms include nausea and stomach cramps together with diarrhoea. Since diarrhoea leads to rapid dehydration, you should drink as much as possible. By following common food safety precautions, you should be able to reduce your risk of diarrhoea. Anti-diarrhoea medication is readily available in Brazil, but you might prefer to bring a supply from home.

Malaria

Malaria is a parasitic disease that affects the liver. It is transmitted by the bite of the infected female anopheles mosquito. Symptoms include sweat, nausea, fever and aches. Malaria occurs in all Amazon states, but the coastal and southern regions are risk-free. For short-term stays in areas with a malaria threat, it is recommended that you take prophylactic drugs. It is best to bring a supply large enough to last for the period of potential exposure. Prophylactic medication needs to be taken several weeks before, during and after a visit to a high-risk area.

Dengue Fever

Dengue (Dengue fever) is a common viral disease. It is transmitted by the Aedes aegypti mosquito, which is most active during the day. Dengue occurs most commonly in urban areas, especially during the rainy season from December through March. Symptoms are headaches, fever, nausea and usually a rash. Dengue fever can last for over a week, and patients sometimes take several weeks to recover completely. Since there is no vaccine, the only way to lower your risk is to avoid being bitten by mosquitoes during the day. If you live in a house with a yard, remove all objects that could collect water and serve as breeding grounds for mosquitoes.

Yellow Fever

Febre amarela (yellow fever) is a viral disease that can cause liver problems. It is transmitted by a mosquito and occurs mainly in the Amazon region, although there are also outbreaks in other areas. Since a vaccine is available, you should not take any risks and get an immunisation. You will be issued an international certificate of vaccination, which is valid for 10 years. Bring this card with you to Brazil. The Brazilian government recommends a yellow fever immunisation for visiting the Amazon. There are immunisation posts with free immunisations along motorways to the Amazon and at airports in major cities. Free yellow fever immunisation is also available at local vaccination posts throughout the Amazon region.

Cholera

Cólera (Cholera) is a bacterial intestinal infection that is contracted by consuming contaminated food and water. The disease is most common in the North-east, due to sanitation problems. Outbreaks are most frequent during the dry season when clean drinking water is not as readily available. Although there is a vaccine, it is not very effective, and is only available in some countries. Following common food safety precautions should significantly reduce the risk of a cholera infection. The number of cholera cases in Brazil has dropped significantly since the early 1990s.

Leishmaniasis

Leishmaniose (Leishmaniasis) is a parasitic disease transmitted by the bite of some species of sand flies. The disease appears in two forms, either affecting the skin in form of sores (cutaneous leishmaniasis), or affecting the internal organs by causing fever, anemia and enlargement of the spleen and liver (visceral leishmaniasis). Infections are more common in rural Brazil, but can occur in urban areas as well. The disease is most common in the North-east, especially the states of Bahia, Ceará and Maranhão. If travelling in an endemic area, the best preventative measure, is to protect yourself against sand flies through insect repellent and clothing. Also, avoid being outside from dusk to dawn.

Leprosy (Hansen Disease)

Hanseníase (Leprosy) is a bacterial disease causing lesions of the skin. Successful treatment depends on early diagnosis and multi-drug therapy. Brazil has the world's second highest rate of leprosy cases, making the disease a growing public health concern. There were over 49,000 new cases of leprosy in 2004, and in response, the ministry of health introduced an ambitious programme to eradicate leprosy in Brazil.

Schistosomiasis

Schistosomiasis is a parasitic disease caused by microscopic worms that live in freshwater, and are spread by snails. The worms penetrate human skin and cause an infection. Common symptoms are fatigue, diarrhoea, fever, nausea and stomach pain. To prevent exposure, you should avoid contact with bodies of water where schistosomiasis is known to exist, or where sanitary conditions are poor. Drying off quickly after contact with water may reduce the chance of infection. Schistosomiasis can be treated with medication.

Chagas Disease

Doença de Chagas (Chagas disease) is caused by a parasite transmitted by contact with the faeces of a reduviid bug, a brown oval-shaped beetle that lives in huts made of mud or palm thatch. The beetle is known as *barbeiro* in Brazil and occurs in rural areas in north-eastern, south-eastern and central states. Chagas disease is a serious illness that can lead to chronic heart or intestinal disease years after the infection. Bed netting can help prevent infection.

Rabies

Raiva (Rabies) is a viral disease transmitted by bites from infected animals, mainly dogs. As a general rule, all animal bites should be treated by a doctor to determine the risk of rabies.

Be Prepared

If you plan on staying in remote rural areas, and are at risk of being bitten by dogs or other animals, consider getting a pre-exposure rabies vaccination.

Hepatitis

Hepatite (Hepatitis) is a viral disease that affects the liver. The main symptoms of hepatitis are chills, fever, nausea, stomach pains and yellowish eyes and skin. Hepatitis A is transmitted by consuming contaminated food and water, or by person-to-person contact. Be especially aware of unsanitary conditions, where the transmission of the disease is much more likely. An active vaccine is now available. Hepatitis B is transmitted by bodily fluids. Immunisation is available, and is recommended for people who might use local health care facilities, have direct contact with blood or have sexual contact with the locals. Hepatitis C, which is transmitted by blood and through sexual contact, is the most serious type of hepatitis. It is often only diagnosed in the advanced stage, when it causes liver cancer and cirrhosis.

Tuberculosis

Tuberculose (Tuberculosis) is a bacterial infection that most frequently affects the lungs. It is transmitted through the air by coughing, or through unpasteurised milk or milk products. Tuberculosis has been on the rise in Brazil since the 1990s, and the government has launched a health campaign to control the disease. Tuberculosis is effectively treated with medication. If you suspect that you might have been exposed, you should get a tuberculin skin test to determine if you have been infected.

Typhoid Fever

Febre Tifóide (Typhoid Fever) is a serious bacterial disease transmitted through contaminated food and water. Although typhoid vaccination is not completely effective, you should add it to your immunisation list, especially if you intend to travel in rural and remote areas. In the case of a prolonged high fever, you should see a doctor, since typhoid fever is highly infectious and can cause other health problems as well. The fever can be treated with antibiotics.

AIDS

AIDS is caused by the HIV virus and is transmitted through blood and sexual intercourse. It is estimated that 660,000 people in Brazil are currently infected with HIV. Government measures, together with public education efforts, have significantly reduced the number of AIDS fatalities and new infections. To reduce the risk of HIV infection, you should always use condoms for sexual intercourse, and avoid sharing needles.

In 1996, the government began to distribute free AIDS drugs and since 2001, in accordance with the World Health Organization, Brazil has been allowed to manufacture its own AIDS medication, which has significantly lowered the cost of treatment.

Healthcare in Brazil

There are about 5,800 hospitals in Brazil, which amounts an average of one hospital bed for every 370 Brazilians. The number recommended by the World Health Organisation (WHO) is one bed for every 250 citizens. Availability and quality of Brazil's health care is largely dependent on income and region.

At the *postos de saúde* (free public health centers), patients wait in line for hours to see a doctor. In large cities, it is not uncommon for people to wait in line, overnight, outside public hospitals, so they can see a doctor, or make an appointment early the next morning. Dental care also varies regionally, and most towns have crowded public dental clinics, as well as private dentists who provide excellent care for insured or paying patients.

About a third of the population is covered under a number of private health insurance plans, which provide comprehensive and high-quality health care at excellent private hospitals and clinics. In contrast, two thirds of Brazil's population uses the free national health care system, known as *sistema único de saúde* (SUS), which provides inadequate and insufficient health services.

Rural Healthcare

In most rural and remote areas, public health centres serve the entire municipal district, and are often overcrowded. These clinics often have only the most basic equipment and supplies, and the number of physicians is small. If you only have a minor health problem, you might try self-treatment, or ask a pharmacist for help. If you plan to travel to areas that are more than a day's travel from a town with medical facilities, plan accordingly, and bring a portable medical kit, including antibiotics, medication to treat malaria, and standard first aid items. A few years ago, I was on an overnight boat trip in the Amazon from a remote village to the nearest town. Among the passengers was a family with a young girl, who was suffering from a severe malaria attack. The local health centre had not been able to help and so the parents decided to take the girl to the nearest hospital 24 hours downriver, in a desperate attempt to save her life. When I woke up the following morning and walked down to the lower deck, the family was holding a wake for the girl, who had died during the night.

Seeking Medical Help

'É melhor gastar um milhão com saúde
do que gastar um milhão com remédio.'
(It is better to spend a million on health,
than spend a million on medication.)
—Brazilian saying

If you only stay in Brazil for a short period of time, you should make sure that your health insurance agency at home will reimburse you for any medical treatment you pay for in Brazil. If that is not possible, you should consider signing up for a traveller's health insurance plan, which will not pay for doctor's visits, but will assume the cost of serious medical emergencies, hospital stays and even evacuation.

If you need medical attention, your consulate in Brazil should be able to refer you to reputable doctors and hospitals in a number of Brazilian cities. It is best to learn a few basic words in Portuguese about your health condition beforehand, so you are prepared to tell the doctor about your problem. When making a doctor's appointment, ask for a *consulta de médico* (medical consultant). Unless you have health insurance in Brazil, payment is usually expected at the time of the consultation.

In case of a medical emergency, it is best to go to the *pronto socorro* (emergency room) of the nearest hospital, or call an ambulance. Most private hospitals require a deposit before admitting a patient without a health insurance plan. Since you will have to pay for all health expenses yourself (unless you have a Brazilian health insurance plan), make sure you get a receipt from the hospital or doctor, explaining the nature of your health problem and its treatment. That way you can bill your insurance company later.

Pharmacies

Farmácias (pharmacies) and *drogarias* (drug stores or chemists) can be found in every neighbourhood and town. Every city district has at least one *farmácia de plantão* (pharmacy on duty), which is open 24 hours, including weekends and holidays. This information is usually posted at pharmacies that are closed. Non-prescription drugs such as pain killers and fever reducers are readily available at pharmacies and chemists, but the selection of over-the counter drugs is modest. All drugs are manufactured in Brazil, but international brands such as Aspirin, and Tylenol are available under the same name. Common drugs such as antibiotics are often sold over the counter without prescriptions. Some injections are routinely given at pharmacies, and pharmacists also give health advice for minor problems.

FOOD AND ENTERTAINING

CHAPTER 6

'Enquanto houver Brasil, Na hora das comidas
Eu sou do camarão ensopadinho com xuxu.'
(As long as there is Brazil,
at mealtime I am all for shrimp stew with okra.)
—from the song *Dizeram que Voltei Americanizada*
('They said I came back Americanised'),
sung by Carmen Miranda

ENJOYING BRAZILIAN FOOD
Daily Meals

Brazilian cooking is rich in traditions and ingredients that reflect the country's diverse ethnic make-up. Dried, salted cod fish is a traditional Portuguese dish and is popular in casseroles and stews. Manioc meal is a daily staple of Brazil's Indians, and is today enjoyed by all Brazilians. The strong *dendê* oil of African origin continues to enrich Bahian cuisine. Despite the different ethnic influences and regional variations in cooking, most Brazilians share similar eating habits.

Breakfast

Café da Manhã (breakfast) is a simple and quick affair. Many people don't eat breakfast or they just have coffee with milk and crackers. Whenever Brazilians take the time for a full breakfast, it usually includes *pãozinhos* (bread rolls), *queijo* (cheese), *frios* (cold cuts), *fruta* (fresh fruit), *sucos* (fruit juices), and *café com leite* (coffee with milk). Breakfast items are also offered at bakeries and *lanchonetes* (cafeterias) everywhere. They usually serve a variety of *docinhos* (sweet pastries) or *salgadinhos* (savoury pastries), *pão de queijo* (cheese rolls), and coffee for people on their way to work.

Lunch

Almoço (lunch) is the biggest and most important meal of the day, and Brazilians usually take at least an hour for lunch.

The main staples are *arroz* (rice), *feijão* (beans) and *farinha de mandioca* (manioc meal), which are served every day in every Brazilian home and restaurant. They are usually accompanied by a *salada* (salad), a *legume* (vegetable), and a *carne* (meat item), often *bife* (beef) or *frango* (chicken), and on Fridays *peixe* (fish). *Macarrão* (pasta) and *mandioca* (fried or boiled manioc) are also sometimes served in addition to rice and beans. A Brazilian lunch is not complete without at least a *sobremesa* (dessert). This could be *fruta* (fruit), *creme* (a fruit creme), *pudim* (custard) or *sorvete* (ice cream). Lunch is usually followed by a *cafezinho*, a black sweetened coffee served in a small cup.

Restaurants fill up quickly between noon and 1:00 pm with hungry workers on their lunch breaks. Most low-priced restaurants offer a *prato do dia* or *prato feito* (daily special), in addition to a-la-carte dishes. These specials provide a filling meal for only a few dollars, and the quantity of food is generally more important than the quality. Those with a little more money choose a restaurant that serves *comida por quilo* (food by the kilogramme), which is buffet-style food sold by weight. Patrons help themselves to whatever they like and then put the plate on a scale. The quality of food at these restaurants is usually excellent, and they always offer a large variety of salads, meat, regional specialities, as well as the standard fare of rice and beans.

Feijoada (bean stew) and *churrasco* (barbecue) are favourite lunchtime dishes, since they take longer to prepare and eat, and are best enjoyed with friends or family, whether at home or at a restaurant.

Weekend lunches are often more elaborate and involved, since everyone has more time, and the extended family often gets together. Brazilian families also enjoy going out to restaurants for lunch, especially when the maid has her day-off.

Supper

Jantar (supper) is a much simpler and lighter meal than lunch, and is often eaten late. It may be leftovers, a sandwich, soup or a variety of light dishes or snacks. *Tapioca* (pancakes of coarse manioc starch), *mingau* (a porridge of corn meal), and *canjica* (a sweet dish of grated sweet corn) are popular evening dishes that are easy to make at home.

ETIQUETTE AT THE TABLE

Brazilian table etiquette is casual and does not follow strict rules. However, there are some customs that foreigners should be aware of, so they can feel more at ease when eating with Brazilians. It is customary to wash one's hands before a meal. A meal at home is a family event, and everyone usually sits at the table together.

Except for soup and dessert, which are served separately, all dishes are laid out together, usually with serving spoons or spatulas. In most homes, the lady of the house does not serve the guests, but invites them to help themselves to as much food as they like. If there are dishes that you don't like, simply don't take any. Brazilians usually finish all the food they put on their plate. Taking more food than you can eat is impolite and might even suggest that you didn't like it. It is common to have second servings, and the host usually asks everyone if they want more. It is okay to decline. Make sure to leave room for dessert and coffee.

When going out to a bar or restaurant at night, *petiscos* (appetisers) with drinks is preferred. *Petiscos* come in a variety of flavours and sizes and are eaten with toothpicks instead of cutlery. Among the most popular items are *bolinhos de bacalhau* (deep fried dried cod balls), *batatas fritas* (french fries) and *mandioca frita* (fried manioc).

Brazilians don't make noises while eating. Smacking, slurping, burping and making noise with plates and cutlery are considered impolite. It is also impolite to reach in front of a person who is eating. Instead, ask the person next to you to pass you the dish. Cutlery may be held in either hand. Food is not usually picked up by hand, and even pizza is eaten with fork and knife. Brazilians use a napkin or toothpick if they can't use cutlery although table etiquette at a home is often more relaxed, and chicken or fried fish may be picked up with fingers. If in doubt, follow the example of your host or ask. To indicate that you have finished your meal, place the knife and fork on the plate. Toothpicks are commonly provided at tables and are used to clean the teeth after meals, while covering the mouth with the other hand. Brazilians rarely smoke at the table and should you like to smoke after a meal, it is best to ask the host, or to excuse yourself and go outside.

Eating At a Restaurant

Eating out is very popular both for lunch during the work week, and for socialising with family and friends at weekends. Restaurants generally post their *cardápio* (menu) at the entrance, and daily lunch specials are often written on a board. In most restaurants, patrons seat themselves. At some fine restaurants, there may be a host who welcomes guests and suggests a table. A waiter will soon bring the menus and take your orders for food and drink.

Waitstaff in Brazil are almost always male. To beckon the waiter to your table, it is customary to lift your hand and motion him to approach you. You can also beckon a waiter by calling out *garçom* (waiter) or simply *moço* (boy, which is used for waiters of all ages). When sitting outdoors, patrons make a hissing sound, a sort of "*psee-oo*," to attract the waiter's attention.

Restaurant Etiquette

- There is usually only one bill per table, and people in a group figure out among themselves their share of the bill.
- Most cheques include 10 per cent for service and tipping is not necessary is this case.
- Payment can be by cash or cheque.
- Even though you might see a credit card symbol on the door, it is best to ask before you order.
- To ask for the bill, beckon the waiter and make a scribbling gesture across your palm.

REGIONAL COOKING

'Experiencing Brazilian cuisine is getting to know the country, and what's more, understanding an important manifestation of Brazilian civilization.'
—Ruth Cardoso, anthropologist and
First Lady from 1995–2002

Due to the country's enormous size and multiple ethnic groups, Brazilian cuisine has its own unique traditions with great regional variations. It would fill a book to list all the regional specialities, and the following selection is only a sampler to encourage you to further explore Brazil's culinary wealth.

The South

Brazil's south is the region of German, Polish and Italian immigrants, but it is also the homeland of the *gauchos*, Brazil's cowboys of European and Indian descent. Due to these unique cultural influences, it has culinary traditions that are distinct from the rest of Brazil.

Churrasco

Churrasco is a Brazilian barbecue, first enjoyed by the nomadic cow-herding *gauchos* who grilled slabs of beef over an open fire. Today, *churrasco* refers to a variety of beef cuts grilled on skewers or a spit, popular throughout Brazil.

The *churrascarias* are restaurants that specialise in barbecued meat often served *rodízio* style, an eat-what-you-can arrangement where servers walk from table to table and cut the desired slices from a large chunk of grilled meat. The most popular cuts are the *filet mignon* and *picanha*, a steak cut from the rump.

Barreado

This is a traditional dish of the state of Paraná and is prepared for festive meals and commemorations. It is a meat stew of layered beef and bacon, topped with a layer of *pirão* (a thick sauce of manioc meal), slowly cooked in a clay pot.

The South-east

The South-east has a very diverse population and this is reflected in the region's cuisine. Espírito Santo, a rural state along the Atlantic coast, north of Rio de Janeiro, is known for its seafood dishes. Rio de Janeiro prides itself in creating Brazil's national dish, and São Paulo is Brazil's most cosmopolitan city with a great variety of international cuisine.

Torta Capixaba

A popular dish in Espírito Santo, *torta capixaba* is a seasoned pie of seafood and palm hearts, topped with beaten eggs and baked till golden brown. It is traditionally prepared at Easter.

Feijoada Completa

The *feijoada completa* is a typical dish of Rio de Janeiro and has its origins as a humble meal of the slaves who mixed leftover meats into their bean stew. Today, *feijoada* is anything but humble. It is a stew of black beans cooked with a variety of meats such as dried beef, smoked sausage and pig's ears. It is traditionally served with rice, sautéed kale, manioc meal and orange slices. The *feijoada* is considered Brazil's national dish and is popular throughout Brazil. Vinicius de Moraes expresses it best in his poem 'Feijoada à minha moda':

> *'Que prazer mais um corpo pede*
> *Após comido um tal feijão?*
> *–Evidentemente uma rede*
> *E um gato para passar a mão ... '*
> (What other pleasure can a body ask for
> After eating such a bean dish?
> —Obviously a hammock
> And a cat to caress with one's hand ...)

Cuscuz Paulista

Originating from São Paulo, this is a dish of cornmeal and marinated shrimp or chicken, steamed in a special dish called the *cuscuzeiro*.

Tutu à Mineira

Popular in Minas Gerais, this is a dish of pork chops, sausage and *tutú*, a thick sauce of mashed beans fried with manioc meal and bacon.

Frango Com Quiabo

Made with chicken pieces and *quiabo* (okra), this is often served with *angú de milho*, a porridge of corn meal, popular in Minas Gerais.

The Central West

Cuisine in this region reflects the abundant supply of beef from its expansive ranches and wealth of fish from its many rivers.

Peixe à Pescaria

This is a popular dish of marinated whole fish, stuffed with a mixture of sautéed vegetables and eggs. The fish is sewn up with string, wrapped in banana leaves, and baked in the oven.

Galinhada Com Pequí

This is a chicken casserole with rice, corn, and the *pequí* fruit (from a regional tree), which adds a distinct flavour. *Pequí* cooked with rice, known as *arroz com pequí*, also accompanies other regional dishes. Be careful when eating the pulp of the *pequí* fruit, since the seeds of some varieties have prickles.

The North-east

The North-east's cuisine is characterised by the proximity of the sea and African influences. One of the main ingredients of Bahian dishes is *dendê* oil, a strong orange-coloured oil, made from the fruit of a palm tree brought to Brazil by African slaves.

Carurú

A popular regional dish, *carurú* consists of okra cooked in a sauce of dried shrimp, ground peanuts, malagueta pepper and *dendê* oil.

Vatapá

One of the North-east's best-known food items, it is used in many dishes. *Vatapá* is a purée made from dried shrimp, ground peanuts, cashews, coconut milk and *dendê* oil.

Ximxim de Galinha

This is a casserole with chicken pieces cooked in a sauce of ground peanuts, cashew, ginger, *dendê* oil and dried shrimp. It is usually served with *farofa*, a roasted manioc meal.

Moqueca

A seasoned stew with coconut milk and *dendê* oil, *moqueca* is prepared with fish, shrimp or other seafood.

Bobó de Camarão

This is a purée of dried shrimp, coconut milk, manioc meal, *dendê* oil and seasonings mixed with fresh shrimp.

The North

The cuisine of the Amazon reflects the abundance of the region's fish, and the variety of indigenous ingredients. Among the Amazon's most delicious fish are the *pirarucu, tucunaré, surubim, pintado, tambaqui, dourado, pacú,* and *piranha*.

Pato no Tucupi

A dish of roasted duck boiled in *tucupi*, a sauce made from an extract of the manioc root, and seasoned with *jambu*, a fresh herb that slightly numbs the mouth.

Tacacá

Often sold on the streets of Amazon towns at night, this broth of manioc starch, *tucupi*, dried shrimp and *jambu*, is served in a *cuia*, a bowl made from gourd, usually decorated with painted designs.

Baianas frying Acarajé fritters made of bean batter.

SNACK FOODS

Lanchonetes (cafeterias or luncheonettes) and street vendors
are a common sight, and they offer a great variety of snacks.
Even if in a hurry, Brazilians will always take their time to
stand at a counter while eating. They rarely eat and walk on
the street at the same time. Each region has its own distinct
snacks, many not available elsewhere.

Acarajé

A dish of African origin and most popular in the state of
Bahia, this appetiser is sold at small vending tables on the
streets, usually by women dressed in the typical regional
Baiana costumes. Acarajé is a ball of bean batter deep fried
in *dendê* oil and filled with thick *vatapá purée*, hot sauce and

dried shrimp. As Bahian songwriter Dorival Caymmi puts it in his song classic, *A Preta do Acarajé*: 'Everybody likes *acarajé*, but how much work it is to make it!'

Cachorro Quente (Hot Dog)

Brazil's version of the hot dog, the term is an exact translation from English. It is also known as *passaporte* (passport) in the North-east.

Empada (or Empadinha)

A small round pie with a variety of fillings such as chicken, palm hearts or shrimp.

An average-sized tambaqui, a tasty fish common in northern Brazil.

Salgadinho

A variety of filled pastries, which vary greatly from region to region, and can be filled with ham, cheese, vegetables, sausages or shrimp.

Pamonha

A very popular snack food in Central Brazil, *pamonha* is made with grated corn, wrapped in corn husks and boiled in hot water.

Pão de queijo

A small roll made with *polvilho* (coarse manioc starch) and cheese, this is usually served hot. A popular snack at any time of the day, often enjoyed with a *cafezinho* (coffee).

Pastel de Queijo

Another favourite quick snack sold all over Brazil. It is a deep fried puff pastry filled with cheese or other fillings such as palm hearts.

Queijo Quente

This is a grilled cheese sandwich with a slice of tomato. When made with cheese and ham, it is called *misto quente*.

Quibe

A snack from the Middle East, *quibe* is a pear-shaped, deep-fried ball of ground beef and bulghur wheat.

Tapioca

Tapioca is a fried pancake made from *polvilho* (coarse manioc starch), and is served with a variety of toppings.

BEVERAGES
Cafezinho

The *cafezinho* is a strong black coffee served in a small cup or glass, and enjoyed with lots of sugar. As a Brazilian saying goes: *'O café deve ser negro como o demônio, quente como o inferno, puro como um anjo e doce como o amor'* ('Coffee has to be black as the devil, hot as hell, pure as an angel, and sweet as love.') The *cafezinho* is an indispensable energy source for most Brazilians, be it in the morning before work, during a business meeting, or in the afternoon at a street corner. During the day, Brazilians rarely sit down to enjoy coffee but usually drink it while standing at the counter of a *lanchonete* or espresso bar, ready to move on. The *cafezinho* is also an important gesture of Brazilian hospitality and is commonly offered to visitors and guests at home, and to business partners and valued customers.

Guaraná

Guaraná is an Amazonian vine whose berries contain a stimulant similar to caffeine. Originally used only by indigenous tribes, *guaraná* is today sold as a soft drink and is manufactured by several companies in Brazil. Known for its medicinal qualities, *guaraná* is also available in health food stores in powder or syrup form. It is also a popular ingredient in *vitaminas* and fruit juices, especially in the Amazon. According to native mythology, the *guaraná* originated by divine intervention.

How Guaraná Began

When a Maué Indian couple lost their only son as a result of a snake bite, they prayed to Tupã, the supreme being, who told them in his language of thunder to bury the boy's eyes separate from his body because an important plant would grow from them.

Soon after the parents buried the eyes, a plant began to grow on the same spot. Its seeds resembled human eyes, which is why the Indians gave it the name *guaraná*, which means 'resembling living people'.

Vitaminas (Fruit Shakes)

Brazil is blessed with a delicious variety of fruits that are great for blended drinks and shakes. These drinks are appropriately called vitaminas and come in amazing combinations of flavours, colours and ingredients, and are often blended with milk. Bananas, oranges, papayas, mangoes, *cupuaçu*, passion fruit, pineapple and cashew fruit are only a few of the many ingredients enjoyed in *vitaminas*.

There are also many fruits that are regional specialities and are not found elsewhere. *Cajá* for example, is the fruit of a tree that grows in the *cerrado* of central and north-eastern Brazil. It is made into a delicious juice and ice cream locally, but is little known elsewhere. Similarly, *açaí*, a thick purple-coloured beverage made from the berries of an Amazonian palm is said to taste so good, those who have tasted it will never leave.

Caldo de Cana
The sweet juice extracted from freshly pressed sugar cane, this is very popular in the sugar growing regions along the north-east coast but is also available throughout Brazil from street vendors and at juice bars.

Água de Coco
Água de coco (the juice of green coconuts) is a natural beverage popular throughout Brazil. Every morning, truckloads of coconuts from the north-eastern plantations arrive in Brazil's large cities to supply thirsty city dwellers with the refreshing drink. The juice is rich in electrolytes and is great for rehydration after a day on the beach.

Chimarrão
Chimarrão, a tea made from the mate herb is the traditional drink of Brazil's southern population the *gauchos*. Boiling water is poured over a few teaspoons of tea inside a *cuia* (gourd). The tea is steeped for a few minutes before it is sipped with a silver straw called *bomba*. After the first person has emptied the gourd, it is handed back to the host who fills it with more hot water and hands it to the next person. This is repeated several times until the tea loses its flavour.

Cerveja (Beer)
Brazilians love beer and enjoy it everywhere from neighbourhood bars and upscale restaurants, to the beach. Brazil's beer market is dominated by a number of large breweries. The main brands available are lager beers such

as Brahma, Antárctica, Skol and Kaiser, but speciality beers such as stouts, German-style malt beers and Pilsners can also be found. Brazilians especially enjoy draft beer known as *chopp*, which is always served ice-cold.

Cachaça

> 'Cachaça tira juízo, mas dá coragem.'
> (Cachaça takes away sound judgement,
> but gives courage.)
> —Brazilian saying

Cachaça is a cheap sugar cane rum also known as *aguardente*, and colloquially as *pinga*. It is a raw liquor that is distilled only once, giving it a somewhat harsh flavour. This is probably why people enjoy it mainly in mixed drinks. For the desperately poor however, a bottle of *cachaça* for less than a dollar, is a cheap way to a night of drunkenness and merriment.

Caipirinha

Caipirinha is a potent mixed drink of *cachaça*, crushed lime, sugar and ice. It is considered Brazil's national drink and is popular at parties, bars and night clubs. A tasty cocktail, its potency is easily underestimated since it is sweet and has a pleasant lime flavour.

Batidas

In addition to *caipirinha*, Brazilians also enjoy other mixed drinks that are based on *cachaça*. These *batidas* (cocktails) are made with a variety of fresh fruit juices usually blended with ice. The most popular *batidas* are *batida de coco* (made with coconut milk), *batida de maracujá* (made with passion fruit) and *batida de caju* (made with cashew fruit).

Licores (Liqueurs)

Brazil produces a variety of liqueurs made from *cachaça*, and flavoured with herbs and fruits. Most regions have their own distinct liqueur traditions and many local fruits find their way into the creative and sometimes pungent concoctions of local liqueur producers. Among the best-known is *jenipapo*, a fruit from the North-east, which is used as a flavouring for a liqueur of the same name.

Vino (Wine)

Brazil is not a traditional wine-drinking country. Vineyards were only introduced in the late 19th and early 20th centuries by Italian settlers in the southern state of Rio Grande do Sul. But since then, wine has gained significant popularity and is today commonly served at dinner parties and festive events. Although Brazilian wines do not compare to those of the world's great wine-growing regions, Brazil's wine producers have greatly improved the quality of their wines and have been awarded several international medals.

ENJOYING BRAZIL

CHAPTER 7

'Gosto de samba, gosto de futebol,
também gosto de praia, nos domingos de sol.'
(I like samba, I like football,
but I also like the beach, on sunny Sundays.)
—from a samba

RECREATION

Owing to the tropical climate and geography of their country, Brazilians have developed a recreational culture based on activities outdoors and near water. Brazilians seem to have an almost mythical attraction to water, which perhaps goes back to the mythological importance of water for Amerindian tribes, and the popularity of African deities associated with water. But on a more profane level, people simply enjoy the refreshing effect of the ocean and the many waterfalls and rivers, especially during the hot summer months.

View of Rio de Janeiro's Copacabana Beach with fishing boats.

Since most of Brazil's population lives close to the coast, beaches are popular playgrounds, especially at weekends. People from all walks of life gather near the ocean, and Brazil's beaches become a colourful kaleidoscope of people who otherwise rarely share the same space. Wealthy couples living in beach-front high-rises sit next to hugging lovers from the *favelas*. Young people from all parts of town play football, volleyball or *futevolei*, a combination of both. People often bring beer, set up a small radio and exchange neighbourhood gossip. Brazil's beaches are also a popular hot spot for flirting. Young women go to the beach to check out the men, and men go there to look at the beautiful women in their string bikinis.

Travel

The main travel season is the Brazilian summer, from Christmas until the end of Carnaval (late February to early March). This is when students are on vacation, and when the whole nation gears up for the revelries of Carnaval. Among the most popular Carnaval destinations are Rio de Janeiro, Salvador, Olinda, Recife and Ouro Preto.

Brazilians love the beach, crowds and parties, and their vacation plans centre mainly around these activities. Most people prefer a day on the beach to a visit to a historical church or museum, but this is gradually changing as more cities and towns are restoring their historical centres and are beginning to promote cultural tourism.

Beach resorts are among the most popular vacation destination for Brazilians, among them Búzios, Cabo Frio and Parati, near Rio de Janeiro, Ubatuba and Ilhabela near São Paulo, and many other towns with beautiful beaches all along Brazil's coastline. There are also several popular vacation destinations inland, among them Ouro Preto (Minas Gerais state), Pirenópolis and Goiás Velho (both in Goiás state).

In addition to its marvellous coastline and architectural treasures from colonial days, Brazil also has a large number of nature reserves and national parks of outstanding natural beauty that offer great recreational opportunities. Although nature and ecological attractions receive fewer visitors in comparison to beaches, Brazilians are beginning to discover the beauty of the country's mountains, forests, rivers and waterfalls far away from the ocean. The increasing interest in eco-tourism encourages the preservation of Brazil's natural heritage and brings visitors to distant regions that lie off the beaten track. Among the most popular nature preserves are Tijuca National Park, a large forest reserve surrounding Rio de Janeiro, the Serra dos Órgãos National Park in the coastal mountains near Rio de Janeiro, the Itatiaia National Park (inland, between Rio de Janeiro and São Paulo) and the Iguaçu National Park with the famous waterfalls (in the south, bordering Argentina). There are several other great nature parks a little more distant from urban centres. Among them are the Chapada da Diamantina National Park in the state of Bahia, the Chapada dos Veadeiros National park (a few hours north of Brasília), and the Chapada dos Guimarães National Park near Cuiabá (Mato Grosso state).

Sports

Brazilians are active people and engage in many different physical activities in their spare time. Beaches are not only popular with sunbathers, but also become athletic playgrounds. Especially in the evenings, esplanades along

There is always room for a game of football, even at high tide.

beaches teem with people who walk, jog, cycle or roller-skate. Some beaches have flood lights where people can play football or volleyball at night. The early morning hours, before the sun gets too hot, are also popular for exercise.

Futebol (football or soccer) is Brazil's favourite sport and is played by people of all ages, races and social classes, and by a growing number of women. Football is also Brazil's favourite spectator sport and is passionately viewed by millions of fans on television and in the many large stadiums. Rio's famous Maracaná football stadium, built for the 1950 World Cup tournament, is the largest in the world with a capacity to seat 200,000 spectators.

The football World Cup is the highlight for every fan of the sport, and Brazilians are very emotional about the performance of their national team. A defeat is somewhat a national tragedy and will keep people in low spirits for days. On the other hand, a victory unites the entire country in a patriotic frenzy and week-long celebration. Brazil won the World Championship in 1958, 1962, 1970, 1994 and 2002. It is the only country that has won five titles and qualified for all World Cup tournaments, including the 2006 tournament in Germany. In addition to international competitions, the matches of the numerous national, state and regional leagues are also followed with devotion and passion. In Rio de Janeiro, a game between the city's two rival teams, Flamengo and Fluminense (Fla-Flu), is a major event. The fans of the winning team celebrate with parades and parties all night long.

Automobile racing is another popular spectator sport and is watched on television by millions of Brazilians. Brazilian race car drivers won several Formula One World Championships, among them Emerson Fitibaldi, Nelson Piquet and the late Ayrton Senna. Senna was Brazil's favourite pilot and his fatal accident in Italy in 1994 was a great national tragedy. In recent years, Rubens Barrichello has ranked among the world's best Formula One drivers, and several other Brazilian race car drivers participate in Formula One events.

Brazilian athletes are not only good football players, but they also excel in other team sports such as basketball and volleyball, winning both Olympic medals and world championships. Beach volleyball, much enjoyed by Brazilians, became an Olympic discipline in Atlanta in 1996, and Brazil's men's and women's teams have shown excellent results. With Brazil's easy access to water, it is not surprising that water sports are also widely practised. Brazilians are excellent sailors and swimmers, and have won several championships and Olympic medals. More and more Brazilians are becoming interested in tennis, especially since Gustavo Kuerten (known as Guga) continues to rank among the world's top professional tennis players.

In urban areas, *academias* (fitness clubs) have become very popular. People work out with stationary bicycles, tread mills, weight lifting equipment and take aerobics classes to stay in shape and build up their bodies to look good on their Sunday outings to the beach.

Capoeira

Capoeira is a martial art that is widely practiced in the form of a stylised dance-fight. The origins of *capoeira* go back to the colonial days when runaway slaves joined *quilombos* (secret African communities), which were founded in remote regions

Performance of *capoeira*, a Brazilian martial art, in Salvador.

in the interior. Since they had no weapons, they used their bodies and developed a highly successful form of combat to defend themselves against the mercenaries sent out to capture them. Eventually, the practice of *capoeira* spread to the plantations, where it was secretly practised by the slaves. In the 19th century, *capoeira* became popular in Rio de Janeiro, Salvador and Recife, but was outlawed because of frequent fighting by street gangs. *Capoeira* continued to be practiced clandestinely until masters in Salvador began to develop a less violent and more stylised form of *capoeira*. It was during this time that *capoeira* evolved into the highly acrobatic and artful sport it is today. In 1937, after impressing President Getúlio Vargas with his skills, the *capoeira* teacher Mestre Bimba was allowed to establish the first *capoeira* school. *Capoeira* was soon legalised and became Brazil's national sport in 1974. It is now practiced, performed and enjoyed in schools, universities and *capoeira* clubs nationwide.

Capoeira in its contemporary form is performed by a group of fighters, called *capoeiristas*, who form a *roda* (large circle) together with the audience. The musical element of *capoeira* consists of instruments of African origin, such as the *berimbau* (a one-stringed instrument made from a gourd), and several percussion instruments. While the audience accompanies the music with clapping, the *capoeiristas* move to the rhythm of the music in a characteristic step, and execute a series of complex acrobatic movements such as somersaults, cartwheels and handstands. During the simulated fight, the opponents never touch each other, but attempt to outdo each other by means of speed and acrobatic skill. After a few minutes, a new pair of dancers enters the circle and continues with the skill demonstration.

NIGHTLIFE

'Quero liberdade pra beber no botequim,
bater papo com os amigos, pois eu sou feliz assim.'
(I want freedom to drink at a bar and chat with friends,
because I am happy that way.)
—from a samba

Brazil's cities offer an endless variety of entertainment options, ranging from the vulgar to the highbrow, and from the intellectual to the sensuous. Rio de Janeiro and São Paulo have an especially diverse cultural programme that is comparable to that of any of the world's great cities. To a lesser degree, you can also expect an interesting nightlife in most state capitals, with fewer events to choose from, but nonetheless an exciting selection of things to do and places to go. Most local newspapers publish a calendar of events, usually on Thursday and Friday, that lists the city's cultural programming for the week. The weekly news magazine *Veja* has a special edition for Rio de Janeiro and São Paulo, which comes with a large pullout listing cultural events.

Bars and Taverns

A favourite place for Brazilians to socialise in the evening after work, are *botecos* or *botequins* (neighbourhood bars or taverns), which is the common people's night entertainment.

> A *boteco* is usually a simple establishment that opens onto the street, where people sit on metal chairs at folding tables, while sharing beer and engaging in conversation. People get together here for an affordable evening of merriment, sometimes watching a football game on TV, or listening to music.

In addition to the simple *botecos*, every town has a variety of slightly more attractive *bares* (bars), which often feature a restaurant menu. They usually offer indoor and outdoor seating in a more pleasant environment, such as a patio instead of the pavement, and may have live music at weekends.

Restaurants

Brazilians enjoy going out to restaurants at night, often just for drinks and appetisers, but on occasion also for a full-course dinner. Since Brazilians dine late, many restaurants have a full kitchen open all evening. Restaurants with outdoor seating are especially popular. If the restaurant is elegant, wine may be more appropriate than beer, and the atmosphere will be a little quieter and more formal. Such places usually have an indoor dining room with air-conditioning. In upmarket restaurants, dinner portions tend to be smaller and prices much higher, but the ambience and food make up for it.

Nightclubs

Boates (nightclubs) are a popular entertainment venue for young Brazilians, and they cater to a variety of audiences, from low-income youth, to university students and the sons and daughters of Brazil's elite. Clubs are usually located near the neighbourhoods whose residents they most appeal to. Upscale nightclubs are more formal and may have a dress code. The *couvert* (cover charge) depends on the programming, but is usually quite high at weekends.

> Brazilians go out late, and it is rare for friends to meet at a club before 11:00 pm. There is no strictly observed closing hour, and most clubs stay open through the night.

Although the age limit to be admitted to a club is 18 years, people are rarely asked to show identification. Many clubs are just discotheques, but they may also feature live music by local bands especially at weekends.

Live Music

Música ao vivo (live music) always attracts large crowds in Brazil. There are not only regular concerts of well-known Brazilian stars, but also internationally famous musicians and bands. Some cities like Rio de Janeiro and São Paulo organise free weekly concerts during the summer and invite well-known Brazilian stars to perform.

In addition to these events, live music can regularly be enjoyed at bars and clubs. Bands play a variety of musical styles, depending on what's most popular from season to season. Among the most popular genres are the *música sertaneja*, Brazilian country music, and *pagode*, a popular form of samba. No matter where you are in Brazil, there will always be live music at weekends, either at a bar or club or at a free concert on a beach, in a park or town square. Each town regularly organises its own regional *bailes* (dances) and *festas* (festivals) with live music, many of them part of religious celebrations.

Dances

Brazilians simply love to dance. Be it in a living room or dance hall, wherever there is music, people will start moving to the beat. In addition to nightclubs and discotheques, there are special clubs and dance halls where people gather to dance to popular rhythms such as samba, salsa, tango, bolero, and *pagode*. *Forró*, a regional music from the North-east has recently become a very popular dance music all over Brazil. It evolved in the 1940s and is traditionally played with an accordion, guitar and percussion instruments.

The *baile funk* or 'funk dance', popular in Rio de Janeiro, is the latest fad among young people from working class neighbourhoods and *favelas*. The predominant rhythm at these dances is the *funk brasileiro* (Brazilian Funk), a Brazilian version of rap.

Performing Arts

Brazil's large cities all have historical theatres, which host large orchestral performances of classical music, opera, ballet and theatre productions. Each city also has a variety of smaller performance venues for theatre, concerts and dance performances. There are also many cultural centres sponsored by public or private organisations, which usually have a small performance space, a movie theatre and art gallery, and sometimes a coffee house and bookshop. The Centro Cultural do Banco do Brasil (CCBB) in Rio de Janeiro and the Centro Cultural de São Paulo are among the largest of these arts centres.

Movie Theatres

Movies are especially popular among the young. Most movie theatres are located in commercial districts and shopping centres. American films dominate the film market, which makes it easy for foreigners to watch a film, because all foreign films are shown in their original language with Portuguese subtitles. Unfortunately, Brazilian films don't get the attention they deserve in their own country. This is gradually changing however, as the local film industry is increasing its production. Although few Brazilian films run at major commercial theatres, many cultural centres have movie festivals screening Brazilian films. Cultural centres, art museums and other cultural institutions also feature international classic and art-house films. Prices of movie tickets go up by as much as 50 per cent at weekends.

Motels

A Motel in Brazil is a love hotel, where rooms are rented by the hour. A well-established and indispensable institution, motels can be found in most cities. They are especially popular at weekends and are usually open 24 hours a day. Quality and prices vary according to the cities and neighbourhoods, but they are generally quite affordable. Most are located along major thoroughfares on the outskirts of towns, and usually feature

> Motels are not only frequented by prostitutes and their clients, but also by young lovers, married couples or anybody else who wants to enjoy a special evening, or a few hours of privacy with a sex partner.

either a walled-in parking lot or parking garage to guarantee their clients' privacy. The rooms are usually equipped with a refrigerator filled with drinks, a mirrored ceiling, radio and TV. Many motels also offer room service, and more elegant establishments even have a swimming pool and sauna.

Strip Clubs

Live nude entertainment is quite popular and every city has at least one *casa de striptease* (strip club). While such places are often frequented by single men and prostitutes in search of customers, you will also find married couples, or men with their girlfriends there.

Brothels

Prostíbulos (brothels) are not officially legal, but they are tolerated by the police and can be found in every city. Quality and style usually depend on the neighbourhood they are in and the clientele they cater to. Some operate as private clubs and allow access only to members. Interested foreigners would be wise to follow the recommendations of a reliable local informant before setting out to explore this unofficial side of Brazil's nightlife. Prostitutes also look for clients on the street and in certain bars and clubs. In addition to the clean and respectable motels on the outskirts, there are usually a number of run-down hotels near city centres that rent out rooms by the hour for the purpose. Foreigners should keep in mind that while Brazil has made progress in the fight against AIDS, there is always a risk of contracting a sexually transmitted disease during intercourse. Condoms are widely used and distributed, but they do not remove all risk factors.

CELEBRATIONS AND FESTIVALS
'O melhor da festa é esperar por ela.'
(The best thing about a celebration is waiting for it.)
—Brazilian proverb

Brazil has an enormous tradition of festivals and holidays both folkloric and religious in nature. The following list gives you an overview of the most popular ones that are celebrated in many towns.

Easter
Páscua (Easter) is among the most traditional of Brazil's Catholic holidays, and is celebrated all over the country. Starting on Palm Sunday, most parishes stage large processions throughout Holy Week until Easter Sunday. Processions may be accompanied by marching bands, and there may also be candlelight processions at night. Many regions and towns have their own traditions.

Festas Juninas
The Festas Juninas (June Festivals) are a series of festivals celebrated all over Brazil, in honour of the three saints, Santo Antônio (St Anthony, on 13 June), São João (St John, on 24 June), and São Pedro (St Peter, on 29 June). While the traditional feasts of Santo Antônio and São Pedro are gradually fading in popularity, the feast of São João remains very popular. The festival of São João is celebrated with music and dances around a bonfire, which is usually lit right after sunset. People drink hot wine and *quentão*, which is

hot *cachaça* flavoured with spices. In some towns, it is still customary to set up tall masts which are scaled by courageous young people for prizes. Another popular tradition is the letting loose of small hot air balloons made of paper, which contain messages and wishes. If the balloon rises, so people say, the wishes contained within will be fulfilled.

Natal

Natal (Christmas) in Brazil is celebrated in similar ways as in other Catholic countries. Traditionally, families put up *presépios* (nativity scenes) in their homes from 24 December– 6 January, but today, many households put up the nativity scenes at the beginning of December. In recent decades, Christmas trees, made popular through international films and television, have been gradually replacing the traditional nativity scenes. The main Christmas event is the *Ceia de Natal* (Christmas dinner), one of Brazil's most festive meals. It is traditionally a turkey dinner served after the midnight mass. Christmas presents are usually exchanged either after the dinner or after returning from mass, depending on family tradition.

New Year's Eve

New Year's Eve is an especially important celebration for Brazilians who never cease to hope for a better year and for better times. The New Year's Eve party is called Reveillon, a word borrowed from the French. It is usually a lively feast with friends and family, centred around a large festive dinner with dancing and music. Brazilians also go out to clubs and ball dances to celebrate the New Year. The festivities usually include traditions that emphasise the beginning of a new period and the end of an old one. Buying new clothes for the Reveillon or wearing white is a popular tradition. A superstition suggests that no poultry should be eaten during the Reveillon, since these animals dig up and throw soil backward, which symbolises a looking back at the old year. On New Year's Eve, people eat grapes, pomegranates and lentils for good luck. It is also customary for Brazilians to put three pomegranate seeds in their wallets or jump over seven waves at the beach for good luck. At midnight, fireworks go off everywhere, and people welcome the new year with toasts of champagne.

Carnaval
'The year doesn't begin until after Carnaval.'
—Brazilian expression

Carnaval came to Brazil in the form of the Portuguese *entrudo*, a merry revelry just before Lent, during which participants threw water, flour and ink at each other. The first documented celebration of Carnaval in Brazil took place in 1641, in honour of the coronation of Dom João IV as king of Portugal. In the 19th century, the *entrudo* led to such excesses that it was finally prohibited by the authorities. Around this time, masked balls were introduced to Rio de Janeiro by Italians, significantly changing the Carnaval culture. These balls were organised by Carnaval societies of the upper class and soon became the central events of Carnaval in Rio de Janeiro. The street revelry also began to take on new forms, as Carnaval groups from different social strata began to organise more disciplined celebrations including processions with costumes and musical bands.

At the beginning of the 20th century, samba became a popular Carnaval music. The first samba school in Rio de Janeiro, Deixa Falar, was founded in 1928, and in 1932, samba schools competed for the first time in a parade. Since then, samba has dominated the Carnaval in Rio de Janeiro, and has evolved into the samba *enredo* (samba narration), composed specifically for the parades. In the 1960s, Rio's Carnaval began to turn into a large commercial spectacle for which tickets were sold. In 1984, the samba schools began to parade in the *sambódromo*, a new stadium built exclusively for Carnaval with seats for 60,000 paying spectators. Today, Rio de Janeiro has the biggest Carnaval in the world and attracts hundreds of thousands of visitors every year. The samba schools have also grown to enormous proportions. Each school of the top division, the *grupo especial*, is made up of about 5,000 costumed participants who parade in different groups between the large allegorical floats that represent a narrative element of the parade theme. The schools are judged by a jury, which evaluates the visual, organisational, musical and narrative elements of the performance. The parades can follow any theme, but they have to relate to Brazilian culture.

With the success and commercialisation of Carnaval in Rio de Janeiro, the samba schools have become a model for Carnaval all over Brazil. Today, most Brazilian cities have

Large *bonecos* at the Carnaval of Recife.

samba schools, including São Paulo whose Carnaval has also grown into a huge spectacle with its own stadium. Many cities and towns also draw from their own regional folkloric traditions and include them in the four-day revelry.

The Carnaval of Salvador is the biggest besides that of Rio de Janeiro, and it attracts enormous crowds every year. Its main element are the *trios eléctricos* (electric trios)—bands that play on stages set up on flatbed trucks with huge mounted speakers. These moving stages parade the streets followed by a large group of revelers. Afro-Brazilian Carnaval groups, known as Afro-blocos, are also very popular. Among the most traditional are Ilê Aiyê and Olodum, which are known for their colourful costumes and fast percussion beat. The parades of Afoxés also form an integral part of the Carnaval in Salvador. They are linked to Candomblé, who parade through the streets and sing in African languages to a fast percussion beat. Among the oldest and best-known Afoxés, is Filhos de Ghandy (The Sons of Ghandi), who wear blue and white costumes with white turbans.

The Carnaval in the state of Pernambuco is considered the most folkloric in Brazil. It includes elements from a variety of traditional folk festivals and celebrations. In the cities of Recife and Olinda, Carnaval is a big street festival where large costumed groups called *blocos* (blocks) parade through the streets. Among the most famous is the Galo da Madrugada (Rooster of Dawn), which attracts over one million revelers during its traditional parade in Recife. The most popular music of the Carnaval in Pernambuco is the fast-paced *frevo* that evolved from marches and polkas. Another popular element unique to Pernambuco is the Maracatu, a theatrical dance performed to a percussion rhythm. Olinda has its own unique Carnaval traditions and the most characteristic element is the parading of large *bonecos*, puppets made of papier-maché. These tall mascots represent popular stars and folk heroes and are part of every *bloco* that parades through the city with its thousands of followers.

In addition to these popular Carnaval destinations, there are also a number of smaller festivals with unique regional attractions. Among them are the historical cities of Minas

Gerais such as Ouro Preto, Mariana, and São João del Rey, which have long-standing Carnaval traditions. These celebrations may not be as large as in Rio, Recife or Salvador, but certainly as much fun.

CALENDAR OF FESTIVALS AND HOLIDAYS

Official Holidays

- 1 January   Ano Novo (New Year's Day)
- March/April   Sexta Feira da Paixão (Good Friday)
- 21 April   Dia de Tiradentes (Tiradentes Day)
- 1 May   Dia do Trabalho (May Day)
- 7 September   Dia da Independência (Independence Day) A celebration of Brazil's independence from Portugal in 1822.
- 12 October   Nossa Senhora Aparecida (Our Lady Aparecida) Brazil's most popular religious festival. Celebrated in honour of Nossa Senhora Aparecida, Brazil's patron saint.
- 15 November   Dia da República (Day of the Republic) Commemorates the proclamation of the Republic in 1889.
- 25 December   Natal (Christmas Day)

Religious and Regional Holidays

In addition to the official public holidays, there are also a number of religious and regional holidays that are observed in many regions:

6 January	Dia dos Reis (Epiphany)
January, second Thursday	Lavagem do Bonfim (The Washing of Bonfim) Celebrated in Salvador.
2 February	• Festa de Iemanjá (Iemanjá Festival) Observed in Salvador. • Nossa Senhora das Candéias (Our Lady of the Candles) Celebrated in Juazeiro do Norte.

February/March	Carnaval. Takes place four days before Ash Wednesday, including Terça Feira do Carnaval (Shrove Tuesday).
May	Ascensão do Senhor (Ascension of Christ). Commemorated 40 days after Easter.
May/June	▪ Festa do Divino Espírito Santo (Pentecost). Celebrates the descent of the Holy Spirit on the seventh Sunday after Easter. Observed mainly in Parati (Rio de Janeiro) and Alcântara (Maranhão). ▪ Domingo da Santíssima Trindade (Sunday of the Holy Trinity). Celebrated on the Sunday after Pentecost, in honour of the Holy Trinity. ▪ Corpus Christi. Observed in honour of the Eucharist on the Thursday after Trinity.
15 August	Assunção de Nossa Senhora (Saint Mary's Assumption)
1 November	Dia de Todos os Santos (All Saint's Day)
2 November	Dia de Finados (All Souls' Day)
8 December	Nossa Senhora da Conceição (Our Lady of Immaculate Conception)

Many towns also have an annual *festa de santo patroeiro*, a festival in honour of their own patron saint. These celebrations are found all over Brazil and are rich in regional folkloric traditions.

Other Commemorations

▪ 12 June   Dia dos Namorados (Day of Lovers) The Brazilian version of Valentine's Day.

- May, second Sunday — Dia das Mães (Mothers' Day) Introduced from the US by the YMCA in 1919, Mother's Day is commonly celebrated throughout Brazil.
- August, second Sunday — Dia dos Pais (Fathers' Day) Also introduced from the Northern Hemisphere.

On a smaller scale, Brazilians also commemorate days dedicated to special events or causes, such as:

- 20 November — Dia Nacional da Consciência Negra (National Day of Black Consciousness)
- 19 April — Dia do Índio (Day of the Indian)

ARTS AND CULTURE
Music

'Cantando eu mando a tristeza embora.'
(With singing I send sadness away.)
—from the song 'Desde Que o Samba é Samba',
by Caetano Veloso

More than any other art form, Brazilian music reveals the influences of all ethnic groups that formed Brazilian society. From the fusion of these diverse folk music traditions evolved the complexity and richness of Brazilian music as we hear it today, a music that uses Amerindian flutes together with European stringed instruments and African drums.

Diverse Roots

From the beginning of Brazil's colonisation, Jesuit missionaries incorporated Amerindian music, rhythms and instruments into their religious plays to convert the natives. This practice resulted in a rich blending of musical influences early on and was later enriched by the music and rhythms brought to Brazil by African slaves. During the 18th century, popular African and Portuguese music gradually began to approach and influence each another. The *lundu*, a sensual and comical song and dance of African origin, became widely popular and was adopted by the Portuguese in an instrumental form. The

A folk music ensemble with traditional instruments in Crato, Ceará.

modinha, a form of Portuguese court dance was adapted to a syncopated rhythm and became a popular musical style around the same time. In the 19th century, polka was brought to Brazil by the Europeans and fused with other musical traditions to create several new urban music genres, among them the *marchinha, maxixe*, and *frevo*, all of which are popular during Carnaval. The *choro*, a rhythmic instrumental music performed by small ensembles with the use of guitars and flutes, became very popular in Rio de Janeiro in the early 20th century.

The Rise of Samba

In the late 19th century, samba began to evolve in Rio de Janeiro from the syncopated rhythms of the *lundu* and *maxixe*, as well as from the musical influences of Bahia. Early sambas were often parodies with comical lyrics and were played during the rowdy Carnaval festivities. After the first gramophone recording of a samba tune in 1917 titled *Pelo Telefone* (*Over the Telephone*), samba became very popular and evolved into the predominant musical style of Rio's Carnaval. Samba dominated Brazilian popular music during the first half of the 20th century and evolved into several genres. During the 1930s, Dorival Caymmi, a musician from Salvador, evolved as one of the leading songwriters of Brazilian music. He not only wrote hit songs for Carmen Miranda, a popular Brazilian star, but his music also influenced Brazilian popular music for generations. His songs are still frequently interpreted by Brazil's contemporary stars today.

Bossa Nova

Bossa nova was born in the early 1960s from samba rhythms and jazz harmonies. Composer Antônio Carlos Jobim (1927–1994), guitarist João Gilberto, his wife Astrud, and poet Vinicius de Moraes (1913–1980) were the driving forces behind a musical style that conquered world audiences with the well-known *A garota de Ipanema* (*The Girl from Ipanema*). Bossa nova was a sophisticated musical style that appealed to intellectuals and the urban middle class. It expressed the optimism of a nation that had just celebrated the inauguration of a new capital and was hoping to join the ranks of developed countries soon. Other important bossa nova musicians were Luis Bonfá, Baden Powell, Roberto Menescal, Carlos Lyra, Ronaldo Bôscoli and singer Nara Leão.

Tropicalismo and MPB

While bossa nova focused on jazzy harmonies and light-hearted lyrics, the Tropicalismo movement of the late 1960s was more socially conscious and became the voice of protest of a young generation that suffered increased repression from the military regime. Caetano Veloso, Gilberto Gil, Maria Bethânia and Gal Costa began to blend elements of rock'n roll with Brazilian rhythms and wrote complex lyrics with encrypted criticism of Brazilian society. Chico Buarque joined the movement later and became one of Brazil's most talented songwriters. One of his songs is titled *Calice* (*Chalice*), which is pronounced the same way as *cale-se* (shut up), a not-so-subtle reference to the censorship during the repression years. By the mid 1970s, the popularity of Tropicalismo had faded, but it was inspiring a new generation of musicians, mainly known by the acronym MPB (Música Popular Brasileira or Brazilian Popular Music). Among the better known interpreters are Milton Nascimento, Rita Lee and her band Os Mutantes, Ivan Lins, Marisa Monte, Cazuza, Djavan, Ney Matogrosso and Leila Pinheiro.

Contemporary Currents

Contemporary Brazilian music continues to draw from the rich traditions of the past, and also incorporates new international elements. Samba reggae, for example, evolved in Salvador and blends samba and reggae elements. Axé, another music genre popular in Bahia, is an upbeat music with samba and strong percussion elements. Funk Brasileiro, popular in Rio de Janeiro, and mangue beat from Recife, combine rap and percussion elements into a Brazilian version of ghetto music, very popular with youths in the *favelas*. In addition to these musical styles, there are a number of folk music traditions that continue to thrive regionally, but are little known elsewhere. This impressive reservoir of musical traditions continues to inspire young generations of musicians, who constantly develop new forms of expression by merging old and new, foreign and familiar elements.

Classical Music

Carlos Gomes (1836–1896) was Brazil's first internationally known composer. Inspired by Verdi, Gomes wrote nine operas. His best-known work is *Il Guarany* (sung in Italian and based on the novel *O Guarani* (1857) by José Alencar), which is still part of the world-wide operatic repertoire today. Starting in the early 20th century, Classical composers began to incorporate folkloric elements into their music, among them Alberto Nepomuceno and Heitor Villa-Lobos (1887–1959). Villa-Lobos participated in the Modern Art Week of São Paulo in 1922, and like his peers from the Modernist movement, he was dedicated to incorporating typically Brazilian elements into his work. His best-known pieces are his nine Bachianas Brasileiras, for which he adapted J.S. Bach's counterpoint technique to Brazilian folk themes. His major symphonic works include *Floresta do Amazonas* and the ballet *Uirapuru*. Brazil's most famous international opera diva was Bidú Sayão from Rio de Janeiro who enraptured audiences at the New York Metropolitan Opera from 1937–1952. After retiring from her operatic career, she worked on several projects with Villa-Lobos, among them the popular *Bachianas Brasileiras No 5*.

Ballet and Modern Dance

Although Brazil has a rich tradition of popular dances derived from Amerindian, African and Portuguese roots, they were strictly distinct from the dance performances in theatres, which followed the European ballet tradition. Starting in the early 1970s, the Ballet Stagium began to incorporate elements from popular dances into their Classical ballet performances. The well-known Grupo Corpo, founded in 1975, and today one of Brazil's best-known Modern ballet troupes, also began to combine Classical ballet with Brazilian folk dances. In addition to Modern tendencies within ballet, Modern dance was introduced in Brazil in the 1970s. Today, there are a large

Maculêlê is a fight dance with sticks or knives, popular in the north-east.

number of Modern dance companies such as Grupo Endança, Grupo Eixo, and O Cisne Negro, all of them with extraordinary professional dancers and an innovative repertoire. In recent years, the Balé Folclórico da Bahia has achieved international fame with their energetic and acrobatic shows. Founded in Salvador in 1987, the group is Brazil's only professional folk dance company. Their repertoire is based on folkloric traditions of the North-east and is a rich collection of regional dances and dance dramas.

FOLK ART TRADITIONS
Handicrafts

The large variety of handicrafts reflects Brazil's cultural diversity, and provides unique insights into the country's folkloric traditions. While some folk art traditions clearly maintain their Portuguese origins, other crafts such as ceramics reveal the rich miscegenation of European and Amerindian influences. The pottery of the lower Amazon for example, shows strong indigenous influences, which is evident in the red, black and white geometric designs that adorn pots and vases. In the Tocantins and Araguaia River valleys, the indigenous influence is noticeable in ceramic vases with spouts in the form of human figures. A popular ceramic tradition in the North-east, which originated in the city of Caruaru in Pernambuco, specialises in painted ceramic figures that enact scenes from daily life. There are numerous other local ceramic traditions and styles that can be found all over Brazil, especially in the North-east.

Basket weaving is a popular folk art with strong indigenous influences commonly practiced in the Amazon and North-east. Women weave baskets, sieves, mats and hats among other common objects for daily use. The materials are always taken from regional plants, mainly palm trees and vines. Lacework came to Brazil from Portugal, and this craft is still practiced today, mainly by women in rural areas. The best-known lacework comes from Ceará and Santa Catarina.

On the São Francisco River, the tradition of carving figure heads is still practiced today. These brightly painted busts in the form of animals with human faces and aggressive

A ceramic market in north-eastern Brazil.

expressions are put on the bows of boats, where they were believed to scare away malicious river spirits. In Minas Gerais, craft traditions evolved from the rocks and minerals abundant in the region. The soft soap stone is a common sculpting material and is made into utilitarian objects such as cups, flasks and bowls, and into decorative objects and religious images.

Weaving is also widely practiced in a variety of regional traditions and fibres. Hammocks, tapestries and rugs are typical in the North-east. In the South, women specialise in weaving ponchos from sheep wool.

Although there are many distinct traditions, handicraft in Brazil is not limited to certain regions, techniques or genres. Wherever you go, you will find unique expressions of the creative spirit of the Brazilian people. In the Amazon, Indian tribes still make traditional utilitarian objects such as bows, arrows, ceramic bowls, simple jewellery and feather hats. *Caboclos* carve beautiful wooden canoe paddles, women of the *sertão* make jewellery and rosaries from the seeds of local plants and painters of Goiás use the myriad shades of regional sandstone as pigments for their paintings, thus enriching Brazil's immense reservoir of folkloric traditions.

Literatura de Cordel

One curious tradition found in the north-eastern states, is the *literatura de cordel* (cord literature), which came to Brazil from Portugal in the 19th century. These booklets, written in verse and illustrated with woodcuts, became a widespread form of popular poetry. The *cordeis* tell of local events and heroes, and helped perpetuate the lore of the famous bandits of the backlands, the Cangaçeiros. The pamphlets were traditionally sold at markets, where they were hung from cords, which gave them their name. The tradition of the *cordeis* was beginning to fade under the influence of modern mass media, but it is now being revived in an effort to preserve regional folk art. Numerous *cordelistas*, as the authors are called, once again publish their satirical and humourous verses.

Folk Dances

Dances are a very popular folkloric tradition, and there are dozens of different folk dances practiced all over Brazil. These folk dances are a rich blend of the country's multi-ethnic heritage and are often characterised by lively dance steps and fast-paced rhythms.

Carimbó

Carimbó is a dance of African origin. It is popular in the Amazon region, especially in the state of Pará, where it is performed at almost every regional festival. In this dance, often performed barefoot, dancers imitate the movements and sounds of animals such as the rooster, turkey and monkey among others.

Coco

The *coco* (coconut) is one of the most popular dances of the North-east. It is a circle dance around a soloist who sings the refrain. The dance is fast-paced and imitates the act of opening a coconut, with rhythmic clapping to imitate the sound of breaking coconuts.

Frevo

This dance is derived from *capoeira* steps and became popular in Recife at the beginning of the 20th century. The *frevo* is a fast-paced dance, and is very popular during the Carnaval in Pernambuco, when dancers perform acrobatic feats with a small open umbrella. The *frevo* is performed by large ensembles, similar to marching bands.

Lundu

The *lundu* is a circle dance of African origin, with sensuous and comical elements that are performed in turn by all dancers.

Folguedos (Folkloric Dance Dramas)

In addition to folk dances, there are many dance dramas that are regularly performed during religious festivals and other folkloric celebrations. They centre around the theatrical performance of a popular theme. The *folguedos* originated in Portugal, but in Brazil they have evolved into a unique tradition of their own, sometimes including themes of African and indigenous origin.

Cavalhada (Knight Tournament)

This folk drama is performed during the Festa do Divino Espírito Santo (Festival of the Holy Spirit), mainly in the Central West and South-east.

A cavalhada is a kind of medieval tournament, where armed knights ride through the streets on decorated horses and re-enact the Christian victory over the Moors. Brazil's most famous *cavalhada* takes place in Pirenópolis, in the state of Goiás.

Bumba-Meu-Boi

Bumba-meu-boi, also known as *boi-bumbá* and by several other names, is a popular dance procession accompanied by percussion instruments and song. The performance tells a simple story with the help of comical theatrical elements. It evolved in the northern state of Maranhão and is today celebrated at different times of the year throughout the North and North-east. The story line has several regional variations, but always centers around a bull, which is killed and brought back to life. The performance includes many characters and the audience often participates in the procession. In some

Boi Bumbá is a dance telling the story of a killed and resurrected bull, popular in northern Brazil.

regions, a lot of work goes into the preparation of the costumes for the festival, not unlike a Carnaval celebration.

Maracatu

The *maracatu* is a theatrical dance performance popular in Pernambuco. It is performed by organised groups called Nações de Maracatu (Maracatu Nations). During the performance, they parade through the streets in colourful costumes, while dancing to a fast percussion rhythm. The *maracatu* evolved from the religious processions of Nossa Senhora do Rosário (Our Lady of the Rosary), the patron saint of Brazil's black population, but is today a secular event performed during Carnaval. The parade's main elements are the king and queen, who parade under a large umbrella. They are surrounded by the members of the court and several other standard characters.

Folia-de Reis

Celebrated between Christmas and Epiphany (25 December and 6 January), this musical procession is held in honour of the Magi, who followed the star to Bethlehem. Groups of costumed singers, called *foliões* (revellers), visit nativity scenes in churches and homes, while singing and praising the birth of Jesus. They are usually accompanied by a group of musicians. Whoever welcomes the visiting kings with food and drink receives a blessing. This tradition is still widely practised in the Central West and South-east.

LITERATURE

> 'Aprendi com meu filho de dez anos,
> Que a poesia é a descoberta,
> Das coisas que eu nunca vi.'
> (I learned from my ten year old son
> That poetry is the discovery
> Of the things I never saw.)
> —Oswald de Andrade, from Pau Brasil (1925)

Colonial Literature

Brazil's history of literature, as well as that of the arts and education, began with the arrival of the Jesuits in 1549. One of the first remarkable literary figures of colonial Brazil was Father José de Anchieta (1534–1597), known for his poetry and plays to convert the Indians. Gregório de Matos (1623–1696) is Brazil's first notable poet whose Baroque poetry was known both for its lyricism and satire. Father Antônio Vieira (1608–1697) was another priest whose literary production was widely respected in colonial Brazil.

During the 18th century, the writers of the mining region of Minas Gerais were Brazil's most prolific poets. Among them were Cláudio Manoel da Costa (1729–1789), José Basílio da Gama (1740–1795) and Tomás Antônio Gonzaga (1744–1810). 'Marília de Dirceu', an epic poem by Tomás Antônio Gonzaga, published in 1792, is the best-known work of the period. It is a collection of poems dedicated to the poet's great love Marília, a girl much younger than himself. Literary critic José Veríssimo wrote about Gonzaga, that 'he was in fact the first one in Brazil, who sang so persistently, so exclusively and so tenderly of love.'

The Birth of Brazilian Literature

When the Portuguese court arrived in Brazil in 1808, the cultural life of the colony began to change. New European literary influences were brought to Brazil, among them the Romantic movement. It was the young Brazilian Romantic writers who first began to establish a national tradition of literature. Castro Alves (1847–1871) was one of the best-known Romantic poets. He wrote about African slaves and was a vehement abolitionist. José de Alencar (1829–1877) is Brazil's best-known Romantic novelist. In his historical novels, the Indians are often glorified and idealised as in *O Guarani* and *Iracema*.

Brazil's most important literary figure of the 19th century was Machado de Assis (1839–1908), a Realist writer whose remarkable psychological portraits had a great influence on Brazilian literature. He is best-known for his novel *Dom Casmurro*, but he also wrote essays and remarkable short stories. Euclides da Cunha (1866–1909), a journalist from Rio de Janeiro, is best-known for his epic work, *Os Sertões* (*Rebellion in the Backlands*) from 1902, which chronicles the defeat of a religious community in the North-east by the Brazilian army. It is a classic work of Brazilian social and cultural history.

The Modernist Movement

The 1922 Modern Art Week (Semana de Arte Moderna) in São Paulo had a long-lasting influence on Brazilian literature. For the first time, Brazilian artists and writers decided to put aside European subject matters and create works of art that were inspired by Brazil's own wealth of folklore, music and traditions.

Mário de Andrade (1893–1945) was one of the most important writers of this movement. He was a novelist, poet, musicologist and essayist, who had a great influence on later generations of writers as well as musicians. His best-known work is the novel *Macunaíma* (1928) in which he combines regional

Poet Oswald de Andrade (1890–1953) was one of the founding members of the Brazilian Modernist movement. In 1928, he published the *Manifesto Antropófago* (*Anthropophagous Manifesto*), a short manifesto in which he suggested that foreign artistic styles must not be copied, but instead had to be assimilated into a uniquely Brazilian form of artistic expression.

idioms and native folklore to create a great metaphor of Brazilian culture.

Modern Poetry

Carlos Drummond de Andrade (1902–1987) and Manuel Bandeira (1886–1968) are among Brazil's best-known Modern poets who wrote poems in free form. Poet Vinicius de Moraes (1913–1980) became famous through his bossa nova lyrics in the 1960s. He also wrote the play *Orfeu da Conceição*, a modern rendering of the story of Orpheus and Eurydice set during the Carnaval in Rio de Janeiro. It was made into the successful film *Orfeu Negro* (*Black Orpheus*, 1959) by French director Marcel Camus. Other important Brazilian poets of the 20th century are Raul Bopp, Murilo Mendes, Jorge de Lima, Ferreira Gullar, João Cabral de Melo Neto and Cecília Meireles.

Modern Literature

Among Brazil's best-known modern novelists is Jorge Amado (1912–2001), whose many novels portray the people of his home state Bahia in a humourous and satirical way. *Gabriela, Cravo e Canela* (*Gabriela, Clove and Cinnamon*) and *Dona Flor e seus Dois Maridos* (*Dona Flor and Her Two Husbands*) are his best-known novels and were made into successful films.

Other important Brazilian writers of the 20th century are Clarice Lispector, Érico Veríssimo, Osman Lins, Lygia Fagundes Telles, Rubem Fonseca and João Ubaldo Ribeiro.

Among the best-known novelists who wrote about Brazil's social realities are Graciliano Ramos (1892–1953), José Lins do Rego (1901–1957) and Rachel de Queiroz (born 1910). Their novels focus on the difficult lives of the inhabitants of Brazil's impoverished north-east. One of Brazil's most complex and accomplished modern writers was João Guimarães Rosa (1908–1967), who used the North-east's regional mannerisms and restrained language as the literary base for his great novel, *Grande Sertão: Veredas* (*The Devil to Pay in the Backlands*).

THEATRE
Colonial Endeavours
The art of theatre came to Brazil in the 16th century, with the Jesuit missionaries who wrote plays to help convert the Indians to Christianity. However, it was not until the gold rush in the 18th century, that theatre became more widely appreciated. At that time, the new class of wealthy citizens in the mining region began to show interest in the performing arts, and several theatres were built. The Casa da Ópera in Ouro Preto, built in 1769, is considered the oldest theatre in Latin America that continues to host performances today.

A Brazilian Theatre
After Brazil's independence in 1822, the first Brazilian theatre troupes were founded, and playwrights began to develop a national theatre tradition. Among Brazil's most prolific poets and writers, is Gonçalves Dias who also devoted himself to theatre, creating the best examples of Brazilian Romantic dramas. During the late empire and early republic, other well-known writers such as José de Alencar, Machado de Assis and Artur Azevedo also wrote plays, expanding the national repertoire at Brazil's growing number of theatres.

Modern Currents
In the 1940s, Brazilian theatre was transformed by the work of Nelson Rodrigues (1912–1980). Many of his plays reveal

the moral hypocrisy of respected Brazilian families. The 1950s were a period of feverish experimentation in the Brazilian arts, that also left its mark on theatre. Playwrights such as Gianfranco Guarnieri, Jorge Andrade and Ariano Suassuna experimented with new means of dramatic expressions and collaborated with several new and dynamic theatre troupes in Rio de Janeiro and São Paulo. Social concerns also surfaced in plays. One of the period's best-known plays is *O Pagador de Promessa* (*To Pay Vows*) by Dias Gomes, which deals with the conflict between the beliefs of the people and religious authorities.

Censorship and Rebirth

The military coup in 1964 and the subsequent censorship which lasted until 1979, stifled most of the creative efforts of Brazilian playwrights. Since the return to democracy, Brazil's theatre has rebounded into a vital and creative art form known for its innovative directors and dynamic theatre troupes. Among the most successful theatre productions of the past few years were contemporary interpretations of classical plays, as well as new works by young playwrights. The plays of Nelson Rodrigues are standard repertoire at Brazilian theatres and are regularly performed in all major cities today. São Paulo and Rio de Janeiro have a particularly diverse theatre scene, and the theatre festival in Curitiba attracts large crowds each year.

BRAZILIAN CINEMA
Early Attempts

The first film made in Brazil was a slow pan of Guanabara Bay, filmed in 1898 from an approaching ocean steamer. It did not take long before the new art form became popular, and by 1906, Rio de Janeiro already boasted 22 cinemas. Humberto Mauro was one of the most prolific directors of the silent era, and some of his films are still shown at film festivals today. In 1933, Carmen Miranda, a popular singer, appeared in her first film. She moved to the U.S. in 1939, where she became a well-known performer on New York's Broadway and performed in a number of Hollywood musicals.

Neorealism

In 1953, *O Cangaceiro* (*The Brigand*) by Lima Barreto won an award at the Cannes Film Festival, and became the first Brazilian film to receive international recognition. It chronicles the adventures of a band of *cangaceiros* (backland bandits) and was inspired by the North-east's most famous outlaw, Lampião. During the 1950s, Brazilian filmmakers began to make films under the influence of Italian Neorealism. Films such as *Rio 40 Graus* (*Rio 40 Degrees*, 1955), *Rio Zona Norte* (Rio North Zone, 1957) and *Vidas Secas* (*Barren Lives*, 1963), all by Nelson Pereira dos Santos, were among the first Brazilian films to take a realistic look at Brazil's social condition and portray poverty, drought and race discrimination.

Cinema Novo

In the early 1960s, a movement known as Cinema Novo (New Cinema) began to emerge, as Brazil's young directors increasingly turned to Brazil's social reality as the subject matter for their films. The first international success of this new form of Brazilian cinema was Anselmo Duarte's film, *O Pagador de Promessa* (*To Pay Vows*), which won the Golden Palm at the Cannes Film Festival in 1962. Glauber Rocha became the leading figure of the Cinema Novo. He made films charged with mysticism and political messages. His dream was to change society through making films, by following his slogan 'an idea in mind and a camera in hand.' His masterwork is the allegorical *Deus e o Diabo na Terra do Sol* (*Black God and White Devil*) from 1963, a film about impoverished peasants, messianic prophets and bandits in Brazil's drought-ridden *sertão*.

The Censorship Years

After the military coup of 1964, Brazilian film makers increasingly suffered from censorship and were no longer able to make films with social or political content. As a result, the films of the 1970s focused on non-political themes. *Dona Flor e seus Dois Maridos* (*Dona Flor and Her Two Husbands*, 1976) by Bruno Barreto, based on a novel by Jorge Amado, is the best-known Brazilian film of that period.

It stands as Brazil's largest box office hit with 12 million viewers worldwide.

Freedom of Expression

Film makers during the 1980s used their freedom from censorship to produce again films about the political and social conditions in Brazil. *Bye, bye Brasil* (1980) by Carlos Diegues is the internationally best-known film of the time. It chronicles the adventures of a group of variety artistes, as they tour the entire country and perform in small villages and towns. Another well-known film is *Pixote—A lei do mais fraco* (*Pixote*, 1981) by Argentinean director Hector Babenco. It is the compelling story of street children in São Paulo.

The Dark Age of Cinema

With the closing of the government film agency Embrafilme in 1991, Brazilian cinema entered a dark period. Few films were made during the early 1990s due to the lack of government funding. But thanks to tax incentives for companies investing in film productions, Brazilian cinema began to make a come-back between 1994 and 1995.

Contemporary Currents

The current cinematic trends show that Brazilian filmmakers are gradually overcoming the strong influence of the Cinema Novo and are looking for new themes and forms of expression. Contemporary films cover diverse topics, from the historical to the personal, and from the lyrical to fast-paced action.

The best-known Brazilian film in recent years is doubtlessly *Central do Brasil* (*Central Station*) from 1998, directed by Walter Salles. It tells the story of a little boy who teams up with a disgruntled school teacher, to search for his father. *Central do Brasil* was Brazil's most successful film of the 1990s and won 50 international awards. A much darker portrayal of contemporary Brazil is the much-acclaimed *Cidade de Deus* (*City of God*, by Fernando Meirelles, 2002), which shows the violent reality of growing up in a Rio de Janeiro suburb.

THE VISUAL ARTS

With the exception of pottery and rock painting, Brazil's Indians produced little durable art before the arrival of Europeans. The first artworks of colonial Brazil were made for the churches and convents established along the coast during the 16th century. Sculpture was limited to the images of saints, and painting was dedicated to biblical scenes. All artistic activity was centred in the coastal cities, until the gold rush in Minas Gerais in the 18th century began to attract artists and artisans to the interior province. Lay confraternities began to build large churches throughout the mining region, and Brazil's most remarkable painters and sculptors of the time worked on the churches that still crown the hilltops of numerous historic towns today.

Brazilian Baroque

Among the earliest masters of Brazilian sculpture was Francisco Xavier de Brito, a Portuguese artist. He worked in Rio de Janeiro and later moved to Ouro Preto, where he worked on several churches. Antônio Francisco Lisboa (1739–1814), nicknamed 'Aleijadinho' (the 'Little Cripple') due to a disfiguring illness, was Brazil's most prolific baroque artist.

Church of Congonhas do Campo in Minas Gerais.

He lived in Ouro Preto (then known as Vila Rica) and worked both as a self-taught architect and sculptor throughout the mining region of Minas Gerais. Aleijadinho took the sculptural traditions of his time a step further and created life-size sculptures with a heightened expressionism and emotional verisimilitude. The wooden sculptures of the Stations of the Cross (1796–1799) and the 12 life-size soapstone sculptures of the prophets (1800–1805) at the sanctuary of Bom Jesus de Matosinhos in Congonhas do Campo are considered Aleijadinho's masterpieces. Other works can be admired in the church of São Francisco de Assis in Ouro Preto and the church of Nossa Senhora do Carmo in Sabará. Poet Carlos Drummond de Andrade expresses the artist's accomplishments in his poem 'O vôo sobre as igrejas':

'This mulatto genius chiseled into soap stone
all of our sins, all of our lasciviousness,
and this confusion of desires,
and this longing to go to heaven,
and to sin more on earth'.

Brazil's best-known painter of this period was Manuel da Costa Ataíde, who collaborated with Aleijadinho on several projects including the Franciscan Church in Ouro Preto, where he painted a mulatto Virgin in the center medallion of the wooden ceiling.

French Influences

During the 19th century, the visual arts received new impulses from the arrival of the Portuguese court in Rio de Janeiro. In 1816, after Napoleon's defeat in Europe, King Dom João VI invited a group French artists (known as the 'French Mission'), to lay the groundwork for Brazil's artistic development. Among the best-known artists were the brothers Nicolas-Antoine and Auguste-Marie Taunay, and painter Jean-Baptiste Debret (1768–1848). Nicolas-Antoine Taunay's oil paintings and Debret's watercolours and drawings were the first comprehensive visual records of colonial life in Brazil.

Due to strong French influence, Brazil's artists remained committed to neoclassicism throughout the 19th century. Victor Meirelles (1832–1903) was Brazil's best-known painter of this period. He painted historical scenes and victorious battles. Among his most famous paintings is *A Primeira Missa* (*The First Mass*, 1861), depicting the first mass celebrated in Brazil by Pedro Álvarez Cabral and his men in 1500. Several of Meirelles' most important works are in the Museu Nacional de Belas Artes in Rio de Janeiro. In the late 19th and early 20th century, visual artists in Brazil followed French artistic styles such as impressionism, art nouveau and symbolism. Among the best-known painters of this period is Eliseu Visconti (1866–1944), who painted the frieze and the ceiling for the Municipal Theater in Rio de Janeiro, which was completed in 1908.

Modernism

Modernist art first came to Brazil with artists such as the Lithuanian-born painter, Lasar Segall (1891–1957) and the Brazilian painter, Anita Malfatti (1896–1964), both influenced by the European avant-garde in Paris. These new artistic ideas culminated in the Semana de Arte Moderna (Modern Art Week) of São Paulo in 1922. This week-long arts event was organised by a group of young Brazilian artists in search of a new artistic identity. Although these artists were influenced by European expressionism, cubism and futurism, they deliberately turned to Brazil's rich culture for their subject matter and inspiration. Among the most notable participants of the Modern Art Week were painters Anita Malfatti, Emiliano di Cavalcanti, Osvaldo Goeldi, John Graz and sculptor Victor Brecheret (1894–1955). This became a seminal event in Brazilian art and sparked an intense investigation into national identity, art and culture throughout the 1920s and 1930s. Tarsila do Amaral (1886–1973) was one of the most successful Brazilian modernist painters of that period. She is known for stylised landscapes with distorted figures. Emiliano di Cavalcanti (1897–1976) is another well-known painter. He mainly painted mulatto women, Carnaval scenes and tropical landscapes. Victor Brecheret is best-known for his Monumento às Bandeiras (Monument to the Bandeira Expeditions), which he completed between 1936 and 1953, based on his model from 1920. This large sculpted scene of an early *bandeira* expedition is located outside São Paulo's Ibirapuera Park. Other noted sculptors were Bruno Georgi (1905–1993) and Alfredo Ceschiatti (1918–1989).

Artistic Diversity

As modernist styles became more widely accepted, artists began to work in a variety of genres and techniques. Cândido Portinari (1903–1962) became Brazil's foremost fresco painter. He is best-known for his masterpiece for Oscar Niemeyer's chapel of St Francis in Pampulha, Belo Horizonte. Many of his paintings were devoted to social criticism and depicted the lives of simple people.

In the 1940s, Brazil's visual arts received new impulses from within. The Art Museum of São Paulo (MASP) was founded in 1947, the São Paulo Museum of Modern Art in 1948 and the Museum of Modern Art (MAM) opened in Rio de Janeiro in 1950. The Biennial of São Paulo (Bienal de São Paulo), an art fair held every two years, was opened in 1951, and it is still Latin America's largest art fair today. Brazilian art is very diverse, allowing for a wide variety of ideas, styles and subject matter, from the figurative to the abstract and conceptional. Rio de Janeiro and São Paulo are Brazil's leading art centres with a lively art scene and a large number of galleries and exhibition venues. Cultural centres and galleries in other cities also have regular shows of both established and emerging regional artists.

ARCHITECTURE

Unlike its Andean neighbours, Brazil has no impressive pre-Columbian temples or palaces. When the Portuguese arrived in 1500, the native tribes were mainly nomadic and their buildings were simple thatched huts. The first permanent structures on Brazilian soil were the Portuguese fortresses and administrative buildings of the mid 1500s, built in the mannerist and later the baroque style. Other notable buildings were the churches and convents that were established along the coast, especially in Salvador and Olinda, where some of the oldest buildings in Brazil can be found.

Baroque Architecture

The gold rush during the 18th century brought new wealth to the colony and caused a building boom in the mining towns of the interior and in the port city of Rio de Janeiro. New government and administrative buildings were erected, and lay brotherhoods in the province of Minas Gerais outdid each other with large and lavishly decorated churches. Among the best-known architects of the late 18th century was Antônio Francisco Lisboa (1739–1814), also known as Aleijadinho, who designed churches in addition to working on sculptures. Although Aleijadinho followed the prevalent baroque and rococo design elements of his time, he was among the first to replace the heavy rectangular designs and stern linear façades with more playful design elements such as curved or scrolled lines and sculpted decorations that adorned both portals, pulpits and balustrades. The architectural and sculptural work of Aleijadinho can still be admired today in the towns of Ouro Preto, Congonhas do Campo, Sabará and São João del Rey, all in the state of Minas Gerais.

Neoclassicism

Brazilian architecture received new impulses starting in 1816, when King Dom João invited a French artistic mission to Brazil. Among the artists was the French architect Auguste Grandjean de Montigny (1776–1850), who built Brazil's first Royal Academy of Arts and began to remodel Rio de Janeiro in the style of French neoclassicism, a style that influenced Brazilian architecture for several decades.

Urban Renewal

At the end of the 19th century, eclectic architecture became popular among the urban elite, who had their mansions built in an extravagant fusion of styles. In 1898, Belo Horizonte was inaugurated as Brazil's first planned state capital, and many of its buildings were designed in the Neoclassical and eclectic styles. In 1906, Rio de Janeiro also received a facelift. The city's major thoroughfare, the Avenida Central (now

Avenida Rio Branco) was designed as the city's showcase avenue with the National Library, Municipal Theater and a number of stately government buildings.

Starting in the 1920s, São Paulo began to develop into a major urban centre. Skyscrapers began to replace the low buildings from the colonial period and the city was modernised according to modern principles of urban planning. In 1929, the Martinelli building was completed, the tallest building in Latin America at the time, and a symbol for São Paulo's rapid economic growth.

Modernist Architecture

In the 1930s, modernist architectural ideas became popular among young Brazilian architects. Lúcio Costa and Oscar Niemeyer were inspired by the French architect Le Corbusier, and they designed the first modern buildings in Brazil. In the 1940s, they were commissioned by Juscelino Kubitschek, then the mayor of Belo Horizonte, to design the new affluent suburb of Pampulha, complete with chapel, casino and yacht club. Other well-known examples of early modern Brazilian architecture are the passenger terminal of Rio de Janeiro's Santos Dumont Airport by the brothers Marcelo and Mílton Roberto (1937), and the Museum of Modern Art (MAM) in Rio de Janeiro by Affonso Reidy (1954).

When Juscelino Kubitschek became Brazil's president in 1956 and decided to build a new capital, the design project was awarded to Lúcio Costa, who invited Oscar Niemeyer and landscape architect Roberto Burle Marx to join him. The city was planned in the shape of a cross and the main axis, called the Eixo Monumental, or Monumental Axis, was dedicated to government buildings while the cross-section was divided into residential blocks. Niemeyer's most notable designs are the cathedral and the Itamaraty Palace (ministry of foreign affairs) with its tall arches and water garden.

Contemporary Challenges

During the military government from 1964–1985, Brazil's architecture was marked by a sterile approach to urban planning and an emphasis on utilitarian and functional architecture. Much of the charm of Brazil's older cities vanished during these years as bland administrative and commercial complexes replaced run-down, but picturesque historical buildings. Brazil's biggest architectural challenges of the new millennium is not so much the construction of new buildings, but the preservation of its architectural past. This task has already been undertaken with the renovation of old city centres in São Luís (capital of the state of Maranhão), the Pelourinho district in Salvador, the old centre in Recife, as well as several other historic cities and towns throughout Brazil. The selection of several Brazilian historic towns as UNESCO World Heritage Sites (Diamantina, Goiás, Olinda, Ouro Preto, Salvador, São Luís) is a sign that these preservation efforts are successful and that they are internationally recognised.

THE MEDIA
Television

Since its introduction in 1950, television has become an integral part of the lives of most Brazilians. It is the most powerful mass medium in Brazil and has long since overtaken the printed news media in popularity and importance as an opinion-maker.

Among Brazil's most popular TV programmes are the *telenovelas* (soap operas). They are sometimes watched by 80 per cent of the television audience, and influence the fashión, attitudes and habits of Brazilians nationwide. In addition to these melodramatic TV shows, Brazilians also enjoy news programmes and talk shows, which are broadcast by all major networks.

The Rede Globo is Brazil's largest TV network. It was founded in 1965 by journalist Roberto Marinho, and has since been built up into a large media empire. Globo has dominated Brazilian TV mainly with its lavishly produced *telenovelas*. The other major TV networks are SBT (Sistema Brasileiro de Televisão), RedeTV, Record and Bandeirantes. There are also two government-owned TV stations, TV Cultura (state of São Paulo) and TV Educativa (state of Rio de Janeiro). These two channels provide educational and cultural programming not usually shown on the commercial channels. All these major networks broadcast their programming throughout Brazil, although in most rural areas, satellite dishes are necessary for reception.

In addition to the open channels, cable television and satellite systems are available by subscription. They include a number of international channels from Europe, US and Latin America.

Radio

Brazil's history of radio began in 1936 with the first broadcast of Rádio Nacional in Rio de Janeiro. Today, there are over 3,400 radio stations all over Brazil which belong to a number of large networks. Several international short-wave radio stations such as Voice of America and BBC World Service can be received in Brazil.

Internet

The Internet usage in Brazil has grown rapidly in recent years, and the number of *internautas* (Internet users) is estimated at twenty million. Although relatively few Brazilians shop online, Internet commerce has seen large growth. With Brazil's sluggish bureaucracy, many Brazilians submit their tax-returns online and prefer online banking to long lines at banks. Internet service providers are available in all cities and most towns. Universo Online (UOL) is Brazil's largest Internet Service Provider, but there are many other national and regional providers offering dial-up and broadband service. The speed of Internet connections varies regionally, but dial-up connections are generally slow, and high-speed internet access is primarily available in large cities.

Newspapers

The history of Brazil's printed media goes back to the royal press that was brought to Rio de Janeiro with the Portuguese court in 1808. While these earliest attempts of journalistic expression are no longer in circulation, the *Diário de Pernambuco*, founded in Recife in 1825, is South America's oldest existing published newspaper. The largest and most reputable among Brazil's 523 daily newspapers are *Folha de São Paulo*, *O Estado de São Paulo*, *O Globo* (Rio), and *O Jornal do Brasil* (Rio). Brazil's largest newspaper with business and economic news is the *Gazeta Mercantil* in São Paulo. These newspapers are distributed nationally and can be purchased in most state capitals either on the same day or the day after. With these exceptions, most other Brazilian newspapers have a very localised scope and focus mainly on news about the respective city, region or state.

Magazines

There are over 1,600 different magazines published in Brazil, with a monthly circulation of over 7 million. These periodicals cover anything from gossip to health, fashion, pornography and sports. There are several weekly news magazines such as *Veja, Isto É* and *Época. Veja* offers the most interesting and in-depth coverage of both national and international affairs.

English Language Publications

Magazines and newspapers in English are hard to find outside São Paulo, Rio de Janeiro and Brasília. *The International Herald Tribune, New York Times, USA Today International, The European, The Financial Times, The Observer*, and *The London Times* are the most common English-language newspapers you may come across at airports and some bookshops or newsstands in Brazil's large cities. Some newsstands in tourist areas might carry *Time Magazine* or *Newsweek*.

Sunday News

The only English-language newspaper published in Brazil is the weekly *Sunday News*, which is available in São Paulo, Rio de Janeiro and Brasília.

Books

Brazilians are not known to be avid readers and only read on average two books a year. Nonetheless, there are numerous publishing houses totaling several thousand new titles every year. Brazil's bestseller lists regularly include many international authors such as John Grisham and Sidney Sheldon, and some popular national authors such as Paulo Coelho. Self-help books, mostly translated, are also immensely popular. English books are difficult to find and are generally only available at airports and large bookshops in major cities.

Bookshops

Bookshops in Brazil are usually small and hard to find. The most common bookshops are those of large publishing houses, as well as chain shops, which can be found in most major cities. Among them are Livraria Curió, Unilivros, Livraria Siciliano, Livraria Kosmos, Saraiva and Editora Vozes. Most cultural centres and art house theatres also have book shops with an interesting selection.

Libraries

All cities have public libraries, but the library system is insufficiently developed, and the selection of books is not always up-to-date. Many small towns don't have libraries at all, but the ministry of education is currently funding the construction of libraries in many small towns. Cultural centres and museums often have archives and libraries that are accessible to the public. Rio de Janeiro's national library, the Biblioteca Nacional, houses Brazil's most impressive collection of books. Curitiba has the nation's most advanced public library system, known locally as *faróis do saber* (lighthouses of knowledge), and they are located all over the city. Universities also have libraries open to the public, although only students can check out books. Many international institutions, as well as foreign language institutes at universities, have small foreign language libraries.

THE COMMUNICATION CHALLENGE

CHAPTER 8

'The Brazilian language is one of the richest and most
sonorous. And it possesses that really splendid sound *ão.*'
—Mário de Andrade, *Paulicea Desvairada*
('Hallucinated City'), 1922

Finding yourself surrounded by people who speak a language that you don't understand is a considerable challenge to most foreigners. Few Brazilians speak English, and the only way to communicate with them is to learn their language. The sooner you start with a Portuguese course at home, the sooner you will master the essentials of basic conversation after your arrival in Brazil. Language is not merely a form of communication; it is the key to a deeper understanding of a foreign culture. With a basic vocabulary, you begin to understand colloquial expressions, the subtleties of humour and start making local friends. Learning Portuguese will enable you to take an insider's look at a fascinating country and a friendly people.

A Good Start

The most important step toward making yourself understood and to understand what others are saying is to start practising. Bring a phrase book and dictionary, and start building an active vocabulary.

Write down words you don't know and look them up later. Don't hesitate to ask people about the meaning of words and phrases, especially colloquialisms and slang, as you won't find them in the dictionary.

Most foreigners are intimidated when they first come to Brazil, and they speak as little as possible so they don't embarrass themselves. While this reaction is understandable, it won't get you very far.

INTRODUCTION TO BRAZILIAN PORTUGUESE

Portuguese is the national language and is spoken by all

Brazilians, except a few isolated tribes in the Amazon. Portuguese belongs to the Romance language family of Indo-European languages together with Spanish, French, Italian and Romanian. It bears a lot of resemblance to Spanish with which it shares common roots, but structurally, Portuguese is more archaic than Spanish and has characteristics not found in other Romance languages. The long Moorish occupation of Portugal in the middle ages also left its traces in the language. There are still many words of Arabic origin in modern Portuguese vocabulary: *alfândega* (customs building), *chafariz* (fountain), *aceite* (olive oil), *garrafa* (bottle), *xarope* (syrup), among others.

With over 185 million people, Brazil is the largest Portuguese-speaking country in the world. Although Brazilian Portuguese is closely related to the Portuguese spoken in Portugal, some variations have evolved over time. It was amusing to watch a film from Portugal at a Brazilian cinema, which had subtitles in Brazilian Portuguese. Apparently, the film distributor found it necessary to help Brazilians understand the different pronunciation of the Portuguese spoken in Portugal. Brazilian Portuguese not only differs in spelling, grammar and pronunciation, but the vocabulary has been enriched with about 10,000 additional words from indigenous and African languages. There are many names of places, fruits and animals that ring with the exotic sounds of the language of the Tupi Guarani, Brazil's most populous tribal group at the time of the Portuguese arrival. Towns such as Curitiba, Parati and Ubatuba, mountains such as Itatiaia and Itacolomy, and rivers such as Tieté, Paraná and Ipiranga, are all names from the Tupi Guarani language.

Many native words describing Brazil's fauna and flora have also entered the Portuguese language. Among them *arara* (macaw), *tatu* (armadillo), *tamanduá* (anteater), *jacaré* (caiman) and most names for native trees such as *umbaúba, copaíba, ipé*, and hundreds more. For the first two centuries after Brazil's discovery, Tupi Guarani served as the *língua geral*, the common language of communication between the Indians and the Portuguese settlers and was used more than Portuguese. Jesuit missionaries compiled grammars and dictionaries of Tupi and spoke the language fluently.

More recently, English words have also made their way into the Portuguese vocabulary, although there are only a handful. Show in Portuguese refers to a live concert and the universal 'okay' is also commonly used. Many English words also entered the Portuguese language through sports although the spelling often changed. Among them are *time* (team), *pênalti* (penalty), and *gol* (goal). Expressions from business and computing have also been introduced from English, such as 'marketing', 'internet' and 'site' among others.

Portuguese has its origins in Latin and shares a large part of its vocabulary with other Romance languages. Since English also has some Latin roots, students of Portuguese will discover many similar or identical words. Here are just a few:

- *hora*   hour
- *capital*   capital
- *exercício*   exercise
- *história*   history
- *montanha*   mountain

There are of course exceptions, and a Portuguese word that looks similar to an English one does not always have the same meaning. Examples are *eventualmente* (accidentally)—eventually and *esquisito* (strange, odd)—exquisite.

PRONUNCIATION

The main challenge of Portuguese pronunciation for English speakers are the numerous nasal sounds. Most other phonemes exist in English in a similar form. In the phonetic transcriptions, I have used capital letters to indicate stress. This introduction is only a rough guideline to the pronunciation of Brazilian Portuguese, and it is best to buy a language course with a cassette or CD to learn pronunciation.

Vowels

The pronunciation of vowels in Portuguese follows more clearly defined rules than in English.

- **a** is pronounced like the *u* in *sun* or the *a* in *father*, e.g. *abacate* ('avocado') is pronounced 'a-ba-KAH-chee'.
- **e** can be open like *e* in *egg*, e.g. *dez* ('ten') is pronounced 'DEZ', or closed like *a* in *state*, e.g. *seco* ('dry') is pronounced 'SAY-co'. When written with an acute accent, the **é** takes the stress and becomes an open vowel: *café* ('coffee') is pronounced 'ka-FEH'. With a circumflex, **ê** also takes the stress, but is a closed vowel as in *três* ('three'), which is pronounced 'trehs'.
- **i** is pronounced as in *idiom* or *eel*: *idioma* ('language') is pronounced 'ee-dee-OH-ma'. With an acute accent, **í** takes the stress: *magnífico* ('magnificient'), which is pronounced 'ma-GNEE-fee-co'.
- **o** is mainly pronounced open as in *cod*: *nove* ('nine'), 'NO-ve' or closed, similar to *boat*: *motor* ('motor') 'mo-TOR'. The definite article **o** ('the') is a short vowel that sounds more like a *u* as in *put*. At the end of a word, **o** also sounds more like *u* as in *put*: *carro* ('car'), pronounced 'KAH-ho'. With an acute accent, **ó** takes the stress with an open pronunciation, as in *avó* ('grandmother'), pronounced 'a-VAW'. When written with a circumflex, **ô** takes the stress and becomes a closed vowel as in *avô* ('grandfather'), pronounced 'a-VOH'.
- **ou** is a closed *o* sound similar to that in *so*: *outro*, pronounced 'OH-troo'.
- **u** is either a long vowel as in *boot*: *burro* ('donkey') pronounced 'BOO-ho' or a short vowel as in *put*: *curral* ('corral'), pronounced 'ku-HAO'. **U** is silent in words with **qu** and **gu** when followed by **e** or **i**: *quebrar* ('to break'), pronounced 'ke-BRAR', *seguir* ('to follow'), pronounced 'se-GEAR'.
  U is written as **ü** after **g** or **q**, and before **e** or **i**, only when it needs to be pronounced. In this position, **u** sounds more like a *w*: *agüentar* ('to tolerate') is pronounced as 'a-gwen-TAR' and *freqüente* ('frequent') is pronounced 'fre-KWEN-chee'. When **u** follows a **g** or **q** and precedes an **a**, it also sounds more like a *w*: *guaraná* (*guaraná* drink) is pronounced 'gwa-ra-NAH' and *quando* ('when') is pronounced 'KWAHN-do'.

Nasal Diphthongs

- **ã** and **ãs** are a nasal *ah* sound: *irmã* ('sister') is pronounced 'eer-MAH' and *irmãs* ('sisters') is 'eer-MAHS'.
- **ãe** and **ães** are a nasal *eye* sound: *mãe* ('mother') is pronounced *my* and *pães* (bread rolls) is pronounced as *pies*.
- **am**, **ão** and **ãos** are a nasal *ow* sound: *olham* ('they look') is pronounced 'OHL-yow', *irmão* ('brother') is pronounced 'eer-MOW' and *irmãos* ('brothers') is 'eer-MOWS'.
- **em** and **ens** are a nasal *ay* sound: *homem* ('man') is pronounced 'OH-may' and *parabéns* ('congratulations') is 'pa-ra-BAYS'.
- **im** and **ins** are a nasal *ee* sound: *motim* ('mutiny') is pronounced 'mo-CHEE', and *botequins* (taverns) is 'bo-te-KEENS'.
- **om** and **ons** are a nasal *o* sound as in the French *bon*: *bom* ('good') is pronounced 'bo' and *sons* ('sounds') is 'sos'.
- **ões** is a nasal *oys* sound: *botões* ('buttons') is pronounced as 'bo-TOYS'.
- **um** and **uns** are a nasal *oo* sound: *um* ('one') is pronounced 'oom' and *alguns* ('some') is 'al-GOONS'.

Consonants

- **b**, **f**, **p**, **v** are generally pronounced as in English.
- **c** is pronounced as in *cat*: *caro* ('expensive') is pronounced 'KAH-ro'. When followed by **e** or **i**, it is pronounced as in *cent*: *cedo* ('early') is pronounced 'SEH-do' and *cinto* ('belt') is 'SIN-to'.
- **ç** is pronounced as in *sit*: *aço* (steel) is 'AH-so'.
- **ch** is pronounced as in *shoe*: *chave* ('key') is pronounced 'SHAH-vee'.
- **d** is pronounced as in English. However, in many regions in Brazil, it is pronounced as *j* in *juice*, when followed by **i**: *diz* ('he/she says') is pronounced 'jeez'.
- **g** is pronounced as *g* in *goal*: *gancho* (hook) is pronounced 'GAHN-sho'. When followed by **e** or **i**, it becomes a melodious *sh* as in *pleasure*: *gengibre* ('ginger') is pronounced 'zhen-ZHEE-bre'.
- **h** is always silent, as in *herb*: *hotel* ('hotel'), which is pronounced 'oh-TEH-oo'.
- **j** is a melodious *sh* as in *pleasure*: *jangada* ('sailing craft') is pronounced 'zhan-GAH-da'.
- **k** is not part of the Portuguese alphabet, but is used in adopted foreign words such as *ketchup*. It is pronounced just as the English *k* in *kind*.
- **l** is normally pronounced as in English, but at the end of a word, it sounds more like *oo* as in *zoo*: *Brasil* ('Brazil') is pronounced 'bra-ZEE-oo'.
- **lh** is pronounced as in *million*: *alho* ('garlic') is 'AHL-yo'.
- **m** is pronounced as in English: *mata* ('forest') is 'MAH-ta'. It is silent when part of a nasal diphthong. (See above).
- **n** is also pronounced as in English: *nariz* ('nose') is 'na-REEZ'. Likewise, it is silent when part of a nasal diphthong. (See above).
- **nh** is a nasal sound pronounced as in *onion*: *ninho* ('nest') is pronounced 'NEEN-yo'.
- **qu** is pronounced as *k* when followed by **e** or **i**: *questão* ('question') is pronounced 'kes-TOW', and *quiabo* ('okra') is 'kee AH-bo'. When followed by **a** or **o**, it is pronounced as *qu* in *question*: *quando* ('when') is pronounced as 'KWAHN-do'.

- **r** is pronounced in a variety of different ways and also has great regional variances. In general, **r** turns into an aspirated sound like the English *h* in *here* e.g. when at the beginning of a word: *rio* ('river') is pronounced 'HEE-o'. **R** is also pronounced as an **h** in the middle of a word when it follows a consonant and is at the beginning of a syllable, e.g. *honra* ('honour') is pronounced 'OHN-ha'. In the middle of a word before a consonant and at the end of a word, **r** is usually rolled as in Spanish, e.g. *perceber* ('to perceive') is pronounced 'per-se-BER'. The double consonant **rr** is pronounced as *h* in *here*, e.g. *carro* ('car') is 'KAH-ho'.

- **s** in general is pronounced as in *sit*: *sapo* ('frog') is pronounced 'SAH-po', and *destruir* ('to destroy') is 'des-troo-EER'. It becomes melodious as in *maze*, when preceded and followed by a vowel: *brasa* ('ember') is pronounced 'BRAH-za', and *desigual* ('unequal') is 'dayz-ee-goo-AOO'; **ss** is pronounced as *sit*: *nosso* ('our') is pronounced 'NOH-so'. In Rio de Janeiro and much of northern Brazil, **s** is mostly pronounced as *sh* in *shoe*: *os cariocas* ('the Cariocas', inhabitants of Rio de Janeiro) is pronounced 'osh ka-ree-OH-kash'.

- **t** is pronounced as in English, but when followed by an **i**, it sounds as *ch* in *child* in most of Brazil: *tia* ('aunt') is pronounced 'CHEE-a'.

- **w** doesn't exist in Portuguese although it occasionally appears in adapted foreign names. It is pronounced like the English *w*: Walter is pronounced 'WOW-ter'.

- **x** is always pronounced as *sh* when it appears at the beginning of a word, as in *shoe*: *xícara* ('cup') is 'SHEE-ka-ra'. When in the middle of a word, **x** can be pronounced as *s* in *sit*: *explorar* ('to explore') is 'es-ploh-RAR', or like the *z* in *maze*: *exercício* ('exercise') is 'ay-zer-SEE-see-o'. In foreign adopted words, **x** is pronounced as in English: *fax*, pronounced 'FAHX' and *taxi*, pronounced 'TAK-see'.

- **y** is only used in some proper names and is pronounced as *y* in *Judy*: *Itamaraty* (Ministry of Foreign Relations) is pronounced 'eeta-ma-ra-CHEE'.

- **z** is mostly pronounced as *z* in *maze*: *doze* ('twelve') is pronounced 'DOH-zee'. In some regions (as in Rio de Janeiro), **z** is a melodious *sh* as in *pleasure*: *feliz* ('happy') is 'feh-LEEZH'.

STRESS

As a general rule, stress falls on the next-to-last syllable when a word ends in the vowels **a**, **e** or **o** and the letters **m** and **s**:

- *casa* ('house') is pronounced 'KAH-sa'
- *alegre* ('joyful') is pronounced 'a-LEH-gre'
- *perto* ('close') is pronounced 'PER-to'
- *homem* ('man') is pronounced 'OH-may'
- *serviços* ('services') is pronounced 'ser-VEE-sos'
  All other words have the stress on the last syllable.
- *comer* ('eat') is pronounced 'ko-MER'
- *quintal* ('backyard') is pronounced 'kin-TAOO'
- *caju* ('cashew') is pronounced 'ka-ZHOO'
- *capaz* ('capable') is pronounced 'kah-PAHZ'
- *abacaxi* ('pineapple') is pronounced 'ah-bah-kah-SHEE'

Exceptions

A syllable with an accent or a tilde always takes the stress:

- *alfândega* ('customs') is pronounced 'al-FAN-de-gah'
- Amazônia (Amazon region) is pronounced 'a-ma-ZOH-nee-a'
- *responsável* ('responsible') is pronounced 'hes-pon-SAH-veoo'
- *polícia* ('police') is pronounced 'po-LEE-se-ah'
- *irmã* ('sister') is pronounced 'eer-MAH'
- *alemães* ('Germans') is pronounced 'a-leh-MAH-ees'
- *sermões* ('sermons') is pronounced 'ser-MOH-ees'.

There are also several other exceptions that follow special rules.

GRAMMAR OVERVIEW

While some of the Portuguese vocabulary will be familiar to English-speakers, Portuguese grammar and syntax are quite different. The following list will give you a brief overview of the most common word groups and their uses.

Nouns

The main difference between Portuguese and English nouns is that Portuguese nouns have a gender. Nouns ending in **a** are usually feminine, while those ending in **o** are masculine. Nouns ending in **e, i, u**, or consonants can be either masculine or feminine. The plural is usually formed by adding an **s**, or, with nouns ending in consonants, by adding the letters **es**. Several other plural forms are also used.

- *casa* (house)   *casas* (houses)
- *carro* (carriage)   *carros* (carriages)
- *bilhete* (ticket)   *bilhetes* (tickets)
- *lugar* (place)   *lugares* (places)

Articles

As in English, the Portuguese language has definite and indefinite articles. But in Portuguese, articles always follow the gender and number of the noun:

Feminine

- *a casa*   the house
- *as casas*   the houses
- *uma mulher*   a woman
- *umas mulheres*   a few (some) women

Masculine

- *o castelo*   the castle
- *os castelos*   the castles
- *um homem*   a man
- *uns homens*   a few (some) men

Adjectives

Most adjectives in Portuguese end in **o** or **a** and need to conform with the gender and number of the noun they modify:

- *a praia bonita*   the beautiful beach
- *os livros velhos*   the old books

Adjectives that end in consonants or the letter **e**, are not gender specific and do not need to adapt to the gender of the noun although they take an **s** or **es** to indicate the plural:

- *o carro azul*   the blue car
- *a camisa azul*   the blue shirt
- *a casa grande*   the big house
- *as casas grandes* the big houses

Verbs

While English verbs hardly conjugate, verb forms in Portuguese vary for every person. It is therefore not always necessary to use personal pronouns with verbs, since the verb form alone indicates who it refers to. There are three main conjugations for verbs, ending in **ar, er**, and **ir**, but there are numerous irregular verbs, where the root vowel changes in the conjugation of the various tenses. Regular verbs ending in **–ar**:

- *falar*   to speak
- *falo*   I speak
- *falas*   you speak; rarely used in Brazil; *você fala* is used instead
- *fala*   he/she speaks; you (*você*) speak
- *falamos*   we speak
- *falam*   they speak; you all (*vocês*) speak

Regular verbs ending in **–er**:
- *comer*   to eat
- *como*   I eat
- *comes*   you eat; rarely used in Brazil; *você come* is used instead
- *come*   he/she eats; you (*você*) eat
- *comemos*   we eat
- *comem*   they eat; you all (*vocês*) eat

Regular verbs ending in **–ir**:
- *abrir*   to open
- *abro*   I open
- *abres*   you open; rarely used in Brazil; *você abre* is used instead
- *abre*   he/she opens; you (*você*) open
- *abrimos*   we open
- *abrem*   they open; you all (*vocês*) open

Between the indicative, subjunctive and conditional verb forms, there are over a dozen different tenses in Portuguese, all with clearly defined usage and countless irregular forms. Mastering the verbs is perhaps the greatest challenge for students of the language since it includes tenses that English speakers are unfamiliar with, such as the frequently used subjunctive and the conjugated infinitive.

Prepositions

Prepositions have the same function as in English but their individual usage varies greatly. Portuguese also has many verbal phrases, but the combinations of verbs and prepositions are very different from English and need to be memorised: *contar com* = to count on; *depender de* = to depend on.

- *a* — to
- *com* — with
- *contra* — against
- *durante* — during
- *de* — of
- *depois* — after
- *em* — in
- *embaixo de* — below
- *encima de* — on top of, on
- *fora de* — away from
- *para* — for
- *por* — by
- *sem* — without
- *sobre* — about

Pronouns

Personal pronouns are as in English:

- *eu* — I
- *você* (tu) — you (tu is rarely used)
- *ele* (masc.sg.), *ela* (fem.sg.) — he, she
- *nós* — we
- *vocês* (*vós*) — you all (*vós*, not used in every-day Brazilian Portuguese)
- *eles* (masc.pl.), *elas* (fem.pl.) — they

Possessive Pronouns

Possessive pronouns follow the noun they modify in gender and number:

- *meu* (masc.sg.)/ *minha* (fem.sg.)/ *meus* (masc.pl.)/ *minhas* (fem.pl.)—my, mine: *meu carro* (my car), *minha mãe* (my mother), *minhas filhas* (my daughters)
- *seu* (masc.wsg.)/ *sua* (fem.sg.)/ *seus* (masc.pl.)/ *suas* (fem.pl.) *(teu/tua/teus/tuas)*—your, yours
- *seu* (masc.sg.)/ *sua* (fem.sg.)/ *seus* (masc.pl.)/ *suas* (fem.pl.)—his, her, hers
- *nosso* (masc.sg.)/ *nossa* (fem.sg.)/ *nossos* (masc.pl.)/ *nossas* (fem.pl.)—our, ours;
- *seu* (masc.sg.)/ *sua* (fem.sg.)/ *seus* (masc.pl.)/ *suas* (fem.pl.)—your, yours (plural)
- *seu* (masc.sg.)/ *sua* (fem.sg.)/ *seus* (masc.pl.)/ *suas* (fem.pl.)—their, theirs

Demonstrative Pronouns

- *este* (masc.sg.), *esta* (fem.sg.), *estes* (masc.pl.), *estas* (fem.pl.)—this, these;
- *esse* (masc.pl.), *essa* (fem.pl.), *esses* (masc. pl.), *essas* (fem. pl.)—that, those;
- *aquele* (masc.sg.), *aquela* (fem.sg.), *aqueles* (masc. pl.), *aquelas* (fem. pl.)—that over there, those over there.

Indefinite Pronouns

- *algo*—something
- *nada*—nothing
- *alguém*—somebody
- *ninguém*—nobody
- *algum* (masc.sg.)/*alguma* (fem.sg.)/*alguns* (masc.pl.) /*algumas* (fem.pl.)—some, several
- *nenhum* (masc.sg.), *nenhuma* (fem.sg.), *nenhuns* (masc.pl.), *nenhumas* (fem.pl.)—none, not any

Adverbs

In addition to the many unique adverbs such as *talvez* (perhaps) or *hoje* (today) any adjective can become an adverb by adding **mente** to the feminine form of the adjective, e.g.

rápido (quick) becomes *rapidamente* (quickly). With adjectives ending in a consonant or letter **e** (and are therefore not gender-specific), the syllable **mente** is simply added to the adjective: *feliz* (happy) becomes *felizmente* (happily) and *triste* (sad) becomes *tristemente* (sadly).

Conjunctions

As in English the conjunction in Portuguese is used to create complex relationships between different sentence clauses. In Portuguese, subordinating conjunctions often require the use of the subjunctive or conditional, which makes them all the more difficult to use correctly.

Coordinating Conjunctions:

- *e*   and
- *ou*   or
- *mas*   but

Subordinating Conjunctions:

- *antes que*   before
- *contanto que*   as long as
- *depois que*   after
- *desde que*   since
- *embora*   although
- *enquanto*   while
- *porque*   because
- *quando*   when
- *que*   that
- *se*   if

SHOWING AFFECTION: THE DIMINUTIVE

The diminutive is a common characteristic of Brazilian Portuguese and expresses affection and familiarity with a thing or person. Most names or words can be used in their diminutive form by adding the syllable *inho* (masc.) or *inha* (fem.) at the end of the word. *Carrinho* instead of *carro* is an affectionate way of talking about a car; *casinha* instead of *casa* is a little house, and *camisinha* (the little shirt) is a familiar term for condom, also known as *camisa de Vénus* (the shirt of Venus). It is also common to create a nickname by using the diminutive of a person's name. *Chico* becomes *Chiquinho,* Antônio becomes Toninho and Teresa turns into Terezinha.

The diminutive is also used to soften verbal statements that might otherwise sound too direct or blunt. Brazilians are rarely confrontational in conversation, and the diminutive allows them to be indirectly direct and to express their opinion or a request in a gentle and harmless way. Instead of saying "Yes", someone may say *"Só um pouquinho"* ("Only a little bit"). When asking someone for money, a person may say *dinheirinho* (a little money) instead of *dinheiro* (money). This does not necessarily indicate a small amount; it only sounds a little friendlier and less urgent. With the diminutive, it is also possible to use words that would otherwise appear as rude. I have overheard conversations where someone called a blind man *ceguinho* (little blind one) and a very small person *baixinho* (little short one), which in neither case was taken as an insult.

GESTURES AND SIGNS

Brazilians are very much in touch with their body, and when observing them in conversation, you will notice they frequently use body language as a natural extension of verbal communication. Gestures are often used as emphasis, but are sometimes used without words.

Be Culturally Aware

There are a great number of gestures and signs, and most of them are understood all over Brazil. Since similar gestures often have different meanings in different cultures, you should be careful with using them until you have a better understanding of their meaning and situational usage.

There are a number of obscene gestures that are best avoided. The following list explains several widely used gestures and sheds some light on Brazilian body language.

Thumb Up

A common gesture in Brazil, this is frequently used in everyday situations. One hand forms a fist and the thumb is pointed straight up. It resembles the American thumbs up gesture, but is executed with only one hand. This gesture signifies approval and means 'okay', 'great', 'fine', or 'thank you', and expresses the inherent optimism of Brazilians. It is also often accompanied by slang words such as *legal* (great), *jóia* (fabulous) or *falou* (agreed).

Do not use the American okay sign, which is an insult in Brazil (*see below*). The American hang loose sign (a fist with stretched-out thumb and little finger) has also become very popular and has the same meaning in Brazil as the thumb up.

Expressing Speed and Emphasis

Hold your middle finger and thumb together (both fingers straight not bent), and shake your hand several times so that the index finger snaps against the middle finger. This gesture means quick, fast, in a hurry, and is also used to add emphasis to a statement or indicate intensity.

A Long Time

This gesture, which is identical to the finger snapping used in Europe and the US, is executed with the thumb and middle finger usually with the palm facing up. It means a long time or a long time ago. The gesture is repeated several times while talking about something that took place a long time ago or lasted for a long time.

The Banana

The forearm jerk is called *dar uma banana* (to give a banana) in Brazil and means 'screw you'. This gesture is performed with both arms. The right arm bends upward at the elbow, the left hand drops down on the right upper arm and the right fist is moved upward in a jerking motion.

Expressing Quantity

With your palm facing up put your fingers and thumb together in a repeated motion. This means that there are a lot of people, that a place is packed or that a bus or taxi is full.

The Obscene O
The index finger and thumb are joined to form an **o**, while the other fingers relax. The hand is lowered to the waist with the palm facing up. This is a gesture of insult and suggests certain bodily orifices.

Expensive
When people express that something is expensive, they hold out their hand and rub the index and middle fingers against the thumb several times, as if handling money.

Pinching an Earlobe
When people want to show appreciation, or express that something is beautiful or clean, or that a meal was delicious, they pinch an earlobe between the thumb and index finger. This gesture means *foi um brinco*—it was great; literally: it was a jewel.

Closeness
To indicate closeness or close friendship between people, hold the index fingers straight next to each other, and rub them back and forth.

Portuguese Self Study
If you decide to study Portuguese by yourself, keep in mind that learning a foreign language on your own is hard work. But with consistent and devoted study, it is possible to acquire a working knowledge of this beautiful language without classes or teachers. There is a growing number of high quality courses available that have made language self-study easy, fun, and efficient. The first step before buying a language course is to determine your learning goals. Do you just want to pick up a few phrases for your vacation? Then a phrase book and cassette will do, and you may only need to put in a couple of weeks of study. But if you plan on spending a few months in Brazil, you probably want to use a programme that goes beyond the basics and builds real conversation skills. In this case you may even want to begin your studies several months or a year before your trip.

The next step is to figure out what language courses you like best. If this is your first attempt at a foreign language, you might want to look for a programme that is well-structured with a clear lesson plan. Course books with cassettes are great for beginners because of their lesson-based structure. Since most speaking situations in real life take place in dialogue, it is important to get a course that teaches dialogue and not just word lists or phrases. It is also important that the dialogues are useful for everyday situations and teach expressions and vocabulary that are used in Brazil today. Listening to native speakers and repeating what you hear is one of the best methods of language learning be it on cassette, CD-ROM, or in a real-life conversation.

No matter what language programme you use for self-study, one method alone won't do. Textbooks don't teach you pronunciation, cassette courses don't teach you grammar, or how to read and write, and most CD-ROMs don't include printed reference materials to deepen your knowledge. The best approach is to use a variety of materials and use them as often and regularly as you can. Different publishers use different methods, which adds variety to your self-study efforts. Keep in mind that Brazilian Portuguese varies significantly in pronunciation from the Portuguese spoken in Portugal.

If available, purchase a course that teaches Brazilian Portuguese. That way you won't have to relearn the pronunciation and various grammatical differences. (*For a list of self-study courses and Portuguese language schools in Brazil refer to the* Resource Guide *at the back of the book).*

WORK AND BUSINESS

CHAPTER 9

'Mais vale uma boa hora de
negócio do que um ano de lavoura.'
(One good hour of business is worth
more than one year of farming).
—Brazilian saying

THE BUSINESS CLIMATE
Economic and Financial Factors

Since the stabilisation of Brazil's currency in 1994, an increasing number of foreign companies have invested in Brazil, lured by the privatisation of many government-owned companies. From 1997–2000, foreign investment amounted to US$100 billion, with US$30 billion in 2000 alone. These figures have dropped since then, due to the end of large-scale privatisations, but still indicate that foreign companies are confident of Brazil's economic growth. Thanks to the privatisations and large foreign investments, Brazil's economy has become more competitive and dynamic, and is better prepared to adapt to new trends and developments in the international marketplace. Experts agree that Brazil's economic growth will continue over the next few years, provided that several urgent reforms take place. Among them is a reform of the social security system, which has a high deficit, and a long-needed tax reform. Brazil has one of the highest tax burdens in the world, which translates into high costs for companies to run operations, a fact that is known as '*Custo Brasil*', or 'Cost Factor Brazil'.

Another factor that greatly affects Brazil's economy are high interest rates. The *taxa SELIC* (government base rate) gradually dropped in the past decade from an annual 38.7 per cent in 1994, to a low 12.4 per cent in 2004, which is still high compared to most industrialised countries. But in order to control inflation which began to increase as a result of higher import and fuel costs, the central bank began to raise the basic interest rate in 2005.

Infrastructure

Foreign businesses have to deal with enormous differences in infrastructure from one region to another. This is one reason why most international companies are located in the South and South-east, where the infrastructure is much better developed. Roads between Brazil's cities in the South and South-east are the best in the country, and suppliers, service and maintenance companies are close-by. Brazil's largest ports with frequent service to the world's major ports are also located in the South and South-east, among them Porto Alegre, Santos and Rio de Janeiro. Electric energy may be in short supply throughout Brazil, depending on the fluctuating capacity of the hydroelectric power plants. There are severe periodic droughts that can cause reservoir levels to drop and create serious energy shortages. Most businesses have uninterrupted power supplies (UPS) for their computers, and many companies in areas with frequent blackouts have generators.

Quality and Productivity

Throughout most of the 20th century, Brazilian consumer goods were manufactured only for the domestic market. Quality was not a big concern, since there was no competition from abroad. This began to change gradually during the 1970s, when Brazil began to export manufactured and industrial goods. The opening of Brazil's markets to foreign products in the early 1990s, and Brazil's growing exports, have further improved the quality standards of Brazil's industry. Today, the quality of Brazilian products such as vehicles, machinery, airplanes and satellites is comparable to those from developed countries.

The productivity of Brazilian companies has improved significantly with the privatisation of government companies such as railroads, banks, telecommunications and steel mills. Inefficient government bureaucrats were gradually

To keep up with the modernisation of Brazil's industry, Brazilian and multinational companies are also investing heavily in the continuous education, training and specialisation of their employees.

replaced by knowledgeable staff from the private sector, who applied modern principles of market economics to improve the efficiency and productivity of both management and production. An increasing number of Brazilian companies are adopting the quality standards of the International Organization for Standardization (ISO). This ISO 9000 certification contains quality guidelines for management, human resources, production and maintenance, and has become an important criteria for Brazilian businesses which want to provide superior services to their domestic customers, and also participate in the extremely competitive export market.

Management

Management practices in Brazilian companies vary according to the size, region and company structure. Most foreigners work for international companies with a global management style. However, smaller companies and businesses with little exposure to the global marketplace often follow more traditional, patriarchal models of leadership. This is especially true for the many family-owned businesses. They often have a hierarchical structure that offers few responsibilities to employees, leaving the decision-making up to the founder or owner of the company. But with the increased globalisation of Brazil's economy, these traditional business practices are gradually changing. There are also many newer Brazilian companies that are eager to adopt modern management concepts.

Labour Market

Brazil's work force is characterised by a low level of education and specialisation, and great regional differences. The skilled labour market is concentrated in large urban areas and state capitals, and it is difficult to find qualified personnel in smaller cities and towns. As a result, the competition for skilled jobs in cities is extremely high. It is not unusual to find several thousand applicants for a small number of trainee positions with multinational companies. This highly competitive situation forces job-seekers to constantly upgrade their knowledge and skills, to increase their competitiveness. They take night courses in foreign languages and undergo any other available training that gives them an advantage over their competitors in their field of work. Though there is an increasing number of Brazilians returning to school to earn a university degree and improve their chances for better employment, the proportion of those with higher education still remains low.

Wages

Wages are low with regard to the overall cost of living. In Brazil, the monthly minimum wage (BRL300 in 2005, ca. US$136) does not only establish the lowest legal salary, but it is also used as an indicator to compute pensions, adjust rent control and determine a number of other indices. It is usually adjusted for inflation and raised once a year. In 2004, the average salary of the employed population was about BRL730 (ca. US$330). Twenty seven per cent of Brazilian workers had an average monthly salary no higher than the minimum wage, and 38 per cent of workers earned between two and three times the minimum wage. Due to these low salaries many Brazilians have difficulties supporting their families and often have several jobs to make ends meet, or to save up some money.

Labour Unions

Unions were outlawed during the military regime. Reborn during the great strikes of the automobile workers in the late 1970s, Brazil's labour unions have made a comeback, and had a significant influence on labour politics during the 1980s and early 1990s. The two largest umbrella organisations among Brazil's unions are the Central Única dos Trabalhadores (CUT) and Força Sindical. In 2004, about 18 per cent of Brazil's employed population were union members. Although Brazil's unions have lost some influence in recent years, they are still engaged in the struggle to increase wages and improve working conditions. The number of strikes has dropped significantly in recent years, but when they take place on a large scale, they can still paralyse an entire city or even the whole country. Among the latest union campaigns is the reduction of the work week from 44 to 40 hours, which has so far been rejected by the leading companies in most economic sectors.

BUSINESS ETIQUETTE AND STYLE
General Considerations
If you come to Brazil on business, it will most likely be in one of Brazil's large metropolitan areas, where business styles and practices are fairly international, and where local business people are familiar with foreigners. Here, people may even speak English, eliminating the need for a translator. But unless you speak Portuguese fluently, or your negotiation partners speak excellent English, it is best to hire an interpreter.

Business Etiquette—Helpful Advice

- It is a good idea to learn some Portuguese before going to Brazil. Being able to speak a few phrases and respond to common greetings and questions, will show Brazilians that you respect their country and culture.
- To make an even better impression, take the time to learn about Brazil and its cultural background before you go. Knowing about a few Brazilian football players, or being able to comment on the performance of the Brazilian football team, will certainly help break the ice at the beginning of a meeting.
- Avoid scheduling a business trip during the Brazilian summer from December through February, as this is the time when most Brazilians take their holidays.

Establishing First Contacts

There are several ways to make business contacts in Brazil. There might be a Brazilian trade office in your country, which you can contact to get information about potential business partners. However, if you come to Brazil in search of business contacts, it is best to contact the chamber of commerce of your country, your embassy, your country's commerce department or foreign trade office. These agencies can provide you with important contacts and information to enable you to break into the local business world. In addition to establishing formal contacts with businesses, personal contacts and references are also very important. Brazilians want to know who they are dealing with, and it can be a big step ahead, if you are introduced or referred to Brazilian business people by someone who is well-known locally. Many business deals are made through personal connections, and it is important to establish a network of personal contacts early on.

Business Meetings

When first introduced to someone at a meeting, it is customary to use the polite form of address, that is, *senhor/senhora* followed by the person's last name. But even at business meetings, people generally prefer more familiar forms of address and may use *senhor/senhora* with the first name or just the first name. When in doubt, use the same form of address as your negotiation partners. Bring a sufficient supply of *cartões de visita* (business cards), since they are commonly exchanged during meetings or when making a contact.

Expect business meetings to begin informally. It is customary to enjoy a *cafezinho* and chat about current events in politics, sports and the economy before talking about business. Your negotiation partners may be interested in learning about your country and your company as well. If business people know each other, they may ask about each other's families, but personal questions are generally avoided. After this initial warm-up, the host will usually initiate talk about business. If foreign negotiators intend to sell a service or product in Brazil, or suggest a business collaboration, they should wait until the Brazilian party approaches business matters.

When making a business presentation, keep in mind that Brazilians take their time to negotiate deals, and they do not like to be pressured. It is important in negotiations not to appear pushy, although pressure can be applied in subtle and indirect ways. You could inform them of the short period of your stay or another important deadline, to indicate that your company cannot wait forever to close a deal. Giving the impression that you are in a hurry, or that you are under pressure to make a deal, will only weaken your position during negotiations. The people you negotiate with are usually not the ones responsible for making the final decision, and business deals are rarely made during the first meeting. You may be asked to come to another meeting, or talk to representatives of a different department, before the company will make a decision.

Business Lunches

Business lunches are a great opportunity to make a first business contact with representatives of the companies you would like to do business with. Lunches are also popular among business associates or partners to check up on the progress of a project, discuss a new one, or simply stay in touch and exchange news and gossip from the local business community. Keep in mind that business matters are usually not discussed until after the meal, usually when coffee is served. Business lunches are held at reputable restaurants, and the inviting party pays the bill. As with any important business meeting, you are expected to arrive on time.

Women and Business

A certain degree of machismo is still common among Brazilian men, and women do not always receive the same respect as men in the business world. Foreign women are not excluded from occasional sexual innuendoes and comments from their male co-workers or business associates. Brazilian women are used to such situations, and have learned to deal with them in a nonchalant way and with a good sense of humour. It is best to follow their example. However, with the increasing number of women entering higher positions in business, these old patriarchal attitudes and prejudices are gradually fading.

Regional Differences

Business practices vary from region to region. When doing business in the interior, expect business etiquettes and styles to be less international, and to follow more traditional and patriarchal patterns. The owner may be the sole authority and decision-maker. He is often a benevolent kind of authority, not unlike a *paterfamilias*, who knows what is best for his business and 'family' of employees. Doing business in small towns depends largely on personal contacts and connections, and deals are often made informally among people who know each other.

Punctuality

Although Brazilians are far from giving in to tropical languor, their concept of timeliness is certainly not as strict as that of most other Westerners. The perception that 'time is money' is not valid here, since Brazilians have quite a laid-back attitude toward punctuality. People are generally not in a hurry to get somewhere, or get things done quickly. What counts is that things get accomplished eventually, but the exact time is irrelevant.

Appointments relating to business and work are not always strictly observed, and arriving 15–30 minutes late for a job interview or meeting is not uncommon. But even though time is a flexible concept, punctuality is expected of everyone at important business meetings and negotiations.

Dressing for Business

Businesspeople in Brazil's large cities are quite fashion-conscious. Men wear dark suits with ties and light-coloured long sleeve shirts regardless of the temperatures. However, some businesses may allow short sleeve shirts to be worn without a tie. Businesswomen dress elegantly in business suits

Since clothing reflects people's social and economic status, you can hardly go wrong with dressing formally for an initial business meeting. It will only increase your credibility. You can adjust to the local level of formality at a later point.

and use light make-up during the day. It is also acceptable for women to wear dress trousers, dresses or skirts with a blouse or jacket. For both men and women, nice shoes are important in all work situations.

What businesspeople wear also depends on where they work. In general, the dress code for business in São Paulo, Belo Horizonte and Brasília is conservative and formal, whereas it is much more casual and relaxed in Rio de Janeiro and other coastal cities. In Brazil's smaller cities, people dress more casually than in large urban centres, and neither politicians nor businesspeople wear a suit to work. In general, foreign businesspeople are expected to dress formally and have a professional appearance.

Social Aspects of Business and Work

It is quite common for co-workers to go out together for lunch or a drink after work. Such drinking sessions are known by the English term 'happy hour'. It is also good practice to invite a business partner or associate to a good restaurant for dinner, or entertain them at a cultural event. Social events are also an important element of successful company management in Brazil. Most companies have *churrascos* (barbecues) from time to time, and organise an annual Christmas party for their employees.

Corruption

Corruption has been an integral part of Brazil's economy and public life for a long time. It is a by-product of Brazil's inflated bureaucracy and of the maze of laws that regulate every aspect of business and public life. In many cases, it is easier to break the law than to pursue a matter through the official channels sanctioned by law. *Propinas* (payoffs) are common practice and so are tax evasion, graft and many other informal and often illegal methods of doing business and conducting public administration. Newspapers are filled with news about politicians under suspicion of enriching themselves with public money. The list of Brazil's corruption scandals is endless and often involves people at high government levels, as was the case with the presidencies of both Fernando Henrique Cardoso and Luiz Inácio Lula da Silva. In 1992, President Fernando Collor was impeached on charges of corruption. But unlike Collor, many officials practically enjoy impunity, especially when they have a large network of connections that protects them. Nepotism, favouritism and cronyism are also long-standing traditions in Brazil and are probably as old as the first colonial Portuguese administration. Even today, elected politicians continue to give important administrative positions to their close family members and cronies. Most people in a position of power will also use their influence to do personal favours, or get a job for a relative or friend.

GETTING THINGS DONE
Jeitinho Brasileiro

'Aos inimigos a lei, aos amigos, tudo'.
(For the enemies the law, for the friends, everything.)
—Brazilian saying, quoted by Roberto da Matta,
in Carnavais, Malandros e Heróis

To deal with the excessive bureaucracy and infinite laws, Brazilians have developed the *jeito* or *jeitinho brasileiro*, which means the 'way around' a bureaucratic or legal obstacle. When Brazilians can't accomplish something by official means, it is common for them to find a *jeito*, a 'way' to get things resolved. The *jeitinho* usually depends on friends and other important contacts who use their power and influence to help someone. As the above quotation shows, the *jeito* is a special way to help friends, whereas all others are confronted with the letter of the law. In everyday situations, the *jeitinho* can help you have your car worked on first, get your doctor's appointment moved up or skip the line at the bank. In more significant cases, it may help you get a car loan approved more quickly, or get a shortcut to obtain a business license. Sometimes all that is necessary is to mention the name of a mutual friend. The *jeito* is also an accepted and widely-used practice in the business world. Many business people contact friends, business associates or government employees they know, to help them find a *jeito*, a way around a little problem.

The Despachante—The Indispensable Middleman

Another way to cut through the red tape of Brazil's overwhelming bureaucracy is a professional consultant or business liaison, who will *dar um jeito*, 'find a way' through the bureaucratic maze for you. This *despachante* is familiar with most legal proceedings, forms and requirements, and will help you get things done quickly, simply by knowing where to go and how to cut through red tape. *Despachantes* charge a fixed fee for their services, depending on the complexity of the task. They handle a variety of bureaucratic matters, including obtaining a driver's license, business permit, property title or any kind of documents that involve government agencies operating with Kafkaesque efficiency. They are indispensable in Brazil's public life, since few people have the time to wait in line for hours or return to the same government agency over and over again.

Despachantes can be especially helpful for newcomers who don't know how to deal with all the red tape regarding their identification cards and other legal matters. If you need to deal with any government agency in Brazil, your consulate may be able to refer you to a reputable *despachante*, to help you get your documents settled quickly.

WORKING IN BRAZIL
Visa Requirements

Every foreigner intending to work in Brazil needs a work visa. This must be obtained in your country of residence by submitting the required documents to a Brazilian consulate, including a signed work contract from a company operating in Brazil, or an offer of employment. The application for a work visa needs to be approved by the Ministry of Labor, and authorised by the Ministry of External Relations. All businesspeople, independent or employed, who intend to do business in Brazil, need to apply for a business visa.

Informal Work

Despite these legal restrictions, there is an informal employment market for foreigners. It is especially easy for native English speakers to find part-time work as English teachers at language schools. It is also possible to recruit students individually for private classes, but this usually takes some time. The classified advertisements in the newspapers list *professor de Inglês* (English teachers) and *escolas*, or *cursos* or *escolas de idiomas* (language schools). Language schools are also listed in the *páginas amarelas* (yellow pages) under the same headings.

Taxes and Withholdings

All foreigners working in Brazil have to pay income tax. Foreigners who have lived in Brazil for over a year, or have a permanent visa, are considered Brazilian residents for tax purposes, and are subject to income tax on worldwide income. Non-resident employees, i.e. foreigners with work contracts for less than six months, are only subject to income tax on income earned in Brazil, or they may even be tax exempt. Brazil has signed tax treaties with a number of countries to eliminate double taxation. You should find out if your home country is among them.

Important Tax Facts

There are three tax rates for residents and this is assessed according to their income levels:

- Income up to BRL1,164 per month is income tax free.
- Incomes between the range of BRL1,164 and BRL2,326 are taxed at a rate of 15 per cent.
- All income above BRL2,326 is subject to a tax rate of 27.5 per cent.
- For non-resident foreign employees, a flat income tax rate of 25 per cent is applicable.

Income tax is usually withheld by the employer on a monthly basis. The tax year is the calendar year and income tax returns are due by 30 April the following year.

Foreigners are also subject to withholdings for Previdência Social (social security), even though most of them will never use the services. The social security tax (7.65—11 per cent) is withheld by the employer. As with income tax, Brazil has reciprocal social security agreements with several countries, and it is worth finding out if your country is among them.

Rights and Benefits

All employees with formal work contracts, i.e. those with a *carteira assinada* (signed card), officially known as Carteira de Trabalho e Previdência Social or CTPS (work and social security card), signed by their employer, are entitled to a number of benefits. This includes a 13th month salary paid in December, a paid vacation and 120 days of paid maternity leave for women. Other benefits include meal coupons, and transportation or fuel subsidies.

Most workers are also covered by *seguro de desemprego* (unemployment insurance) for up to five months, which amounts to one or two times the monthly minimum wage. When they lose their jobs, employees are also entitled to a one-time payout from the FGTP (Fundo de Garantia por Tempo de Serviço or Guarantee Fund for Time of Service). This is a fund to which the employer makes monthly contributions during the employee's period of employment. Foreign professionals in Brazil can expect to receive several other benefits such as health insurance, a company car, private pension plan, bonuses and profit-sharing.

FAST FACTS
ABOUT BRAZIL

'It is impossible to completely know such an immense world as Brazil. I know only now that a whole lifetime would not be sufficient to be able to say: I know Brazil.'
—Stefan Zweig, in *Brazil, Land of the Future.*

Official Name
República Federativa do Brasil
(Federative Republic of Brazil)

Capital
Brasília

Flag
The Brazilian flag is green in colour with a yellow diamond at the centre. The green represents Brazil's lush green forests while the yellow represents Brazil's rich mineral reserves. There is a blue globe in the centre of the diamond which has twenty-seven stars. The stars represent the twenty-six federal states and one federal district. Across the globe is a white band with the motto 'Ordem e Progresso' which means 'Order and Progress'.

Time Zones
Brazil has four time zones. The islands of the Fernando de Noronha Archipelago in the Atlantic Ocean are two hours behind Greenwich Mean Time (GMT). All of the Atlantic and central states including major cities such as São Paulo, Rio de Janeiro, Salvador, Belo Horizonte and Brasília, are three hours behind GMT. The states of Mato Grosso, Mato Grosso do Sul, Rondônia, most of Amazonas, Roraima, and the western half of the state of Pará are four hours behind GMT.

The state of Acre and the south-western corner of the state of Amazonas are five hours behind GMT. The central and southern states observe daylight saving time, which is in effect from October through February. Clocks go back one hour during this period.

Telephone Country Code
+55

Land
Brazil is located in the eastern region of South American and shares common boundaries with almost all the South American countries except Ecuador and Chile. It borders the Alantic Ocean.

Area
8.5 million sq km (3.2 million sq miles)

Highest Point
Pico da Neblina (3,014 m / 9,888.5 ft)

Climate
Brazil is characterised by a mostly hot and humid climate, with regional variations. Since Brazil is situated south of the equator (except its northernmost corner), the seasons are reversed. The Brazilian winter lasts from June to September and the summer from December to March. The coastal region with cities such as Rio de Janeiro, Salvador and Recife is hot and humid. The proximity of the ocean brings moisture all year and leads to frequent rainfall. High temperatures in the summer are around 30°C (86°F), but can climb to 38°C (100°F) in Rio de Janeiro. The inland plateau with cities such as Belo Horizonte and São Paulo is slightly cooler than the coast, with average highs in the summer around 30°C (86°F) and the average lows in the winter around 15°C (59°F). Southern Brazilian cities like Porto Alegre and Curitiba experience a subtropical climate with hot summers and cool winters with occasional frost. Central Brazil is marked by a hot climate with less frequent rainfall and a distinct

dry season. The seasonal variation in temperature is low. Temperatures can reach a high of 35°C (95°F). The inland region of the North-east, known as the *sertão*, experiences severe periodic droughts. In the Amazon river basin the temperatures don't vary much between the coldest and warmest months, and the weather is usually hot and humid with frequent rainfall. The high temperatures rarely exceed 35°C (95°F).

Temperature

In Brazil, temperatures are measured in *graus centígrados*, which are degrees centigrade or Celsius (written as °C). When talking about temperature, Brazilians simply use the term *graus* (degrees): "*A temperatura é trinta e cinco graus*"—"The temperature is 35 degrees".

0°C (32°F) is the freezing temperature of water. 100°C (212° F) is the boiling point of water. To convert Fahrenheit to Celsius, subtract 32 and multiply by 5/9. To convert Celsius to Fahrenheit, multiply by 9/5 and add 32.

Celsius	Fahrenheit
-20	-4
-10	14
0	32
5	41
10	50
15	59
20	68
25	77
30	86
35	95
40	104
100	212

Population
185 million (2005)

Natural Resources

Bauxite, gold, iron, ore, manganese, nickel, phosphates, plantinum, tin, uranium, petroleum, hydropower, timber.

Ethnic Groups

White: 53.7 per cent
Mulatto (mixed white and black): 38.5 per cent
Black: 6.2 per cent, as well as Japanese, Arab and Amerindian minorities.

Religion

Roman catholic (nominal): 73.6 per cent
Protestant: 15.4 per cent, as well as spiritistic, syncretistic and Afro-Brazilian cults.

Official Language

Portuguese

Government Structure

Federative republic

Administrative Divisions

See Chapter 2, *A Look At Brazil*

Currency

real (BRL)

Gross Domestic Product (GDP)

Brazil's GDP in 2004 was US$600 billion (at year-end exchange rate).

Agricultural Products

Coffee, soybeans, wheat, rice, corn, sugarcane, cocoa, citrus, beef

Industries

Textiles, shoes, chemicals, cement, lumber, iron ore, tin, steel, aircraft, motor vehicles and parts and other machinery and equipment.

Exports

Transport equipment, iron ore, soybeans, footwear, coffee and autos.

Imports

Machinery, electrical and transport equipment, chemical products and oil.

Airports

Rio de Janeiro International Airport Galeão
Santos Dumont Airport, Rio de Janeiro (Domestic Flights)
São Paulo International Airport Congonhas
Sao Paulo International Airport Guarulhos
Brasília International Airport Presidente Juscelino Kubitschek

FAMOUS PEOPLE

- **Ayrton Senna**
  Brazil's most successful Formula I race car driver, who died in a racing accident in 1994.
- **Caetano Veloso**
  A key figure of Brazilian popular music in the 1960s and 1970s, and still one of Brazil's most famous musicians and song writers.
- **Daniela Mercury**
  A famous singer of the popular Axé music, she is also an ambassador for UNICEF working to prevent AIDS in children.
- **Dorival Caymmi**
  A key songwriter of samba and popular music, who has written innumerable great songs since the 1930s.
- **Fernanda Montenegro**
  One of Brazil's most famous actresses, with a long career. She was nominated for an Oscar for her role in *Central do Brasil* ('Central Station', 1997).
- **Frans Krajcberg**
  A Polish-born sculptor, who creates large pieces from found organic materials and strongly promotes environmental protection in Brazil's North-east.

- **Gisele Bündchen**
  Brazil's best-known supermodel of international fame.
- **Helô Pinheiro**
  A beloved Rio de Janeiro celebrity, she inspired António Carlos Jobim to compose the famous song *The Girl from Ipanema* back in 1962.
- **Jorge Amado**
  Among Brazil's most popular novelists, who portrayed the lives of the people of his home town of Salvador.
- **José Wilker**
  One of Brazil most versatile actors, who has left a permanent imprint on Brazilian cinema.
- **Letícia Spiller**
  A famous actress for the Globo TV network, starring mostly in popular soap operas.
- **Maria Bethânia**
  The sister of Caetano Veloso, and a successful singer of popular Brazilian music.
- **Paulo Coelho**
  Brazil's best-known writer abroad, he is also widely read in Brazil.
- **Pelé**
  Brazil's greatest football player of all time, who participated in three World Cup tournaments and helped the Brazilian team win two championships.
- **Rachel de Queiroz**
  Writer and first woman to be admitted to the Brazilian Academy of Letters.
- **Roberto Carlos**
  Brazil's most popular romantic singer of the past few decades.
- **Ronaldo**
  One of Brazil's most successful football stars today, who has played in Europe's best teams. Of humble background, he is today a Goodwill ambassador of the United Nations Development Program, and is involved in fighting poverty around the world.
- **Sebastião Salgado**
  Brazil's best-known photographer, whose haunting images

of landless peasants, refugees and migrants, have become known all over the world.

- **Xuxa**
A popular singer and star of the Globo TV network, best known for her children's variety shows.

ACRONYMS

DF	Distrito Federal (the Federal District of Brasília)
MERCOSUL	Mercado do Cone Sul (the Mercosur common market, including Brazil, Argentina, Uruguay and Paraguay)
CPF	Cadastro de Pessoas Físicas (personal tax identification card)
RNE	Registro Nacional de Estrangeiros (National Registry of Foreigners, the registration card of foreigners)
ONG	Organisação Não-Governamental (non-governmental organisation)
IBAMA	Instituto Brasileiro do Meio Ambiente e dos Recursos Naturais Renováveis (Brazilian Institute of the Environment and Renewable Natural Resources)
MST	Movimento dos Trabalhadores Rurais sem Terra (Rural Landless Workers' Movement)
FUNAI	Fundação Nacional do Indio (National Indian Foundation)
MPB	Música Popular Brasileira (Brasilian Popular Music)
MASP	Museu de Arte de São Paulo (São Paulo Art Museum)
MAM	Museu de Arte Moderna (Museum of Modern Art in Rio de Janeiro)
DETRAN	Departamento de Transportes (Brazilian Transportation Department)
ALCA	Área de Libre Comércio das Américas (FTAA, Free Trade Area of the Americas)
INCRA	Instituto Nacional de Colonização e Reforma Agrária (National Institute of Colonization and Agrarian Reform)
PM	Polícia Militar (Military Police)

CULTURE QUIZ

SITUATION 1

It is Sunday evening and you are at home watching *Fantástico*, your favourite television news programme. All of a sudden, the maid enters the room and tells you that one of your employees is at the door, waiting to talk to you. Irritated by the fact that the TV programme is being interrupted, and knowing that this employee has been testing your patience for some time, do you:

Ⓐ Tell the maid to say that you are already asleep?

Ⓑ Talk to him at the door and tell him to see you on Monday because you don't want to talk about work on Sunday night?

Ⓒ Invite the man into the living room and hear what he has to say, without mentioning a word about the inconvenience of his visit?

Comments

Ⓐ is probably a common excuse, since it avoids a confrontation altogether. But at the same time, you don't know if your employee has a serious problem that he needs help with. ❸ is not a good solution. Brazilians are polite and rarely reject people or express criticism directly. If you reacted that way, the employee would consider you inconsiderate, and he would let all his co-workers know about the incident. ❸ is the preferred solution. You remain on good terms with your employee, and appear to be helpful and interested in what he has to say, even though it may not be very important.

SITUATION 2

The sister of your Brazilian spouse just called, asking if a few friends of hers can put up at your house for a few days. You are already expecting guests the following week. Do you tell her:

❹ You already have guests coming but her friends are of course welcome too. The more the merrier?
❸ There is no more room in your apartment, since there is only one guest room?
❹ Her friends are welcome to stay, but only for two days?

Comments

❹ is the most common response. Brazilians customarily visit with friends and family of friends. Sometimes every square inch of an apartment is taken up by the foam mattresses of visitors. Brazilians readily open their homes, but also expect to find doors open to them elsewhere. ❸ is a cheap excuse, since everyone knows that there is always room on the living room floor. ❹ is an ambiguous answer. Either someone is welcome or not. Setting limits for a visitor's stay goes against the Brazilian tradition of hospitality. This does not mean however, that guests are happily accommodated for weeks at a time.

SITUATION 3

You make arrangements to buy a used pick-up truck, which is still being restored at the garage. A few weeks later, you take the truck for a test drive and show it to a friend. In addition to having the handbrake and windscreen wipers missing, your friend tells you that the truck has a completely wrong engine installed. When you finally arrive back at the dealer, do you tell him that you:

Ⓐ Don't like the vehicle and apologise for having caused an inconvenience. You shake the dealer's hand, pat him on the shoulder, and leave with a friendly face?

Ⓑ Have discovered the truck's defects and insist that he change the engine, fix the brake, and windscreen wipers etc., and sell you the truck at a discount, because of the inconvenience he caused you?

Ⓒ Will let everyone in town know about his business practices. You call him names in front of his employees, and threaten to file a complaint with the consumer protection agency?

Comments

Ⓐ is the most diplomatic answer and probably the best solution, since Brazilians avoid open conflict. The fact that the truck is returned with hardly a comment, already indicates that you know more than you say, while maintaining a diplomatic and jovial attitude. **Ⓑ** is not a good idea, since the dealer has already proven that he is not trustworthy. **Ⓒ** is the wrong approach. Open conflict in which one party loses face, is never a desired solution. A loud argument also makes you appear as irrational and bad-tempered. Threats and insults create bad blood, and never help to resolve a problem. Seeking help with government agencies rarely brings the desired results in Brazil and is not worth considering.

SITUATION 4

It is the beginning of the month and you have to go to the bank to take care of some important financial matters. Bank lines are extremely long this time of the month, but you really don't have the time to wait in line. Faced with this difficult situation do you decide to:

Ⓐ Plan your day so you have time to get to the bank half an hour before it opens, and be the first in line?

Ⓑ Go to the bank on your lunch break and hope that the line will move quickly?

Ⓒ Go to the branch in a different city district, where the wife of a friend works and simply walk up to her desk and ask her to help you with your 'problem'?

Comments

Ⓐ is a reasonable option for someone who is organised and plans out their day well. **Ⓑ** is what most people end up doing, which is why the lines are so long. **Ⓒ** is the preferred choice. Brazilians will always take advantage of the fact that they know someone who knows someone who can help them. Choosing this option will also give you the opportunity for a quick chat and to find out how the family of your friend is doing.

SITUATION 5

A close business associate is requesting that you to lend him some important equipment from your company, which he needs right away to get a project completed. You realise that the requested item is needed by your own company for an important task that needs to be completed this week. In this situation, do you tell your business associate that:

Ⓐ You are really sorry, but that you need the equipment in your own company this week. Maybe you'll be able to help him out next time?

Ⓑ The equipment is in use, but that you will see to it that it becomes available in a few days?

Ⓒ The business equipment is in use, but since he is a good friend, you'll lend it to him right away. You just need it back as soon as possible?

Comments

Ⓐ is the reaction to avoid. Business associates do each other favours all the time, and it would be very unwise to refuse to help him. ❸ could be an appropriate answer, since it aims for a compromise. The person gets what he asks for, but has to wait for a few days, in order for you to clear your priorities first. Although not always feasible, ❸ is the best answer, because business associates form a network of important contacts. Helping him out in this manner will insure the best future collaboration and business relationship, and you can count on his assistance at a later time.

DO'S AND DON'TS

DO'S

- Do shake hands when greeting someone. Brazilians customarily shake hands with everybody present.
- Do use the polite form of speech to address people older than you and those whose position demands respect.
- Do ask about the well-being of their family, spouse, girlfriend, etc., when talking to Brazilian friends, since family life is important to Brazilians.
- Do avoid making sarcastic and sardonic commentaries in conversation. Brazilians are an inherently optimistic and light-hearted people. Their sense of humour and manner of speech is mostly light and inoffensive. Wit, irony and sarcasm are not as much part of Brazilian conversation and dialogue as in other cultures.
- Brazilian women expect men to treat them with courtesy and respect, and to act as gentlemen. Do open car doors for women, hold doors open for them and help carry their bags or luggage.
- Do take your hat off when entering a church, especially in the case of men.
- Do wear long trousers and appropriate clothing when visiting government offices, or entry may be denied.
- Do offer your seat to the elderly, to pregnant women and women in general, when riding on public buses. It is also common for seated passengers to offer to hold a bag for a passenger who is standing.
- Do accept a complementary cup of *cafezinho* (black coffee) offered, unless you have a good reason to refuse. Coffee is a symbol of hospitality. Likewise, do offer a *cafezinho* to anybody who comes to your home.
- Do be patient when waiting for appointments and guests etc. Brazilians customarily arrive late for all but the most important business meetings.
- Do give street kids a few coins for watching your car while it is parked. This is not compulsory, but rather an unofficial and widely-accepted form of charity.

- Do round up the fare when taking a taxi.
- Do give porters and chambermaids a small tip.
- Do learn a little bit about football, Brazil's national passion, before arriving in Brazil. Knowing a few of the best players and teams by name will help break the ice, and impress Brazilians.
- Do keep in mind that poverty is widespread in Brazil. Giving a few coins to street kids or buying gum from them will make a small difference in their lives.
- Do be patient when waiting in line. This is an inevitable part of daily life in Brazil. Accept it with the same upbeat attitude as the people around you. Read or engage in conversation with the other people in line.

DON'TS

- Don't be alarmed when people stand close to you in public or in conversation. Personal space is not very important for Brazilians.
- Don't use gestures unless you know exactly what they mean and when to use them, since some gestures in Brazil have different and unexpectedly strong meanings.
- Don't use the American okay sign. It is considered an obscene gesture.
- Don't use slang expressions, unless you know exactly what they mean and when to use them. Although proliferated by the media and through music, the slang of Rio's shantytowns is inappropriate in most common social settings.
- Don't be alarmed when people, especially men, pat you on the shoulder or touch your arm in conversation. It is normal behaviour during conversation.
- Don't shy away from kisses. In greeting, women commonly offer both cheeks to men and women alike, for a light kiss.
- Don't criticise the government, culture or society in front of Brazilians, or point out how backward Brazil is compared to other countries. Brazilians are very sceptical and critical of the merits of their government and society, but criticism from a foreigner may be interpreted as an insult.

- Don't take photographs of government or military installations without permission.
- Don't curse in public. It is considered a sign of bad manners and low social status. If you need to use swear words, make sure that a Brazilian has initiated you into their exact meaning and usage.
- Don't use blasphemous language. Brazilians are a religious and spiritual people, and they may be offended.
- Don't be alarmed by people randomly talking to you in public. Brazilians are a sociable and communicable people. A casual conversation with strangers is normal, mostly without any other intention than to pass time.
- Don't eat food with your fingers. Even when eating on the street, people use napkins or toothpicks to pick up food.
- Don't visit a shantytown or slum unless invited and accompanied by a resident. Explorations on your own are dangerous, since many shantytowns are controlled by drug traffickers.
- Don't make noises while eating. Smacking, slurping, burping and making noise with plates and cutlery is considered a sign of bad manners.
- Don't eat food with your hands, unless encouraged to do so by your host.
- Don't be offended when called a gringo in public. It is generally used as a nickname for foreigners of European descent, and is not intended as an insult.

GLOSSARY

CONVERSATION BASICS

The following words and phrases provide a basic vocabulary for daily situations. But in order to be well-prepared for the challenges of communicating in Portuguese, you should buy a phrase book with a variety of conversation topics, as well as a small dictionary.

Greetings and Basic Phrases

Bom dia	Good morning
Boa tarde	Good afternoon
Boa noite	Good night
Adeus	Goodbye
Tchau (from the Italian ciao)	Bye bye
Oi (also used when answering the telephone)	Hi
Olá	Hello
Tudo bem?	Everything's fine?
Até logo; Até mais	See you soon; See you later
Sim	Yes
Não	No
Por favor	Please
Obrigado (when the speaker is male); Obrigada (when the speaker is female)	Thank you
Como está? Como vai?	How are you?
Estou bem, muito obrigado/ obrigada	I am fine, thank you
De nada	You are welcome
Não há; não tem de que	Don't mention it
Não tem importância	Never mind
Desculpa; Perdão	I am sorry

Parabéns!	Congratulations!
Com licença; used when attracting someone's attention	Excuse me
Feliz aniversário!	Happy birthday!
Boa viagem!	Have a good trip!
Boa sorte!	Good Luck!
Muito prazer; prazer em conhecé-lo	Glad to meet you
Fala inglês?	Do you speak English?
Não falo Português	I don't speak Portuguese
Entende?	Do you understand?
Não entendo	I don't understand
Não sei	I don't know
Pode falar mais devagar?	Could you speak more slowly?
Qual é o seu nome? / Como se chama?	What is your name?
Meu nome é ...	My name is ...
Que?	What?
Porque?	Why?
Quem?	Who?

On the Telephone

Alô or Oi	Hello
A Maria está?	Is Mary there?
Quem fala? Quem está falando?	Who is talking?
Queria falar com ...	I would like to talk to ...
É da parte de quem?	May I ask who is calling?

Getting Around

Onde é ...? Onde fica ...? Onde está ...?	Where is ...?
o banheiro	the bathroom
o terminal rodoviário	the bus terminal
a estação ferroviária	the railroad station
o centro	the city centre
o ponto de ônibus	the bus stop
o metrô	the subway (underground station)
o shopping	the shopping centre
o correio	the post office
o Museu Nacional	the National Museum
Onde tem ...?	Where is there ...?
um restaurante	a restaurant
um hotel barato	a cheap hotel
um banco	a bank
A que horas abre ...?	At what time does the ... open?
a banca	the newsstand
a livraria	the bookshop
a casa de câmbio	the money exchange office
Qual é a taxa de câmbio?	What is the exchange rate?
Queria trocar dinheiro	I would like to change money
Quando chega o ônibus?	When does the bus arrive?
O ônibus vai para ...?	Does the bus go to ...?
a praia	the beach
o jardim botânico	the botanical garden
Quanto é a passagem?	How much is the fare?
Quero ir ao aeroporto	I would like to go to the airport

Quero ir ao Teatro Municipal	I would like to go to the Municipal Theater
A que hora sai ...	At what time does the ... leave?
o avião	the airplane
o barco	the boat
a balsa	the ferryboat
a excursão	the excursion
o trêm	the train
Quanto tempo demora?	How long does it take?
Onde está o telefone mais próximo?	Where is the nearest telephone?

Shopping

Quanto custa? Quanto é isto?	How much is it?
Queria comprar ...	I would like to buy ...
uma calça	a pair of trousers (pants)
uma saia	a skirt
uma camisa	a shirt
uma camiseta	a T-shirt
Meu tamanho é ...	My size is ...
Queria provar isto	I would like to try this on
Eu gosto disso	I like that
Tem desconto?	Is there a discount
barato	cheap
caro	expensive
bom	good

Eating and Drinking

Queria ...	I would like ...
um cafezinho	a small coffee
uma cerveja	a beer

um refrigerante	a soft drink
Posso ver o cardápio?	Can I see the menu?
Qual é o prato do dia?	What is the daily special?
A conta, for favor!	The bill please!
O serviço está incluido?	Is the service included?

Time and Date

In daily conversation, Brazilians use the 12-hour clock. Therefore 9:00 am is *nove horas da manhã* (9 o'clock in the morning), 3:00 pm is *três horas da tarde* (3 o'clock in the afternoon) and 9:00 pm is *nove horas da noite* (9 o'clock at night). The official 24-hour clock is more commonly used for arrival and departure times, and on television. Time is expressed in the plural (except when saying *É uma hora*—It is 1 o'clock). For example:

São sete horas da manhã—It is 7 o'clock in the morning (plural), but: *É meio dia*—It is noon (singular).

São dez horas da noite—It is 10 o'clock at night (plural), but: *É meia noite*—It is midnight (singular).

Useful Expressions

Que horas são?	What time is it?
São duas horas e meia da tarde.	It is 2:30 pm
São oito e quinze da manhã.	It is 8:15 am
São onze e quarenta e cinco da noite	It is 11:45 pm
São quinze para as onze da noite	It is 11:45 at night or it is 15 minutes before 11 o'clock at night
ontem	yesterday
hoje	today
amanhã	tomorrow
a manhã	morning
a tarde	afternoon

a noite	night
meio dia	noon
meia noite	midnight

Days of the Week

The week starts with Sunday. Ordinal numbers are used for weekdays:

segunda feira (second day)	Monday
terça feira (third day)	Tuesday
quarta feira (fourth day)	Wednesday
quinta feira (fifth day)	Thursday
sexta feira (sixth day)	Friday
sábado	Saturday
domingo	Sunday
Que dia é hoje?	What day is today?
Hoje é quarta feira, onze de outubro	Today is Wednesday, 11 October
final de semana	weekend
feriado	holiday
Natal	Christmas
Ano Novo	New Year
Páscoa	Easter

The Months of the Year

janeiro	January
fevereiro	February
março	March
abril	April
maio	May
junho	June
julho	July
agosto	August
setembro	September

outubro	October
novembro	November
dezembro	December

Years are expressed as simple numbers:
1999 is *mil novecentos noventa e nove*—one thousand nine hundred and ninety-nine; 2002 is *dois mil e dois* etc.

Numerals

um	one
dois	two
três	three
quatro	four
cinco	five
seis, or meia (from meia dúzia meaning 'half a dozen')	six
sete	seven
oito	eight
nove	nine
dez	ten
onze	eleven
doze	twelve
treze	thirteen
quatorze	fourteen
quinze	fifteen
dezasseis	sixteen
dezassete	seventeen
dezoito	eighteen
dezanove	nineteen
vinte	twenty
vinte e um	twenty-one
trinta	thirty

trinta e um	thirty-one
quarenta	forty
cinqüenta	fifty
cem	hundred
cento e um	one hundred and one
cento e dez	one hundred and ten
cento e vinte	one hundred and twenty
duzentos	two hundred
trezentos	three hundred
mil	one thousand
dois mil	two thousand
um milhão	one million
um bilhão	one billion

A List of Food Items
Meat

bife	beefsteak
camarão	shrimp
caranguejo	mud crab
carne de sol (or carne seca)	salted, sun-dried meat, also known as *charque* or *xarque*
carneiro	mutton
costela	rib
filé	steak
filé mignon	filet mignon
frios	general term for cold cuts
frango	chicken
galinha	hen, chicken
langosta	lobster
lingüiça	sausage

lombo	pork loin
pato	duck
peixe	fish
peru	turkey
picanha	beef steak from the rump
porco	pork
presunto	smoked ham
salsicha	small sausage, such as hot dog
siri	sea crab

Vegetables

abóbora	pumpkin, squash
alface	lettuce
alho	garlic
banana pacova	plantain
beringela	aubergine / eggplant
beterraba	beet
bróccoli	broccoli
cebola	onion
cenora	carrot
chuchu (or xuxu)	a pear-shaped, light-green squash
couve	kale
couveflor	cauliflower
jilô	a green vegetable shaped like a small fig
maxixe	a small, green, squash-like vegetable with soft spines
moranga	winter squash
palmito	palm hearts
pepino	cucumber
pimenta malagueta	small, red, hot pepper

pimentão	green pepper
pupunha	peach palm fruit
quiabo	okra
repôlho	cabbage
tomate	tomato

Starches

aipim (or mandioca doce)	the sweet, non-poisonous manioc root, known in the North-east as macaxeira
arroz	rice, usually white rice
batata	potato, often served as batatas fritas (french fries)
farinha de mandioca	grated manioc meal that is lightly toasted; it is usually sprinkled on beans or sauces
arofa	coarse manioc meal roasted in oil or butter with garlic, bits of ham or meat
feijão	general term for Brazil's many varieties of beans
mandioca	manioc root, mostly served cooked; mandioca frita, fried manioc is a popular petisco (appetiser) at bars and restaurants
pirão	a thick sauce made from fish broth and manioc meal, often served with fish

Condiments and Spices

aceite	olive oil
canela	cinnamon
cravo	cloves
dendê	an orange-coloured strong oil from a palm tree of African origin, used in Bahian cookery.
gengibre	ginger
molho de soja	soy sauce
molho de pimenta	hot sauce
pimenta de cheiro	chilli pepper, used for hot sauce
pimenta do reino	black pepper
sal	salt
vinagre	vinegar

Desserts and Sweets

doce de leite	a sweet dessert made from boiled milk and sugar, resulting in a caramel-coloured sweet creme
doce de goiaba	a paste similar to a preserve made from the guava fruit, also called *goiabada*
creme de abacate	a sweet paste made from sugar and avocado
creme de cupuaçu	a milky pudding made from the sweet pulp of the *cupuaçu* fruit

brigadeiro	a truffle-like candy made with chocolate and condensed milk, especially popular at children's birthday parties
canjica	a popular dessert made with grated sweet corn, coconut milk, condensed milk and peanuts; also known as *munguzá*.
pé de moleque	a peanut brittle

Fruits

abacate	avocado
abacaxi	pineapple
açaí	a black, berry-like palm fruit, made into a thick juice of the same name
acerola	barbados cherry
amendoim	peanut
banana	banana; there is a wide variety of bananas with different flavours; some are only edible when cooked
cacau	cocoa fruit; the pulp is used in fruit juices and ice creams
caju	cashew fruit, used for juices
carambola	star fruit
castanha de cajú	cashew nut
castanha do pará	brazil nut
coco	coconut, used in desserts and for a variety of flavourings

cupuaçu	similar to the cocoa fruit; used in fruit juices, ice creams and desserts
fruta do conde (ata, pinha)	sweetsop or sugar apple
goiaba	guava
graviola	soursop, used in juices
imbu (or umbu)	the Brazilian plum, yellow-green in colour
jaboticaba	a purple berry that grows on the trunk and branches of its tree, similar in flavour to the black currant and gooseberry
jaca	jackfruit
jambo	rose apple
jenipapo	an oval fruit from the North-east, used in liqueurs and ice cream
laranja	orange
lima	sweet lime, similar to a grapefruit in size, shape and colour, but closer to an orange in flavour
limão	small, tart lemon, more like a lime
mamão	a large and less sweet variety of papaya
maçã	apple
manga	mango, eaten raw and made into juice and dessert
maracujá	passion fruit, used in juices
melancia	watermelon
melão	melon
papaia	papaya

pitanga	suriname cherry
saboti	sapodilla

COLLOQUIAL PORTUGUESE
Slang and Colloquial Expressions

Brazilian slang, known as *jíria*, is widely used in daily conversation everywhere in Brazil, especially by young people. Some colloquial expressions remain fashionable for a long time, while others are only popular for a season. Rio de Janeiro is known as Brazil's capital of slang, and television and song lyrics have helped spread new slang to every corner of Brazil. The following list only gives a few examples of the wealth of colloquial expressions in Brazilian Portuguese that continue to enrich the language.

legal	all right, great
maneiro	easy-going, cool, hip
massa	great, fabulous, excellent
sangue bom	a good, trustworthy person; literally: 'good blood'
descascar um abacaxi	to solve a difficult problem, to get out of a difficult situation; literally: 'to peel a pineapple'
ter dor de cotovelo	to be lovesick; literally: 'to have elbow pain'
segurar a vela	to be superfluous, to be the third wheel; literally: 'to hold the candle'
encher o saco	to annoy someone; literally: 'to fill the sack'
estar duro	to be broke; literally: 'to be hard'
pisar na bola	to make a mistake; literally: 'to step on the ball'

quebrar o galho	to make do, to find a way around a problem; literally: 'to break the branch'

Exclamations and Curses

caramba	Darn!; expression of dislike or surprise.
caralho	literally: penis; strong exclamation of dislike or surprise.
cacete	literally: stick, club, also penis; often used in the expression *pra cacete* (or *pra caramba* or *pra caralho*) meaning 'a lot', *trabalhei pra cacete* means 'I worked a hell of a lot.'
que saco!	What a drag!
é uma facada!	What a rip-off!
opa!	oops!
oba!	exclamation of joy, encouragement, and agreement.
qual é?	expression of disbelief, something like: What's that?
puxa!	expression of surprise
credo!	expression of disbelief
meu Deus!	oh my God!
Deus me livre!	God forbid!
nossa Senhora!	Our Lady!
se Deus quiser!	God willing!

PROVERBS

Portuguese is also rich in proverbs and sayings that express both folk wisdom and the Brazilian sense of humour:

- *Cada macaco no seu galho*—every jack to his trade; literally: every monkey on its branch. This is an admonition to express the belief that everyone has a place in society where they belong.
- *A esmola, quando é muita, o santo desconfia*—when there's a lot of alms, the saint becomes suspicious. This refers to someone who is doing a lot of good to make up for something bad that he has done.
- *Cautela e caldo de galinha não fazem mal a ninguém*—caution and chicken broth do not harm anybody; this is an admonition to be cautious.
- *A verdade é como o azeite, sempre vem à tona*—truth is like olive oil, it always comes to the surface.
- *Não se chora pelo leite derramado*—one doesn't cry over spilled milk; what has happened, has happened. There is no need to cry over something that is past.
- *De raminho em raminho, o passarinho faz seu ninho*—little by little, the bird builds its nest; things are accomplished little by little.

EMERGENCIES

Isto é uma emergência	This is an emergency
Preciso de ajuda	I need help
Estou perdido/perdida	I am lost
Pode me ajudar?	Can you help me?
Socorro!	Help!
Onde posso encontrar um médico?	Where can I find a doctor?
Onde tem um médico que fale inglês?	Where is there a doctor who speaks English?
Chame ...	Call ...
a polícia	the police
os bombeiros	the fire department
uma ambulância	an ambulance
pronto socorro	the emergency room/first aid clinic

Onde tem um hospital por aqui?	Where is there a hospital nearby?
Estou doente	I am sick
Dói aqui	It hurts here
Tenho ...	I have ...
um resfriado	a cold
dor de cabeça	a headache
dor de estômago	a stomachache
uma dor nas costas	a backache
dor de garganta	a sore throat
uma ferida	a wound
cólicas	cramps
dor de dente	a toothache
Estou com febre	I have a temperature
Tenho diarréia	I have diarrhoea
Estou sangrando	I am bleeding

RESOURCE GUIDE

EMERGENCIES AND HEALTH
Emergency Telephone Numbers

Polícia Militar (Military Police)   190
Pronto Socorro (Municipal ambulance/first aid)   192
Corpo de bombeiros (Fire department)   193

Hospitais (Hospitals)
São Paulo

Hospital Israelita Albert Einstein
Av Albert Einstein, 627/701, Morumbi
Tel: (11) 3747-1233; emergency unit: (11) 3747-0200
Ambulance: (11) 3747-1000/3747-1100
Website: http://www.einstein.br

Hospital das Clínicas FMUSP
Av Dr Enéas de Carvalho Aguiar 255, Cerqueira César
Tel: (11) 3096-6000; ambulance: 192
Website: http://www.hcnet.usp.br

Hospital Samaritano
Rua Conselheiro Brotero, 1486, Higienópolis
Tel: (11) 3821-5300
Website: http://www.samaritano.com.br

Rio de Janeiro
Hospital Municipal Miguel Couto
Rua Mario Ribeiro 117, Gávea
Tel: (21) 3111-3800
Emergency unit: (21) 3111-3600 or (21) 3111-3610 or
(21) 3111-3712

Hospital Samaritano
Rua Bambina 98, Botafogo
Tel: (21) 2537-9722; emergency: (21) 2535-4000
Website: http://www.hsamaritano.com.br/

Belo Horizonte
Hospital Municipal Odilon Behrens
Rua Formiga, 50, São Cristovão
Tel: (31) 3277-6231

Hospital João XXIII
Av Alfredo Balena, 400, Santa Efigênia
Tel: (31) 3239-9200 / 3239-9260

Health Information
**US Center for Disease Control, Traveler's Health
Home Page**
Provides information on vaccinations and other health
precautions. The section on 'Tropical South America' includes
information on Brazil.
Website: http://www.cdc.gov/travel/tropsam.htm

World Health Organization, Brazil Country Guide
Contains information on vaccination requirements and
health advice.
Website: http://www.who.int/countries/bra/en/

USEFUL ADDRESSES
Foreign Embassies and Consulates in Brazil

Canadian Embassy (Brasilia)
Av das Nações, Quadra 803, Lote 16,
70410-900, Brasília
Tel: (61) 3424-5400; fax: (61) 3424-5490
Email: brsla@international.gc.ca
Website: http://www.dfait-maeci.gc.ca/brazil

Canadian Consulate General (São Paulo)
Av das Nações Unidas, 12901-16° andar,
04578-000 São Paulo
Tel: (11) 5509-4343; fax: (11) 5509-4262
Email: spalo-immigration@dfait-maeci.gc.ca

Canadian Consulate (Rio de Janeiro)
Av Atlântica, 1130-5° andar, Atlântica Business Center,
Copacabana, 22021-000 Rio de Janeiro
Tel: (21) 2543-3004; fax: (21) 2275-2195
Email: rio@international.gc.ca

British Embassy (Brasilia)
Setor de Embaixadas Sul
Quadra 801, Lote 8, Conjunto K, 70408-900, Brasilia
Tel: (61) 3329-2300; fax: (61) 3329-2369
Email: contato@reinounido.org.br or
contact@uk.org.br

British Consulate General (São Paulo)
Rua Ferreira Araújo 741, 2° andar, Pinheiros,
05428-002, São Paulo
Tel: (11) 3094-2700; fax: (11) 3094-2717
Email: saopaulo@gra-bretanha.org.br

British Consulate Rio de Janeiro
Praia do Flamengo 284 (2nd floor),
22210-030, Rio de Janeiro

Tel: (21) 2555-9600; fax: (21) 2555-9672
Email: consular.rio@fco.gov.uk

US Embassy (Brasilia)
Av das Nações, Quadra 801, Lote 03,
70403-900, Brasília
Tel: (61) 3312-7000; fax: (61) 3225-9136
Email: contact@embaixadaamericana.org.br
Website: http://www.embaixada-americana.org.br

US Consulate General (São Paulo)
Rua Henri Dunant, 500, Chácara Santo Antônio,
04709-110 São Paulo
Tel: (11) 5186-7000; fax: (11) 5186-7199
Website: http://www.consuladoamericanosp.org.br

US Consulate General (Rio de Janeiro)
Avenida Presidente Wilson, 147,
20030-020, Rio de Janeiro
Tel: (21) 3823-2000; fax: (21) 3823-2003
Website: http://www.brasilia.usembassy.gov

US Consulate Recife
Rua Gonçalves Maia 163, Boa Vista, 50070-060, Recife
Tel: (81) 3421-2441; fax: (81) 3231-1906

USEFUL WEBSITES
Business and Money
US Commercial Service (São Paulo)
Rua Thomas Deloney, 381-Chácara Santo Antonio,
04710-110, São Paulo. Mailing address: Rua Henri Dunant,
700-Chácara Santo Antonio, 04709-110, São Paulo
Tel: (11) 5186-7440; fax: (11) 5186-7399
Website: http://www.focusbrazil.org.br (English and
Portuguese versions)
There also also branches in Rio de Janeiro, Brasilia, Belo
Horizonte and Porto Alegre. See website for contact info.

American Chamber of Commerce (São Paulo)
Rua da Paz 1431 CEP 04713-001, São Paulo
Tel: (11) 5180-3804; fax: (11) 5180 3777
Website: http://www.amcham.com.br
Email:business@amcham.com.br
There are also branches in Belo Horizonte, Brasília, Campinas, Curitiba, Goiânia, Porto Alegre and Recife. See website for contact info.

Classic 164 Currency Converter
Website: http://www.oanda.com/convert/classic
Provides current exchange rates for 164 different currencies.

ATM Locators
Mastercard/Maestro/Cirrus
Website: http://www.mastercard.com/atmlocator/index.jsp

Visa/Plus
Website: http://visa.via.infonow.net/locator/global/jsp/
SearchPage.jsp

American Express
Website: http://maps.americanexpress.com/expresscash/
PrxInput.aspx

Education

WWTeach—International Education, Schools & Living
Website: http://members.aol.com/wwteach/Teach.htm
Provides resources for teachers, students and parents.

International Schools Services
Website: http://www.iss.edu
Provides listings of international schools.

Information about Brazil
Website: http://www.brazil.gov.br
Brazilian Government Website. Provides a wealth of information on Brazil. English version available.

InfoBrazil
Website: http://www.infobrazil.com
Independent analysis and opinion on Brazilian current affairs.

Brazzil
Website: http://www.brazzil.com
Breaking news and analysis from Brazil.

Welcome to Brazil, (Bem Vindo ao Brasil)
Website: http://darkwing.uoregon.edu/ ~ sergiok/brasil.html
Facts and information about Brazil's cities, history and culture.

MariaBrazil
Website: http://www.maria-brazil.org
Provides a lot of useful cultural information.

BrazilBrazil
Website: http://www.brazilbrazil.com
Information on Brazil's culture, travel, business, art, sports and history.

BrazilMax
Website: http://www.brazilmax.com
An informative e-zine with articles, links and information.

Language
Travelang
Website: http://www.travlang.com
Provides language-related services to travellers, and hosts translating dictionaries and on-line phrase books. Also available in Portuguese.

News Media
Brazilian Newspapers and Magazines
- *Jornal do Brasil*
  Website: http://jbonline.terra.com.br
- *Estado de São Paulo*
  Website: http://www.estado.com.br

- *O Globo*
  Website: http://www.oglobo.com.br
- *Época*
  Website: http://www.epoca.com.br
- *Veja*
  Website: http://vejaonline.abril.com.br

Safety Information and Travel Advisories
US Bureau of Consular Affairs
Website: http://travel.state.gov

World Factbook
Website: http://www.odci.gov/cia/publications/factbook
Compiled by the CIA, with country profiles and basic information.

Foreign and Commonwealth Office
Website: http://www.fco.gov.uk
The homepage of the British Government department responsible for overseas relations and foreign affairs. Contains basic information for travellers.

Canadian Department of Foreign Affairs and Int Trade
Website: http://www.dfait-maeci.gc.ca
Provides travel and safety information.

Cultural and Expatriate Organisations
British Council
Headquarters: Ed Centro Empresarial Varig, SCN Quadra 04 Bloco B, Torre Oeste Conjunto 202, 70710-926 Brasília
Tel: (61) 2106-7500; fax: (61) 2106-7599
Email: brasilia@britishcouncil.org.br
A British cultural organisation with offices in Brasília, Rio de Janeiro, São Paulo, Curitiba and Recife.

American Society of São Paulo
Website: http://www.americansociety.com.br
An English-speaking club for expats in São Paulo.

São Paulo Athletic Club (SPAC)
First location: Av Robert Kennedy, 1448-Socorro, São Paulo
Tel: (11) 246-2220
Second location: Rua Visconde de Ouro Preto,
119-Consolação, São Paulo
Tel: (11) 256-5944
Website: http://www.clubeingles.com.br

The British Commonwealth Cultural Club
Rua Ferreira de Araújo, 741-1st Floor-Pinheiros, São Paulo
Tel: (11) 3819-0135
Email: bcccmanager@uol.com.br
Website: http://www.bccc-fundacaobritanica.org.br

International Women's Club of Porto Alegre
Email: iwcpoa@yahoo.com.br
Website: http://br.geocities.com/iwcpoa

LIVING ABROAD

Overseas Jobs
Website: http://www.overseasjobs.com
Features international job opportunities for professionals, expatriates and adventure seekers.

International Real Estate Digest
Website: http://www.ired.com
The Brazil page provides links to real estate agents, relocation services in Brazil, some links in English.

Escape Artist
Website: http://www.escapeartist.com
Provides links, and information about immigration, overseas careers, investing, retirement, worldwide moving companies and more.

Expat Exchange
Website: http://www.expatexchange.com
A wealth of resources and articles for expatriates, as well as a discussion forum.

Meetup
Website: http://www.meetup.com
A listing of group meetings in cities around the world to help bring people with common interests together.

Network for Living Abroad
Website: http://www.liveabroad.com
Acts as a network to link expatriates. Provides a useful source of information and resources. Also features a newsletter for expatriates.

Transitions Abroad
Website: http://www.transitionsabroad.com
Popular and useful alternative travel directory with resources for living, working and studying abroad. They also publish *Transitions Abroad* magazine.

Gringoes.com
Website: http://www.gringos.com.br
Is a portal for the foreign community in Brazil, with articles, links and information.

VOLUNTEER ORGANISATIONS
Associação Iko Poran
Av Nilo Peçanha, 50/1709-Centro-Rio de Janeiro 20 044-900
Tel: (21) 3084-2242; fax: (21) 3084-1446
Email: lfmurray@ikoporan.org
Website: http://www.ikoporan.org
Offers volunteer programmes in Rio de Janeiro

Amigos de las Américas (AMIGOS)
Amigos de las Americas, 5618 Star Ln.,
Houston, TX 77057-7112
Tel: 800-231-7796, fax 713-782-9267
Email: info@amigoslink.org
Website: http://www.amigoslink.org
Is an international organisation providing community-based volunteer opportunities in Brazil

Amigos de Iracambi

Fazenda Iracambi, Caixa Postal No. 1, Rosário da Limeira, 36878-000 Minas Gerais
Tel: (32) 3721-1436; fax: (32) 3722-4909
Email: iracambi@iracambi.com
Website: http://www.iracambi.com
Volunteer opportunities with rainforest preservation efforts.

Cross-Cultural Solutions

For USA and Canada:
2 Clinton Place, New Rochelle, New York 10801
Tel: 800-380-4777 or 914-632-0022
Email: info@crossculturalsolutions.org
For UK and all other countries:
Tower Point 44, North Road, Brighton BN1 1YR;
Tel: 0845 458 2781 or (0) 1273 666392
Email: infouk@crossculturalsolutions.org
Website: http://www.crossculturalsolutions.org
Offers volunteer opportunities in Brazil.

Volunteers for Peace

1034 Tiffany Road, Belmont, Vermont 05730 USA
Tel: 802-259-2759; fax: 802-259-2922
Email: vfp@vfp.org
Website: http://www.vfp.org
Offers affordable volunteer opportunities in Brazil.

Institute for International Cooperation and Development (IICD)

117 Hancock Road - Williamstown, MA 01267 USA
Tel: 413 441-5126
Email: info@iicd-volunteer.org
Website: http://www.iicd-volunteer.org/
Offers volunteer opportunities with street children in Brazil.

Global Vision International, GVI

- *GVI UK*
  Amwell Farmhouse, Nomansland, Wheathampstead, St Albans, Herts, AL4 8EJ, UK
  Tel: (44) 0870-608-8898 / 870-608-8898
  Fax: (44) 0870-609-2319
  Email: info@gvi.co.uk
- *GVI North America*
  PO Box 25256, Prescott Valley,
  AZ 86312, USA
  Tel: 1-888-653-6028 or 1-561-282-6992
  Email: info@gviusa.com
  Website: http://www.gvi.co.uk

Offers volunteer conservation work in Brazil.

INTERNATIONAL SCHOOLS

Website: http://www.state.gov/m/a/os
Department of State, Office of Overseas Schools, lists American International Schools in Brazil.

British Schools Around the World

Website: http://www.cobisec.org/index.htm
Lists British schools in Brazil.

International School of Curitiba

Av Dr Eugênio Bertolli, 3900, Santa Felicidade,
82410-530 Curitiba, Paraná
Tel: (41) 3364-7400; fax: (41) 3364-9663
Email: isc@iscbrazil.com
Website: http://www.isc-cic.com.br

American School Belo Horizonte

Avenida Deputado Cristovan Chiaradia 120, Bairro Buritis,
Caixa Postal 1701, 30575-440 Belo Horizonte
Tel: (31) 378-6700; fax: (31) 378-6878
Email: eabh@eabh.com.br
Website: http://www.eabh.com.br

American School of Brasília
SGAS 605, Conjunto 'E' Lotes 34/37, 70200-650 Brasília
Tel: (61) 442-9700; fax: (61) 244-4303
Email: lsantana@eabdf.br
Website: http://www.eabdf.br

American Elementary and High School São Paulo
Street address: Av Presidente Giovanni Gronchi, 4710,
05724-002, São Paulo
Mailing address: Caixa Postal 1976, 01059-970 São Paulo
Tel: (11) 3747-4800; fax: (11) 3742-9358
Email: drandall@graded.br
Website: http://www.graded.br

American School of Campinas
Rua Cajamar, 35-Jardim Alto da Barra, PO Box 978,
13012-970 Campinas
Tel: (19) 2102-1000; fax: (19) 2102-1016
Email: talktous@eac.com.br
Website: http://www.eac.com.br

American School of Recife
Rua Sa e Souza, 408, Boa Viagem, 51030-060 Recife
Tel: (81) 3341-4716; fax: (81) 3341-0142
Email: info@ear.com.br
Website: http://www.ear.com.br

American School of Rio de Janeiro
Estrada da Gavea 132, 22451-260, Rio de Janeiro
Tel: (21) 2512-9830; fax: (21) 2259-1606
Email: peter.cooper@earj.com.br
Website: http://www.earj.com.br

Pan American School of Bahia
Loteamento Patamares S/N CEP:41680-060 Salvador
Tel: (71) 3367-9099; fax: (71) 367-9090

Portuguese Courses in Brazil

For those who plan on studying Portuguese in Brazil, the following section provides a list of Portuguese language schools in several cities. Rio de Janeiro and São Paulo have the largest selection of language schools, and several international language schools also have branches in Brazil, making it easy to start a course in your home country, and continue after your arrival in Brazil. Request detailed information before making a decision, since prices and quality vary.

Berlitz International, Inc

Website: http://www.berlitz.com
http://www.berlitz.com.br
Berlitz has over twenty language schools throughout Brazil, including fourteen in São Paulo. Check website for addresses.

CIEE (Council on International Educational Exchange)

7 Custom House Street, 3rd Floor, Portland, ME 04101
Tel: 1-207-553-7600; toll-free: 1-800-40-STUDY
Fax: 1-207-553-7699
Website: http://www.ciee.org
Email: studyinfo@ciee.org
CIEE offers Portuguese courses at university level as well as student exchanges at universities in São Paulo and Salvador.

PUC-Rio (Pontifícia Universidade Católica de Rio de Janeiro)

- *For Portuguese courses for foreigners, contact the extension office:*
  CCE (Coordenação Central de Extensão), Casa 15,
  Rua Marquês São Vincente 225, Gávea, 22453-900, Rio de Janeiro
  Tel: 0800-90-9556
  Email: info@adm.cce.puc-rio.br
  Website: http://www.puc-rio.br/
- *For international student exchange programmes at PUC-Rio contact:*

CCCI-Coordenação Central de Cooperação Internacional
(International Programs Central Coordination Office)
Rua Marquês de Sao Vicente 225, Edifício Padre Leonel
Franca-8° andar, Gávea, 22453-900, Rio de Janeiro
Tel: (21) 3114-1578; fax: (21) 3114-1094
Email: inter@ccci.puc-rio.br
Website: http://www.puc-rio.br/ensinopesq/ccci/

IBEU (Instituto Brasil-Estados Unidos)
Caixa Postal 12154, Avenida N. S. de Copacabana 690, 5°
andar, Copacabana, Rio de Janeiro, RJ, CEP 22050-000
Tel: (21) 2548-8430
Website: http://www.ibeu.org.br
IBEU has 14 branches in Rio de Janeiro.

Bridge Linguatec
915 South Colorado Blvd., Denver, CO 80246, USA
Tel: 1-303-777-7783; toll-free: 1-800-724-4210 (USA &
Canada) and 0-800-028-8051 (UK); fax: 1-303-777-7246
Website: http://www.bridgelinguatec.com
Bridge Linguatec offers Portuguese language programmes
in Rio de Janeiro.

Diálogo Language School
Rua João Pondé, 240, 1° andar, Barra 40120-411 Salvador
Tel: (71) 3264-0007; fax: (71) 3264-0053
Email: info@dialogo-brazilstudy.com
Website: http://www.dialogo-brazilstudy.com

Fast Forward Language Institute
Rua Dep José Lages, 507-Ponta Verde,
Maceió-Alagoas 57035-330
Tel: (82) 3327-5213; fax: (82) 3337-2737
Website: http://www.fastforward.com.br
Email: info@fastforward.com.br
Fast Forward also has a branch in São Paulo:
Rua Cardoso de Almeida, 313 conj. 91/92/93,
Perdizes 05013-000 São Paulo
Tel: (11) 3667-8782; fax: (11) 3667-8782

FURTHER READING

RECOMMENDED READING
Art and Architecture

Oscar Niemeyer and the Architecture of Brazil. David Kendrick Underwood. New York, NY: Rizzoli International Publications Inc, 1994.

Brazilian Cinema. Ed. Randal Johnson and Robert Stam. New York, NY: Columbia University Press, 1995.
- This anthology of Brazilian cinema covers the development and history of filmmaking from its beginning in 1898 to the present.

The New Brazilian Cinema. Ed. Lucia Nagib. New York, NY: I B Tauris & Company, Ltd, 2003.
- A survey of Brazilian cinema since the mid 1990s.

The Art of Brazil. Ed. Carlos Alberto Cerqueira Lemos and José Roberto Teixeira Leite. New York, NY: Harper Collins Publishers, 1983.

- Including painting, sculpture, and architecture, this comprehensive volume covers Brazilian art from the early colonial period to Brazil's diverse contemporary art scene.

Journal of Decorative and Propaganda Arts No. 21: Brazil Theme Issue. Miami, FL: The Wolfson Foundation of Decorative and Propaganda Arts, March 1995.
- This issue takes a look at the past and present of Brazil's architecture, design, and the arts.

Business

Brazil Company Handbook 2005/2006: Data on Major Listed Companies. Austin, TX: Hoover's Inc, 2005.
- A guide for investors, updated annually.

Brazil Business Law Handbook. US: International Business Publications USA, 2005.
- A useful manual for Brazilian law relating to business.

Brazil Business Intelligence Report. US: International Business Publications USA, 2003.
- Provides information on exporting, importing, business strategies, investment in Brazil, and more.

Culture

Bodies, Pleasures and Passions. Sexual Culture in Contemporary Brazil. Richard G Parker. Boston, MA: Beacon Press Books, 1991.

Soccer Madness: Brazil's Passion for the World's Most Popular Sport. Janet Lever. Long Grove, IL: Waveland Press, 1995.
- This book investigates Brazilians' passion for their favourite national sport.

Samba in the Night: Spiritism in Brazil. David J Hess. New York, NY: Columbia University Press, 1994.
- This book is an investigation of popular Brazilian religions such as Spiritism, Kardecism, Umbanda and Candomblé, and their followers.

The Brazilian People: The Formation and Meaning of Brazil.
Darcy Ribeiro. Gainsville, FL: University of Florida Center
for Latin American Studies, 2000.
- Portuguese title: *O povo brasileiro–a formação e o sentido
  do Brasil.* This in-depth study by one of Brazil's best-
  known 20th century scholars reveals and analyses the
  complex roots that formed Brazilian society and the
  Brazilian people.

Capoeira: A Brazilian Art Form: History, Philosophy, and Practice.
Bira Almeida. Berkeley, CA: North Atlantic Books, 1986.
- An introduction to the history and development of Brazil's
  fascinating national sport.

Brazilian Mosaic: Portraits of a Diverse People and Culture.
Ed. G. Harvey Summ. William H. Beezley and Judith Ewell.
Woodbridge, CT: Scholarly Resources Inc, 1995.
- Containing 44 excerpts from a variety of authors,
  both historical and contemporary, this book
  provides an in-depth look at both Brazilian history
  and culture.

Food and Cooking
Brazil (Food and Festivals). Mariana Serra. Austin, TX: Raintree
Steck-Vaughn Publishers, 1999.

Brazilian Foods and Culture. Jennifer Ferro. Vero Beach: FL:
Rourke Press Inc, 1999.
- An introduction to Brazilian food and festive meals, with
  recipes.

Brazil: A Cook's Tour. Christopher Idone. New York, NY:
Clarkson N Potter Publishers Inc., 1995.
- This is an introduction to Brazilian cooking which
  includes 100 recipes and over 100 colour photographs.

*Eat Smart in Brazil: How to Decipher the Menu, Know the
Market Foods & Embark on a Tasting Adventure.* Joan and David
Peterson. Madison, WI: Gingko Press Inc., 1995.

- A comprehensive guide to Brazilian food and cooking, including regional dishes and recipes.

History and Politics

A Concise History of Brazil. Boris Fausto. New York, NY: Cambridge University Press, 1999.
- Portuguese title: *História concisa do Brasil.* This thorough account provides insights into Brazilian history, from her discovery in 1500 to the present.

Red Gold: The Conquest of the Brazilian Indians. John Hemming. New York. NY: Macmillan Publishers Ltd, 1995.
- The history of the Brazilian Indians from 1500–1760.

Amazon Frontier: The Defeat of the Brazilian Indians. John Hemming. New York, NY: Macmillan Publishers Ltd., 1995.
- This is the sequel to *Red Gold: The Conquest of the Brazilian Indians.* It covers the history of the Brazilian Indians from 1760–1910.

The Brazil Reader—History, Culture, Politics. (Ed.) Robert M Levine and John J Crocitti. Durham, NC: Duke University Press, 1999.
- An interesting selection of historical writings and documents from Brazil's discovery to the present.

The Golden Age of Brazil: 1695–1750, Growing Pains of a Colonial Society. Charles R Boxer. New York, NY: St Martins Press, 1995.
- An authoritative work about Brazil's gold rush and its colonial history.

Rebellion in the Backlands. Euclides de Cunha. Chicago, IL: University of Chicago Press, 1990.
- Portuguese title: *Os sertes.* First published in 1902, this classic social and historic commentary chronicles the military campaign against the religious community of Canudos from 1893–1897.

Language Learning

Cassette Courses:

501 Portuguese Verbs : Fully Conjugated in All the Tenses in a New Easy-To Learn Format. Alphabetically Arranged. John J Nitti and Michael J Ferreira. Hauppauge, NY: Barrons Educational Series, 1995.

Lonely Planet Brazilian Phrasebook. Mark Balla. (Lonely Planet Language Survival Kit, Victoria, Australia: Lonely Planet, 1993.
- A compilation of important conversational phrases and a basic working vocabulary for travellers.

Brazilian Portuguese. Pimsleur Language Method (4 cassettes),. New York, NY: Simon & Schuster Audio, 1996.

Brazilian Portuguese Complete Course. Living Language. New York, NY: Crown Publishing Group, 1998.
- An introductory course for beginners, based on the course book and audio cassettes. Includes a dictionary.

Teach Yourself Brazilian Portuguese, Complete Course. Sue Tyson-Ward. California, US: NTC Publishing Group, 1997.

Colloquial Portuguese of Brazil: The Complete Course for Beginners. Esmenia Simões Osborne, João Sampaio. and Barbara McIntyre. London, UK: Routledge, 2004.

CD-ROM Programs

Rosetta Stone Portuguese.
- A comprehensive CD-ROM course based on the method of associating spoken words and phrases with images. Published in two volumes. Fairfield Language Technologies,
  Email: info@RosettaStone.com
  Website: http://www.RosettaStone.com.

PortugueseNow! 8.0
- A CD-ROM programme on how to speak, listen, read and

write Portuguese. Transparent Language, Inc.
Email: info@transparent.com
Website: http://www.transparent.com.

A + Portuguese Language Lessons
- A comprehensive CD-ROM programme for beginners. Transparent Language, Inc.
  Email: info@transparent.com
  Website: http://www.transparent.com.

Literary Anthologies

An Anthology of Twentieth-Century Brazilian Poetry. Ed. Elizabeth Bishop and Emanuel Brasil. Lebanon, NH: University Press of New England,1994.
- An introduction to Brazilian poetry, including works by Brazil's best-known poets of the Modernist generation.

Three Contemporary Brazilian Plays. Plínio Marcos, Leilah Assunção, Consuelo De Castro. Austin, TX: Host Publications Inc, 1988.

Urban Voices: Contemporary Short Stories from Brazil. Ed. Cristina Ferreira Pinto. Lanham, MD: University Press of America, 1999.
- An anthology of 18 short stories that focus on urban Brazil with its ethnic, economic and cultural diversity.

Literature

The following titles have been published in English. Some of them are out of print, but may be available at libraries or used book shops. All of these titles are available in Portuguese at bookshops in Brazil.

Jorge Amado

Dona Flor and Her Two Husbands. New York, NY: William Morrow & Co., 1998.
- Portuguese title: *Dona flor e seus dois maridos*. The ghost of Dona Flor's deceased first husband returns and joins Dona Flor and her new husband in their marriage.

The War of the Saints. New York, NY: Doubleday Dell Publishing Group, 1995.
- Portuguese title: *O sumiço da santa*. A valuable statue of St Barbara disappears, causing much confusion in the city of Salvador.

Gabriela, Clove and Cinnamon. New York, NY: William Morrow & Co., 1988.
- Portuguese title: *Gabriela, cravo e canela*. This is the endearing story of Gabriela, a cooking instructor from north-eastern Brazil, who has become one of Brazil's best-known literary figures.

Mário de Andrade
Macunaíma. New York, NY: Random House Inc, 1984.
- Portuguese title: *Macunaím–o herói sem nenhum caráter*. This satirical and humourous novel tells of the adventures of Macunaíma, the 'hero without any character', as he travels from his native Amazon region to different parts of Brazil, and discovers the idiosyncrasies of his fellow Brazilians.

Machado de Assis
Dom Casmurro. New York, NY: Oxford University Press, 1998.
- Machado de Assis's most important novel, Dom Casmurro was first published in 1899. It tells a moving story of love, deception, and betrayal in the author's unique narrative style.

The Posthumous Memoirs of Brás Cubas. New York, NY: Oxford University Press, 1998.
- Portuguese title: *Memórias póstumas de Brás Cubas*. First published in 1881, the novel's narrator, Brás Cubas, tells the story of his life from beyond the grave.

Autran Dourado
The Bells of Agony. London, UK: Peter Owen Publishing, 1988.
- Portuguese title: *Os sinos da agonia*. This novel portrays Brazil's interior province of Minas Gerais at the end of the

18th century, when the gold rush came to an end and the region began to fall into decay.

Rubem Fonseca

High Art. New York, NY: Carroll & Graf Publishers, 1987.

- Portuguese title: *A grande arte.* The lawyer Mandrake, one of the great characters of contemporary Brazilian fiction, sets out to solve a tough murder case that takes him to the shady side of urban Brazil.

João Guimarães Rosa

The Devil to Pay in the Backlands. New York, NY: Alfred Knopf, 1971.

- Portuguese title: *Grande sertão: veredas.* This classic of modern Brazilian fiction, first published in 1956 and often compared to James Joyce's *Ulysses* for its innovative use of language, tells of the lives of bandits in the backlands of Brazil's North-east.

Clarice Lispector

The Hour of the Star. New York, NY: New Directions Publishing Co. 1992.

- Portuguese title: *A hora da estrela.* Written shortly before Lispector's death in 1977, this novel tells the story of Macabéa, a girl from rural, interior Brazil, as she tries to survive in urban São Paulo.

The Foreign Legion: Stories and Chronicles. New Directions Publishing Co., 1992.

- Portuguese title: *A legião estrangeira.* This book includes 13 stories exploring Lispector's existentialist themes such as loneliness and isolation.

Graciliano Ramos

Barren Lives. University of Texas Press, 1990.

- Portuguese title: *Vidas secas.* One of the masterpieces of Brazilian social realism, the novel chronicles the life of a peasant family who flees a severe drought in Brazil's North-east.

Rachel de Queiros
The Three Marias. Austin, TX: University of Texas Press, 1990.
- Portuguese title: *As três Marias*.

João Ubaldo Ribeiro
An Invincible Memory. New York, NY: HarperTrade, 1989.
- Portuguese title: *Viva o povo brasileiro*

Sergeant Getúlio. Houghton Mifflin Company, 1977.
- Portuguese title: *O sargento Getúlio*.

Music
Masters of Brazilian Contemporary Song: MPB 1965–1985. Charles A Perrone. Austin, TX: University of Texas Press, 1993.
- Provides an overview of contemporary Brazilian music with a special focus on Chico Buarque, Caetano Veloso, Gilberto Gil, Milton Nascimento, João Bosco and Aldir Blanc.

Samba. Alma Guillermoprieto. New York, NY: Vintage Books, 1991.
- The author partakes in the preparations for Rio's carnaval as a member of one of the most famous Samba schools.

The Brazilian Sound: Samba, Bossa Nova, and the Popular Music of Brazil. Chris McGowan and Ricardo Pessanha. Philadelphia, PA: Temple University Press, 1998.
- This comprehensive introduction to Brazilian music covers all the well-known musical styles such as Samba, Bossa Nova, MPB, as well as regional trends and new developments. Includes numerous photographs.

Nature and Environment
A Neotropical Companion–An introduction to the Animals, Plants, & Ecosystems of the New World Tropics. John Kricher. Princeton, NJ: Princeton University Press, 1997.
- A practical and in-depth guide to the animals, plants and ecosystems of tropical America including Brazil. With colour photographs and numerous drawings.

Amazon Journal: Dispatches from a Vanishing Frontier. Geoffrey O'Connor. New York, NY: Dutton/Plume, 1998.

- This travel account by a documentary filmmaker investigates the conflict between native tribes and gold miners in the Brazilian Amazon.

The Amazon River Forest: A Natural History of Plants, Animals and People. Nigel J H Smith. New York, NY: Oxford University Press, 1998.

Social Issues

At Home in the Street: Street Children of North-east Brazil. Tobias Hecht. New York, NY: Cambridge University Press, 1998.

- This investigative study, based on the author's fieldwork among street children in Recife, portrays the struggle of Brazil's most neglected citizens.

Death Without Weeping–The Violence of Everyday Life in Brazil. Nancy Scheper-Hughes. University of California Press. 1992).

- An anthropological study of the lives of women in a shantytown in north-eastern Brazil.

Racism in a Racial Democracy: The Maintenance of White Supremacy in Brazil. France Winddance Twine. Piscataway, NJ: Rutgers University Press, 1998.

- Based on the author's extensive field research, this book investigates the continuing socioeconomic disadvantages of Brazil's dark-skinned population and reveals racial attitudes and prejudices.

The Masters and the Slaves: A Study in the Development of Brazilian Civilization. Gilberto Freyre. Berkeley, CA: University of California Press, 1990.

- Portuguese title: *Casa grande e senzala*. This classic of Brazilian social history investigates how the patriarchal plantation society has formed Brazilian society.

The Mansions and the Shanties: The Making of Modern Brazil. Gilberto Freyre. Berkeley, CA: University of California Press, 1986.
- Portuguese title: *Sobrados e mucambos.* This book is a sequel of *The Masters and the Slaves* and further investigates the roots of Brazilian civilisation.

Child of the Dark. Carolina Maria de Jesus. New York, NY: New American Library, 1989.
- Portuguese title: *Quarto de despejo.* The personal diary of a woman about her life in a São Paulo slum during the 1950s.

Travel and Adventure

A Naturalist on the River Amazon. Henry Walter Bates. New York, NY: Viking Penguin, 1989.
- The journals of a 19th century British naturalist, who spent several years in the Amazon.

Brazilian Adventure. Peter Fleming. Evanston, IL: ern University Press, 1999.
- In 1932, the author went in search of the lost Amazon expedition of English adventurer Colonel P H Fawcett.

History of a Voyage to the Land of Brazil. Jean de Léry. Berkeley, CA: University of California Press, 1993.
- A protestant missionary writes about his two-year stay in Brazil in the 1550s.

Tristes Tropiques. Claude Levi-Strauss. New York, NY: Random House Inc., 1997.
- This classic anthropological travelogue describes Levi-Strauss' trip to Brazil in the 1930s.

Travelers' Tales, Brazil. Ed. Annette Haddad and Scott Doggett. Palo Alto, CA: Travelers' Tales Inc, 1997.
- A collection of stories and observations about Brazil by a number of authors.

Through the Brazilian Wilderness. Theodore Roosevelt, New York, NY: Cooper Square Publishers Inc, 2000.

- A fascinating account of Roosevelt's Amazon expedition in 1914.

Travel Guides

Brasil 2006, Guia Quatro Rodas (in Portuguese). Brazil: Editora Abril, 2005.

- This detailed and resourceful travel guide is intended for travel by automobile. It includes all of Brazil's popular travel destinations, but focuses on places accessible by car.

Insight Guide: Brazil. Jane Ladle. Duncan, SC: Langenscheidt Publishers Inc, 1999.

- Provides an informative introduction to Brazilian history, culture and travel destinations with many colour photographs. This is the most colourful of all travel books about Brazil.

The Rough Guide to Brazil. David Cleary, Oliver Marshall, Dilwyn Jenkins. New York, NY: Rough Guides Ltd, 2003.

- This is the most readable guide for intrepid budget travellers. The practical travel information contained within is not as extensive as in other budget guides, but the cultural, social and historic background information is superior.

Lonely Planet Brazil. Regis St. Louis, Andrew Draffen, Molly Green and Thomas Kohnstamm. Victoria, Australia: Lonely Planet Publications, 2005.

- Geared toward youthful budget travellers. Lonely Planet Brazil provides a general round-up of where to go, what to see, and where to stay.

Brazil Handbook. Alex Robinson. Bath, UK: Footprint Handbooks, 2005.

- Provides in-depth information for those who want to explore Brazil on their own.

ABOUT THE AUTHOR

Volker Poelzl is an Austrian-born freelance writer, photographer, and world traveller who lives in the US. His interest in Brazil was inspired by the country's wealth of music which he discovered playing the guitar. He lived in Rio de Janeiro to study Portuguese and was involved in an agroforestry project in the Amazon.

Volker Poelzl has travelled extensively all over Brazil and returns every year to explore the hidden parts of this beautiful and fascinating country. He also enjoys travelling in the footsteps of explorers and has descended several jungle rivers in his canoe.

INDEX

Titles in the CULTURE**SHOCK**! series:

Argentina	Hawaii	Pakistan
Australia	Hong Kong	Paris
Austria	Hungary	Philippines
Bahrain	India	Portugal
Barcelona	Indonesia	San Francisco
Beijing	Iran	Saudi Arabia
Belgium	Ireland	Scotland
Bolivia	Israel	Sri Lanka
Borneo	Italy	Shanghai
Brazil	Jakarta	Singapore
Britain	Japan	South Africa
Cambodia	Korea	Spain
Canada	Laos	Sweden
Chicago	London	Switzerland
Chile	Malaysia	Syria
China	Mauritius	Taiwan
Costa Rica	Mexico	Thailand
Cuba	Morocco	Tokyo
Czech Republic	Moscow	Turkey
Denmark	Munich	Ukraine
Ecuador	Myanmar	United Arab
Egypt	Nepal	Emirates
Finland	Netherlands	USA
France	New York	Vancouver
Germany	New Zealand	Venezuela
Greece	Norway	Vietnam

For more information about any of these titles, please contact any of our Marshall Cavendish offices around the world (listed on page ii) or visit our website at:

www.marshallcavendish.com/genref